VEILS AND DAGGERS

A CENTURY OF
NATIONAL GEOGRAPHIC'S
REPRESENTATION OF THE ARAB WORLD

VEILS AND DAGGERS

A CENTURY OF

NATIONAL GEOGRAPHIC'S

REPRESENTATION OF THE ARAB WORLD

LINDA STEET

TEMPLE UNIVERSITY PRESS
Philadelphia

Temple University Press, Philadelphia 19122
Copyright © 2000 by Temple University
All rights reserved
Published 2000
Printed in the United States of America

⊗ The paper used in this publication meets the requirements of the American
National Standard for Information Sciences—Permanence of Paper for Printed
Library Materials, ANSI Z39.48-1984

Library of Congress Cataloging-in-Publication Data

Steet, Linda, 1949-
    Veils and daggers : a century of National Geographic's representation of
the Arab world / Linda Steet.
        p.   cm.
    Includes bibliographical references (p. -) and index.
    ISBN 1-56639-751-0 (cloth : alk. paper). -- ISBN 1-56639-752-9 (paper :
alk. paper)
        1. Arab countries--History--1798-   2. National Geographic.
I. National Geographic.   II. Title.
DS38.9.S73   2000
910'.917'4927--dc21   99-37257

This is dedicated to my wonderful parents,
Joseph G. Steet and Mary A. Steet

CONTENTS

LIST OF ILLUSTRATIONS

CHAPTER FOUR

CHAPTER FIVE

ACKNOWLEDGMENTS

Virginia Woolf advised that to write, a woman needs a room of one's own. I have many people to thank for agreeing to have a relationship with a person who also needs a chair of one's own, a coffee mug of one's own, a phone of one's own, a subscription of one's own, a remote control of one's own, a place in the car of one's own. . . .

I want especially to thank my son Joey for being a constant source of pleasure and surprise in my life. Throughout this project, he has shown himself to be a fine example of good humored, low-maintenance offspring. I have relied on Jeffrey Liles for innumerable eleventh hour tasks during this project and I am grateful for his making peace with my work habits and sense of personal space.

I want to thank Joann Capozzi and Richard Capozzi for giving me a house key, figuring out how to use a typewriter, and letting me rely on them. Their friendship and warm hospitality have made accomplishing this and other projects so much easier. I am grateful to Diane Becerra and Leila and Lena for unselfishly sharing their space with us and making us feel missed when we left. I want to thank Bette Adams for suggesting we look through her family photo albums, again and again and again.

For many years, I have depended on Sari Biklen for advice, inspiration, and friendship, and she has always come through for me. I am grateful to my dear friend Pat Russo for thinking I am so much better than I am. The energy and determination with which she approaches her work have been an important model for me. I thank Susan Laird for being an unselfish source of kindness and support whom I can count on even when her own affairs need tending. I want to thank Bill Bain for giving me so much of his time to participate in magazine hunts and endless discussions that went all over the place, or was that no place? I appreciate Shanti Menon for being my faithful phone companion.

I am very thankful to Vera Nofal for playing cards with me, taking afternoon walks, and being like a sister during some remarkable times. I am grateful to Anita Abdullah for always laughing with me at the most inappropriate moments—her appreciation of the humor in it all has been soothing. And I thank her for keeping a perspective I tend to lose.

I am indebted to Lois Patton at Temple University Press for taking such good care of this project. I would still be knee deep in *National Geographic* magazines if it were not for her wise guidance.

I have dedicated this book to my parents, but it is hardly enough to express my gratitude for their love, support, and generosity throughout all the different directions I have taken. Thank you.

VEILS AND DAGGERS

A CENTURY OF
NATIONAL GEOGRAPHIC'S
REPRESENTATION OF THE ARAB WORLD

INTRODUCTION

A few years ago, I came upon a picture postcard of a white, adult hand holding a tiny, severely emaciated black hand. It was captioned: "Priest of the Verona Fathers holds the hand of a starving boy, Uganda." The photograph haunted me because I felt certain I had seen it before but could not place where. Finally, it came to me. I had not, in fact, previously seen that photograph. I was confusing it with one from the Benetton Company's clothing advertisements. The Benetton image was a close-up of a white, adult hand holding that of a black child. The only difference between the postcard and the clothing ad images was that in the latter, the child's hand looked chubby and well nourished.

I was not only intrigued by these overlapping images employed for very different purposes; I once again sensed that I had seen the image somewhere else. The Verona Fathers' postcard and the Benetton clothing ad, in turn, brought to mind *National Geographic* magazine. It was not any particular picture I remembered when I made the initial link to *National Geographic,* but by way of an abstract reference I recognized a mood or dimension of otherness created within the pages of the magazine. Though I had not picked up a copy of *National Geographic* in years, these apparently unrelated images jogged my memory of it. While discourses of Christian charity, fashion advertising, and popular geography are distinct from one another, and each has its own territory, the visual images revealed shared assumptions and practices. At the intersection of these images, a place where one realizes the strong associations between areas with seemingly hard boundaries of separation, I began to reread *National Geographic* magazine—specifically, one hundred years of the magazine's representation of the Arab world.

National Geographic magazine is an American popular culture icon and an educational journal that, since its founding in 1888, has been on a nonstop tour classifying and cataloguing the peoples of the world, again and again. With more than ten million subscribers, *National Geographic* is the third-largest magazine in America following *TV Guide* and *Reader's Digest,* respectively. Having been given privileged educational space that material from popular culture is generally denied, *National Geographic* has long been a staple of school, public, and home libraries across the country.

Gilbert H. Grosvenor, editor of the magazine from 1899 to 1954 and, following that, president–editor and chairman of the Board of Trustees until his death in 1966, noted that more volumes of the magazine are bound than any other and are "constantly consulted by students, teachers, travelers, artists, scientists, persons in a hundred walks of life."[1] In 1936, he asked: "Who can even begin to estimate the cultural results of distributing this readable, easily understood, humanized, and picturized knowledge among millions of people ... decade after decade?"[2] More than half a century later, this study takes up Grosvenor's challenge to "begin to estimate the cultural results" of *National Geographic* magazine.

The longevity, American cultural niche, educational reputation, and mass popularity of *National Geographic* magazine make it a phenomenon in print media. As Catherine Lutz and Jane Collins have well demonstrated, it is a phenomenon that needs to be seriously critiqued "not as a single artifact but a powerful voice" in the cultural discussion of difference.[3] We too often take for granted the magazine's claims about itself and allow it to bypass the critical scrutiny that ought to be given to educational material. This examination of *National Geographic* embarks on a process of demystification that helps develop an overall guarded reading and viewing position toward ideas, images, and practices that masquerade as common sense or objective knowledge. Such an approach regards neither text nor visual image in *National Geographic* as natural or self-evident. Rather, everything needs to be interpreted for underlying assumptions. Developing and sustaining a skepticism toward that which claims neutral, factual ground is a productive and intensive activity requiring decoding strategies that in operation resist oppressive arrangements of gender, race, sexuality, ethnicity, and so on. These arrangements and their scaffolding of meanings are created and reinforced in sites of popular culture and education.

Up until the mid-1960s, *National Geographic* magazine carried the slogan: "Mention *National Geographic*—It Identifies You." Beyond an appeal to middle-class elitism, the slogan is on target in that the magazine actually does play an important role in the construction of identity related to gender, race, and nation. Yes, *National Geographic* does "identify" you, and that is why I am "mentioning" it. For more than a century, Americans have learned something of their sense of self and other by way of *National Geographic*'s worldview. Recognizing the magazine as both site and vehicle for the complex social processes of identity formation and the establishment of hierarchies of difference is crucial. A feminist and multicultural critique of *National Geographic* can unpack it to reveal the particular ideological perspectives that, guarded under its seemingly objective, educational surface, have guided the magazine throughout its long history.

It is a history that, as this book shows, has not altered much in some of its broad strokes. Indeed, this is a proud claim made by the magazine itself. Commenting on Washington's Corcoran Gallery of Art marking the National Geographic Society's centennial year, 1988, with an exhibition of the magazine's photographs, editor Wilbur E. Garrett said: "It inspires us to keep on covering stories the way we always have."[4] The way *National Geographic* always has includes the early-established stated policy to "portray people in natural attire—or lack of it"— that is, "in their natural state."[5] The unchanging face of *National Geographic* is perhaps most obvious in this particular policy producing a century of images of bare-breasted non-Western women. What could be called the magazine's impossible weaning began with its first photograph of a bare-breasted woman in 1896 (Photo 1) and continues more than a century later. From the picture of a "Zulu Bride and Bridegroom" shaking hands to more recent breast shots, the magazine claims to be practicing its policy of presenting people "in their natural state."

The accompanying text also speaks to peoples' "natural state." The photograph of the Zulu couple is part of an article that informs readers that Zulus "are horribly cruel when once they have smelled blood" and, along with other tribes, wage "furious inter-tribal wars" resulting in "unsparing slaughter," which makes it remarkable that any considerable number remain. "Nothing but the phenomenal fecundity of the race has kept up its numbers."[6]

Lest anyone think such images no longer appear, a peek into the 1990s shows that the important place occupied by breasts in *National Geographic* can still be charted. The focus of a December 1991 photograph can be lost on no one: It is a half-page photograph of a bare-breasted woman from Mali whose image is cropped at the neck and hips. In the background of this torso close-up are

PHOTO 1

"Zulu Bride and Bridegroom," November 1896

three children, visually confirming the continued "fecundity of the race." The context of this picture is an article retracing the route of the fourteenth-century Arab traveler Ibn Battuta. The woman represents a sight Ibn Battuta would have seen during a journey through Mali six centuries ago. Thus, in a confusion of context and pretext, we are to imagine that we are viewing what an Arab man looked at in the fourteenth century, not what *National Geographic* looked at in 1991.

Staying with the example of Mali, in May 1998 another bare-breasted woman from that country appeared in the magazine—this time with head intact and sound asleep alongside her children on a sandy mat. The photograph's context was an article on global weather trends, with Mali offered as an example of drying conditions. Whether articles on Ibn Battuta's world travels or world climate, it seems that bare-breasted women (with children) best illustrate Mali. These two examples on either end of the decade proceeding the period of this study, 1888–1988, will suffice to demonstrate the continued place of breasts in *National Geographic*.

Returning to the Arab world and the magazine's first one hundred years, what will be examined? By tracing the magazine's journeys through the Arab world, this book not only demonstrates the magazine's unchanging character. It also examines the conscious choices made in its structures of representation and their consequences. Donna Haraway comments that following the Spanish–American War, in 1898, the importance of geography for U.S. citizens grew and *National Geographic* articles "stressed the benefits of colonialism, geography, and the commercial possibilities of America's new possessions."[7] She goes on to state that policies initially set by Gilbert Grosvenor have essentially continued into the present time. Echoing this position, Alison Devine Nordstrom's work finds that the magazine has had an "unchanging role as a vehicle for capitalist and imperialist ideology" and maintained a "remarkable consistency of theme, approach and choice of illustrations."[8] And, again, *National Geographic* itself makes the same claim proudly. Looking back at the magazine's one-hundred–year history, an editor-at-large said: "At the end of its first century the magazine remains unmistakably its original self."[9]

Making up that unmistakably original self are the resilient and bonded discourses of Orientalism and primitivism at work in *National Geographic* throughout its history of contact with the Arab world. This book examines those discourses in their popular incarnations as they are taken up by the magazine in its construction of *the* Arab man and *the* Arab woman. Moreover, this study maps gender through an elaboration of the specific roles women play within Orientalism and primitivism. Marianna Torgovnick maintains that "the real secret of the primitive in this century has often been the same secret as always: the primitive can be—has been, will be (?)—whatever Euro-Americans want it to be. It tells us what we want it to tell us."[10] My research examines what it is *National Geographic* wants the primitive—in this case, *the* Arab man and *the* Arab woman as constructed within Orientalism—to be.

My critique of popular Orientalism includes an examination the magazine's masculinist rhetoric, the one-directionality of its cross-cultural contact, its claim of objectivity, and representations that build layers of a West-to-Arab-world hierarchy. And I demonstrate how decontextualizing and emblematizing strategies work to create spectacles and markers of difference. In short, this work on one hundred years of *National Geographic*'s representation of the Arab world deciphers that which we too often do not take to be coded.

When I critique *National Geographic,* I am situating myself as an Arab-American feminist and educator. Gayatri Spivak asserts that "there are many subject positions which one must inhabit; one is not just one thing."[11] Identifying my speaking position as an Arab-American feminist and educator is in itself several positions. It is important to put these subject positions forth from the outset because it is part of a perspective on knowledge and representation crucial to the meaning of my project as a whole, which I discuss in detail in the next chapter. I am declaring my speaking locations because I agree with Russell Ferguson when he points out that "recent critical debate has taught us, systems of discourse are themselves implicated in real social and political relationships of power. Explanations inevitably privilege one set of interests over others, and today few of those engaged in critical work would claim to speak from a neutral or objective place. . . . The most insidious explanations are the ones which see no need to explain themselves."[12] It is without a pretense of speaking from nowhere for everyone, an imaginary place, that I am locating myself for the reader.

During a 1972 conversation that touched on counter-discourse, Giles Deleuze said to Michel Foucault that his work on confined individuals taught us "something absolutely fundamental; the indignity of speaking for others. [And] to appreciate the theoretical fact that only those directly concerned can speak in a practical way on their own behalf."[13] In a broad understanding, counter-discourse includes work that Mary Louise Pratt calls "autoethnography" or "autoethnographic expression," referring to colonized subjects engaging the colonizers through texts constructed "in response to or in dialogue with those metropolitan representations."[14] It is also what bell hooks calls "back talk" or "talking back." In the southern black community where hooks grew up, this "meant speaking as an equal to an authority figure. It meant daring to disagree."[15] And counter-discourse is what Michel Leiris pointed to in the 1950s when, according to James Clifford, he spoke of a situation "in which the 'objects' of observation would begin to *write back* [my emphasis]. The Western gaze would be met and shattered."[16]

In his work on crass French colonial postcards of Algerian women, Malek Alloula says that his project would be unnecessary if there were photographs of "the gaze of the colonized upon the colonizer." It is "in the absence of a confrontation of opposed gazes" that Alloula sees his work as an attempt, "lagging far behind history, to return this immense postcard to its sender."[17] With that wonderful image in mind, I can look at a 1924 *National Geographic* picture of Muslim pilgrims on their way to Mecca and think of my project as an attempt to slap the hand entering from the photograph's left frame and holding open the woman's robe, exposing her breast (Photo 2).

Edward Said points out that the act of representing others "almost always involves violence of some sort to the subject of the representation. . . . Whether you call it spectacular image, or an exotic image, or a scholarly representation . . . [it] inevitably involves some degree of violence, decontextualization, miniaturization, etc." And he argues that the discourse of representation of an inferior other "depends on the silence of this Other."[18] Counter-discourse, autoethnography, talking back, writing back, directing an oppositional gaze, and so on break this silence and resist the violence. This is how and why, as an Arab-American feminist and educator, I approach a century of American popular education about Arabs from *National Geographic.*

PHOTO 2

"Pilgrims Bound for Mecca," January 1924
(Photo: National Geographic Society Image Collection)

My approach to the areas known as the Occident and the Orient is in step with Said's. He argues that the line separating the two "is less a fact of nature than it is a fact of human production" and is "imaginative geography." Said insists that "the Orient and the Occident are facts produced by human beings, and as such must be studied as integral components of the social, and not the divine or natural, world."[19]

Understanding the Occident and the Orient as "imaginative geography" opposes *National Geographic*'s relentless drive to essentialize the relationship between people and place—indeed, to collapse people and place into one natural Arab state of being.

Facing the enormity and complexity of sorting through a century of *National Geographic*'s textual and visual representations of the Arab world, I was once again inspired to the task by Gilbert Grosvenor's words. During the celebration of his fiftieth anniversary with the magazine, Grosvenor was presented with a gold medal carrying his image. Upon receiving it, he said: "Every morning when I look into my mirror . . . I am going to say to my mirror, 'You lie.' Then I shall take this beautiful medal, look at the idealized Grosvenor face on it . . . and chuckle to myself! My descendants happily will not know the difference between fact and fiction."[20]

This book takes a look into that mirror and begins to sort through the fact and fiction of *National Geographic*'s imaginative geography.

1

WHAT WOULD I BE
WITHOUT YOU?

The significance of offering a coherent, alternative interpretation of *National Geographic,* specifically, lies in understanding and treating this kind of mainstream educational material on a serious level of critical engagement. Too often the requirements of rigorous critique practiced in other areas of study, such as literature or film, are not applied to the area of popular educational texts and visual images. As Elizabeth Ellsworth and Mariamne Whatley point out: "Research into the ideological work of educational media has been virtually nonexistent."[1]

Recognizing and analyzing such educational materials, materials that must be redefined in light of their ideological interests and consequences, contributes to work in critical educational theory. Examining *National Geographic* offers a view of the interrelationships among popular education, schooling, mass media, and dominant ideology. These interrelationships are neither haphazard nor new, as is evidenced by this study.

From the outset, it must be made clear that I am not attempting to construct an encyclopedic record of *National Geographic*'s textual and visual representations of Arabs. Such a project would amount to little more than a cumulative index of the sort that the magazine itself produces regularly. Rather, this study should be understood as discourse analysis, with popular Orientalism as its primary concern. Edward Said says, "Orientalism is fundamentally a political doctrine willed over the Orient because the Orient was weaker than the West."[2] This book aims to understand what this political doctrine looked like in its popular configurations; therefore, articles and pictures selected for close attention in this project are those lodged within Orientalist discourse. I am not interested in the possibility of finding a sentence or page or article or picture that could stand as an example of the magazine's representing Arabs outside of Orientalism. I am interested in Orientalism. The portrayal of Arabs that unfolds in this study cannot be erased, softened, or minimized by collecting counter-representations that could be read as complimentary or sensitive to Arabs. Representations do not cancel one another out like a math equation. Therefore, a collection of both so-called positive and negative images of Arabs would not mean that the overall portrayal in *National Geographic* is a balanced one. That is to say, a racist statement is not balanced by also finding a non-racist statement. For example, saying that Arabs are naturally violent is not made less racist by also saying that Arabs are fine coppersmiths.

Additionally, as a feminist researcher, I have read for patriarchal discourse running through and alongside *National Geographic's* popular Orientalism. Again, I did not pursue the possibility of finding examples of non-sexist photographs or text because I am interested in examining patriarchal discourse. If analyzing representations could be reduced to mathematical treatment, then we could determine how many pictures of fully clothed women cancel out one photograph of a bare-breasted woman and read the final numbers to decide whether *National Geographic* was a gender-sensitive journal. But then again, even our math equation would rest first upon finding agreement over interpreting the equivalent value of a picture of a bare-breasted woman.

Just as this book is not concerned with counter-examples, let there be no confusion that, as this study demonstrates, *National Geographic* is positively steeped in Orientalism and patriarchy. Citing exceptions would in no way negate the rule of these discourses. I have determined what is typical in the representation of Arabs, and it is that which I am presenting—not the atypical. How did I establish the typical?

The sheer quantity of a century of material on the Arab world in *National Geographic* makes identifying the typical quite a task. Once the initial sorting was accomplished, texts and photographs that best exemplify designated themes or categories—the most typical of the typical, if you will—were chosen. (These photographs were later sifted again based on practical publishing concerns.) Handling the mass of material produced by the long period of time and wide geographical area that this study covers was made messier by *National Geographic's* particular style. This style is an eclecticism that gathers a diverse range of subjects within one magazine issue and, further, covers a given subject by stringing together a wide range of topics. For example, the contents of typical *National Geographic* magazine issues containing articles examined in each of the four time periods of this study are:

- August 1925—"Waimangu and the Hot-spring of New Zealand"; "Tripolitania, Where Rome Resumes Sway"; "Under Italian Libya's Burning Sun"; "Toilers of the Sky"; "From England to India by Autombile"; and "The MacMillan Arctic Expedition Sails."
- December 1946—"Oregon Finds New Riches"; "Where Rolls the Oregon"; "Syria and Lebanon Taste Freedom"; "Ali Goes to the Clinic"; "Paris Lives Again"; "Mending Dykes in the Netherlands"; and "Fairy Terns of the Atolls."
- January 1966—"Saudi Arabia"; "Stalking Seals under Antarctic Ice"; "Profiles of Presidents: Part V"; "Finding Rare Beauty in Common Rocks"; and "Brazil's Waura Indians."
- May 1988—"Wool: The Fabric of History"; "India's Unpredictable Kerala"; "Supernova—Death of a Star"; "The Persian Gulf: Living in Harm's Way"; and "Fleas: The Lethal Leapers."

Between the covers of one issue, *National Geographic* offers its readers an array of completely unrelated subjects. Clearly, there is no common theme at work in the articles and photographs about Oregon, Arabs, Paris, dikes, and birds collected in a single issue. The magazine's contents are typically a potpourri, with something for everyone. Given this characteristic of the magazine, it is with absolutely no loss of context that articles on Arabs have been extracted from their particular *National Geographic* issues and gathered together here for examination.

Although I organized the book's chapters chronologically, I did not tie myself to a rigid movement through a century of *National Geographic*'s history. Beyond not wanting to produce what Said would call a "mindlessly chronological order,"[3] I gave serious consideration to developing a research design around themes of Orientalism in the manner of Malek Alloula's *The Colonial Harem*. His work on French postcards of Algerian women is arranged according to topics such as Women's Quarters; Couples; Inside the Harem: The Rituals, Song and Dance; and The Figures of the Harem: Dress and Jewelry.

Deciding that the specific needs of this project would not be served by adopting either a straight historical or thematic approach, I chose to combine the two by looking at themes within time periods. So while preserving the tone of different time periods, we can simultaneously hear certain themes echoing through the whole one hundred years. This keeps a sense of the magazine's and the Arab world's histories, but does not mindlessly chain us to it. It allows us to follow the themes of Orientalism and watch them function, rather than chop everything up according to a tedious timetable that would result in great loss of meaning. That settled, the quantity and eclectic material of *National Geographic* made additional demands on the course of research and presentation.

A second layer of eclecticism appears within the articles themselves. Assorted pieces of information are collected and arranged in *National Geographic* articles, with a heavy reliance on abundant subtitles—on average, one subtitle per half-page of text. Each article on the Arab world examined in this study touches on anywhere from half to all, or more, of the following array of topics: food, architecture, markets, landscape, ceremonies, behavior, sanitation, economy, trade, family, political system, history, marriage laws and customs, dress, physical and mental characteristics of the people, manners, crafts, natural resources, animals, religion, tourist facilities and sights, climate, education, and entertainment. Such a string of topics, multiplied hundreds of times, obviously creates a bundle from which to sort and select. (I did put this eclectic store of data to additional use as a source for the chapter titles and subtitles that are quotations from *National Geographic.*) Before describing criteria for my overall selection process, I must first introduce another layer of complexity that influenced the lines of this study.

Further discontinuity or fragmentation is met because *National Geographic*'s visits to Arab countries do not follow any regular patterns. For example, within the period of my study, 1888–1988, the last article on Libya was published in 1944. Among articles on Algeria, two appeared in 1943, but in the 1970s and 1980s there was a lapse of fourteen years between articles. In 1982, there were three trips to Egypt, but none between 1967 and 1977. In 1958, there were three trips to Iraq, but there have been none since 1985. The last article on Syria appeared in 1978. Between 1967 and 1985, there was only one article on what was then the People's Democratic Republic of Southern Yemen. Tunisia was covered four times in 1911, but not at all between 1946 and 1960 and was last visited in 1980. The very first article on Kuwait appeared in 1952, and so on.

Thus, there is no pattern to Arab world coverage in *National Geographic,* which means that this study is also, necessarily, devoid of such a pattern. The magazine does not dole out equal space or treatment to the various Arab countries, nor does it conduct regular visits. This is not surprising, because *National Geographic* is an educational journal covering "the world and all that's in it," not an international airline. But this means that the book does not plot straight courses between time and the countries of the Arab world. True to my object of study, I follow *National Geographic*'s meandering tracks. Because these tracks are an integral part of the magazine's successful formula, one could hardly dismiss or try to work around them.

National Geographic's overall eclecticism, or curio-cabinet style (with its fragmented lineup and content of articles and irregular coverage), combined with my wide research scope (the Arab world over a century) demanded that select themes be discerned and tracked through the whole of this seeming chaos. Some questions I pursued while reading more than 220 *National Geographic* articles, averaging thirty to forty pages each, were: What are common threads? What are typical representations in place over long periods of time? What are *National Geographic*'s symbols for the Arab world? What figures of speech are regularly used? What are the magazine's cultural stereotypes of Arabs? Do Arabs ever participate in the representation of Arabs in *National Geographic?*

The methodological procedures I chose for setting and examining such questions in this book are directly informed by particular projects of Alloula, Ellsworth, Whatley, Catherine Lutz and Jane Collins, Alison Devine Nordstrom, and Said. Of these, I most heavily relied upon Said's works on Orientalism (1979, 1981, 1985, 1990). It is his analysis of Orientalist discourse that theoretically (as I will elaborate in the section on research strategies) and practically informs my project on popular Orientalism in *National Geographic*. I tracked well-known tropes of Orientalism, such as Oriental violence, Oriental sensuality, Oriental excess, and Oriental timelessness. I looked for what Said refers to as "summational statements"—those bits of material used to confirm something about the Orient as a whole.[4] I gave attention to the magazine's representations of Islam, Muslims, and religious fanaticism. I listened for information on "the Arab mind," "the Arab character," and "the Arab personality." I looked for predictable markers of Orientalism, such as harems, angry men, dancers, dirt, jewelry, veils, and daggers. I read for reductiveness and generalizations on the Arab world. I looked for examples that established cultural difference and distance. And I tracked signs of what Alloula calls "cultural belatedness."[5]

Alloula's work in interpreting French picture postcards of Algerian women has been critical to my study of *National Geographic*'s visual representations. In reviewing more than 3,000 pictures and finally selecting those included in this book, I depended on Alloula's interpretive work focusing on Orientalism and gender. Following his example, I examined the photographs for self-conscious attitudes, forced realism, redundant signs of backwardness, pose repetition, women's adornment, expressions of eroticism, "naturalness," ridiculous poses, suggestions of intimacy, trespassing private quarters, and voyeurism.

In addition, I analyzed each picture's "ethnographic alibi"—that is, its avowed purpose and its "rhetoric of camouflage," or caption. Alloula explains that captions carry a disavowal that, paradoxically, work to establish the avowed purpose. Thus, for example, captions to photos of bare-breasted women identify the picture in any number of ways, but never by mentioning the exposed breasts. And like Alloula, I noted the anonymity of the models who, without individual identity, serve to produce a generality.

In addition to Alloula's work on photographs, I depended on Said's book *After the Last Sky,* which contains 120 photographs of Palestinian life taken by Jean Mohr in various locales throughout the Middle East. The photographer, a Swiss man whose work with John Berger had impressed Said, brought back pictures of Palestinians about which Said says: "He saw us as we would have seen ourselves."[6] I agree with Said. More important, Said's critique of Mohr's photographs is an extremely significant statement because it says there is the possibility of overcoming distance and difference, and representing others well—as they see themselves.

I compared and found an enormous gulf between Mohr's pictures of the Arab world and those of *National Geographic* magazine. I have lived in the Middle East and fondly recognize the culture and the people in Said's book, but *National Geographic*'s representation of the Arab world makes me uncomfortable. When I put my visual memories of the Arab world against *National Geographic*'s images, there is dissonance. And when I compare my personal collection of photographs from the Arab world with *National Geographic*'s representations of the Arab world, there is a discrepancy in the overall picture. Since Mohr successfully and sensitively worked across cultures, this difference cannot be attributed to Arab identity or gender identity. When sorting and analyzing *National Geographic* pictures of Arabs, I asked: Have the editors and photographers seen us as we would see ourselves? Have they achieved the level of intimacy with the culture that Mohr did? Could a picture with this meaning be found in my photo album? When *National Geographic*'s pictures of Arabs disturbed me, I asked, Why? And while posing these questions, I was fair to *National Geographic* by consciously trying not to overanalyze the pictures. I attended to the general impression given by a picture, the overall meaning being delivered by it, rather than carve it up and over-read isolated bits of it.

As an Arab-American woman, a twelve-year resident of the Arab world, and someone who knows the language and culture firsthand, my personal biography offered another source for this study. Including my personal background as a source should not be overestimated or underestimated. We have learned from work done in women's studies, African-American studies, gay studies, Native American studies, and so on that one's identity does not contaminate, distort, or weaken research. We know that traditional social-science assertions that researchers from outside a group can best study the group lack a historical understanding of the interplay among identity, interest, and representation. As Joan Acker and Kate Barry remind us, "the assumption that the researcher must and can strive to be a neutral observer standing outside the social realities being studied" has been challenged by feminist critiques of social science which have documented the bias in theory and research previously taken as neutral accounts of society.[7] We recognize that those from outside a group do not, thereby, carry better instruments of research than those inside. No one stands as the objective observer of the rest of us. As Donna Haraway puts it, "that view of infinite vision is an illusion, a god-trick."[8]

Said is an example of scholars who lay out the personal dimension in their work as part of a necessary inventory to compile. He is a researcher set apart from those who would claim the impossible, to speak from objective, innocent locations. Also, Said's perspective is very different from that of those who adopt essentialist positions on identity that produce isolationist research. The difference between these sorts of researchers and Said is that he maintains a methodological self-consciousness that submits to critical scrutiny. Said makes his inventory, knows the instruments and sources he uses, and then maintains a critical consciousness in his work and invites response. By including something of my personal inventory that informs this work, I attempt the same— nothing more, nothing less. And this is done from an understanding of identity that agrees with Haraway's when she says, "Identities seem contradictory, partial, and strategic."[9]

At the same time that I take seriously the need to identify oneself rather than attempt invisibility to serve a claim to objectivity, I am working from a perspective on experience that relies on Joan Scott's analysis. She argues that "experience is at once always already an interpretation and is in need of interpretation. What counts as experience is neither self-evident nor straightforward; it is always contested, always therefore political."[10] This means I am neither privileging my personal background nor essentializing identity. I am simply recognizing my experience as a source, not uncontested evidence, that may lend in rereading *National Geographic*.

In my study I also relied on Ellsworth's[11] work interpreting educational films and Whatley's[12] on textbook photographs. Both women analyze educational material from the understanding that choices made in any given representation are not neutral. Employing methods for ideological analysis used by Ellsworth and Whatley, I engaged text and image in *National Geographic* to tease out patterns by asking: What is included in and what is excluded from this representation? What meanings or ways of knowing are being privileged? How are ideological positions encoded as "natural" ways of looking? How are readers and viewers being encouraged to relate to those being represented; for example, is difference or similarity suggested? What relationship is being set up between the viewer and reader as "self" and those being represented as "other"—for example, one of equality or hierarchy? And what are the assumptions on which the privileged reading depends?

This book's research was also directly informed by the work of Lutz and Collins and of Nordstrom on *National Geographic*. Nordstrom analyzed the representation of Samoans in the magazine and, with only eight articles produced on Samoa in more than one hundred years, she points to the manageability of her case study. At the same time, Nordstrom says that her case study "offers, in microcosm, the same lessons about [*National Geographic*'s] role as would . . . a similar study of a larger country."[13] Nordstrom is right. Her small study does, in fact, correspond to what I saw in my much larger case study on the Arab world. Adopting some of Nordstrom's methods of examination, I looked for change, or the lack of it, in the representations; the technical needs of the photographer modifying an event (particularly in the earlier days of photography when, for example, we find people doing outdoors what they would normally do indoors); a form of comparison being made in terms of Western values; using posed pictorial shots; static images of the same few categories of subject matter; and the process of creating markers by using certain images repeatedly.

Lutz and Collins have produced a detailed study of the National Geographic Society that includes a store of information on the whole process of choosing and presenting subjects in the magazine. Their inside view of *National Geographic*'s structure and dynamics helped to explain and confirm some of my findings on the representation of Arabs. The two authors follow the magazine's step-by-step procedure for putting an article together (text, images, and captions) and give a useful overview of the magazine's coverage of the Third World since the 1950s.[14]

Together, the research methods of Said's work deconstructing Orientalist discourse; Alloula's study of Orientalist and colonialist visual images of Arab women; Ellsworth's and Whatley's ideological analyses of educational film media and textbooks, respectively; Nordstrom's case study on Samoa in *National Geographic;* and Lutz and Collins's broad study of the National Geographic Society offered me a wide range of procedures needed for a study that overlaps all of these areas of research. I will further frame that research by giving some general background and context to *National Geographic* pertinent to the specifics of my project and, following this, discuss my overarching research strategies.

A SKETCH OF THE OBJECT OF STUDY

The National Geographic Society was formed in Washington, D.C., on January 13, 1888; Gardiner G. Hubbard became its first president. In January 1898, following Hubbard's death, his son-in-law Alexander Graham Bell took over the presidency. With the society in debt and with insufficient subscriptions to its magazine, Bell decided that the organization could not possibly succeed unless it hired a full-time, salaried assistant editor. In April 1899, Gilbert H. Grosvenor—who married Alexander Graham Bell's daughter Elsie the following year—became assistant editor of *National Geographic* and editor in 1903, a position he retained until 1955. His son, Melville Bell Grosvenor, became editor in 1957, while the senior Grosvenor remained highly connected to the society, serving as chairman of the Board of Trustees until his death in 1966. In 1970, another generation of the Grosvenor family took over the editor's desk, with Gilbert M. Grosvenor taking the helm until 1980, at which time he became president of the National Geographic Society and chairman of the board, positions he held beyond Wilbur Garrett's tenure as editor from 1980 to 1990.

The Grosvenor family—Gilbert H. Grosvenor, in particular—has shaped *National Geographic* magazine throughout its history. In 1914, G. H. Grosvenor set down *National Geographic*'s "Guiding Principles," which remain in place. The very principles said to guide the magazine are those against which *National Geographic* will be measured in this book. We will see how well the magazine lives up to its self-representation by using the following guiding principles as a backdrop to reading and viewing the magazine's representation of the Arab world (the italics are mine):

1. The First principle is *absolute accuracy.* Nothing must be printed which is not *strictly according to fact.* The Magazine can point to many years in which not a single article has appeared which was not *absolutely accurate.*
2. Abundance of *beautiful, instructive, and artistic* illustrations.
3. Everything printed in The Magazine must have *permanent value,* and so be planned that each Magazine will be as valuable and pertinent one year or five or ten years after publication as it is on the day of publication. The result of this principle is that tens of thousands of back numbers of The Magazine are *continually used in school rooms.*

4. All personalities and notes of a *trivial* character are avoided.
5. Nothing of a *partisan* or *controversial* character is printed.
6. Only what is of a kindly nature is printed about any country or people, everything *unpleasant or unduly critical* being avoided.
7. The content of each number is planned with a view of being *timely*. Whenever any part of the world becomes prominent in public interest, by reason of war, earthquake, volcanic eruption, etc., the members of the National Geographic Society have come to know that in the next issue of their Magazine they will obtain the latest geographic, historical, and economic information about that region, presented in an *interesting and absolutely non-partisan* manner, and accompanied by photographs which in number and excellence can be equaled by no other publication.[15]

These were the stated principles to be upheld by all involved with the magazine, but in practice they were not self-evident. *National Geographic* readers learned that Gilbert H. Grosvenor was a "strong-minded editor ... [and] he reserved the right to decide what was controversial and what was not." Additionally, principle number six "had a certain built-in elasticity, and the Editor determined the amount of stretch. There was never any doubt about that."[16] Thus, it is clear from *National Geographic* itself that these seven principles were a matter of interpretation. My research examines the magazine's understanding of "absolute accuracy," "beautiful and instructive illustrations," "fact," and "non-partisan" information by tracking these claims along winding routes through the pages on the Arab world. Even though Gilbert H. Grosvenor said he wanted the text in *National Geographic* to be made "so simple that a child of ten can understand it," a critical reading of the text is not so simple.[17]

The magazine described Gilbert H. Grosvenor as a "strong-minded editor" who had the last word on interpreting the seven principles while, at the same time, *National Geographic* insisted on its reputation as an objective, educational journal offering totally factual material to its readers. Readers were informed that both text and photography were "verified—double- and triple-checked by a research staff second to none."[18] And the magazine's rigorous verification standards meant "each statement to be published in the *National Geographic* Magazine must pass the test of thorough research. If it doesn't, out it goes." Readers were told that when they received their copy of the magazine, "just about every word bears an invisible check mark." The magazine described itself as a "lasting reference work in thousands of libraries, in millions of homes." So accurate is its information that: "Over the years, the *Geographic*'s research has changed books, museum labels, even plaques on historic buildings."[19] And twice, in August 1949 and November 1958, *National Geographic* quoted for its readers the words of a South Dakota governor who said: "Wherever it circulates, it has become a part of family life and education. 'I saw it in *The Geographic*' carries practically conclusive and absolute confirmation."[20]

National Geographic also shared with readers examples of how the magazine served its varied audience. When a housewife's life seems "dull, walled in by monotonous repetitions," she goes "traveling" by reading *National Geographic*. A father wrote in that the magazine gave him "adventure and business perspective." A mother said that she used the magazine for her women's club and that her children used it for school assignments. Another reader reported that the magazine helped him "to interpret world news." In sum, editor Gilbert Grosvenor declared: "For 'armchair traveling' there is no substitute for *The Geographic*"[21] and that

> Nowhere in the world is there another magazine exactly like the *National Geographic*. . . . Its purpose is and always has been to promote science and education, and it educates in the most effective way by portraying this thrilling world and its life in clear, vivid, comprehensible manner, stripped of dull, technical verbiage, and mirrored in many striking pictures.[22]

National Geographic pointed to itself as having something for everyone—a source for doing school assignments, interpreting world news, armchair traveling—and educating through vivid language and mirrored images. These claims were tied to presenting the magazine as an objective, factual transmitter of information, and require us to think of language and visual images as neutral and undistorted reflections of reality.

But from the outset, this description of the magazine becomes problematic if we try to square it with the typical composition of *National Geographic*'s Board of Trustees. For example, in October 1966, upon the death of Gilbert H. Grosvenor, *National Geographic* published a tribute to him that included a photograph and roll of his board colleagues. During the mid-1960s, in addition to four men from the society itself, the members of *National Geographic*'s Board of Trustees were:

Chief of Staff, U.S. Air Force
Vice Admiral, U.S. Navy, Ret.

Deputy Administrator of NASA
Rear Admiral, U.S. Coast and Geodetic Survey, Ret.
Former Assistant Secretary of the Navy for Research and Development
Chairman, Board of Governors, Federal Reserve System
Former Director, National Park Service
Chief Justice of the United States
Research Associate, Smithsonian Institution
Editorial Chairman, *Washington Star*
Director, Folger Shakespeare Library
President, Carnegie Institution of Washington
Chairman of the Board, Rockefeller Brothers, Inc.
Chairman of the Board, E.I. duPont de Nemours & Company
Honorary Board Chairman, Chesapeake & Potomac Telephone Co.
Vice-President, American Telephone & Telegraph Co., Ret.
Advisory Chairman of the Board of Riggs National Bank
Chairman of the Board, Pan American World Airways[23]

This reads like most any year's Board of Trustees in that, as Lutz and Collins have also noted, big business, military branches, and government were regularly represented.[24] Instead of 1966, I could just as well have chosen to introduce a board from 1926, 1936, 1946, 1956, 1976, or 1986 and produced a membership list with only minor variations. I found the 1966 board especially telling in its composition because the 1960s saw the Vietnam war and were a time of mass social movements in the United States. Other boards boasted a membership of important national personalities that included, for example, U.S. Vice-President Charles Gates Dawes in 1926 and Mrs. Lyndon B. Johnson, former First Lady of the United States, in 1976. How can an institution with a Board of Trustees made up of members directly linked to the offices and interests of dominant groups in industry and government produce "absolutely correct" and "absolutely non-partisan" information, as claimed in the guiding principles?

National Geographic took special pride in its connections to the highest offices in the United States, to Britain, and to Christianity. This was communicated, for example, by informing readers that during Gilbert Grosvenor's editorial tenure (more than a half-century), twelve U.S. presidents "honored the Society by presiding over its functions, supporting its causes, or presenting its medals. Six contributed articles to the magazine."[25] And in 1964, reporting on U.S. President Lyndon B. Johnson's dedication speech for the new headquarters of the National Geographic Society in Washington, D.C., the magazine quoted the president's suggestion that *National Geographic* should, "in this land and around the world, serve as a clearing-house for knowledge."[26]

Similarly, clear military and government links were relayed during the 1960s through articles such as "The FBI, Public Friend Number One," which included a friendly interview with the director of the Federal Bureau of Investigation, J. Edgar Hoover, and "U.S. Air Force: Power for Peace," written by General Curtis LeMay, chief of staff of the United States Air Force. (LeMay was also a *National Geographic* board member for more than twenty-five years.) In 1965, "Of Planes and Men: U.S. Air Force Wages Cold War and Hot," written by the *National Geographic* senior staff member Kenneth Weaver, focused on the role of the Air Force in the Vietnam war and concluded with the words: "And an airman put it in the simplest of terms: 'I feel like I'm promoting Uncle Sam.' You may call it what you will, but it adds up to patriotism."[27]

Regarding Britain, *National Geographic* readers learned in a 1966 tribute to Gilbert Grosvenor that "always patriotic, Dr. Grosvenor also believed strongly in the importance of our British heritage and unity of purpose among the free peoples of the English-speaking world."[28] In 1918, Grosevenor wrote: "I intend to use the *Geographic Magazine* to the best of my ability to promote a better understanding between Great Britain and the United States." And to that end, Grosvenor was said to have "labored with special care and pride" over the April 1949 single-subject issue of *National Geographic* "devoted wholly to 'The British Way,' recounting the British Isles' great gifts to mankind." It was reported to readers that he chose "every picture and personally edited every word" to the piece he had been planning for five years.[29]

The magazine's Christian thread was also clear in its 1966 tribute to Grosvenor. The man who "charted the dynamic course . . . followed for more than half a century" by *National Geographic* was described as "a devout and lifelong Christian." The tribute recalled Grosvenor's love of birds and remarked: "It must make the Almighty especially happy when people appreciate His world so much."[30] The magazine's Christian tie was also communicated by Melville Grosvenor, editor from 1957 to 1970, who told *National Geographic* readers that while visiting Jerusalem in 1967, he was inspired to have the Society produce a book that would re-create biblical times for them. Melville Grosvenor declared that ever since his boyhood, his imagination had been fired by Paul, and that when walking in his birthplace he could feel Paul's presence. He said this feeling was one that he hoped others could share by way of the book, *Everyday Life in Bible Times,* which included "thirty-six Biblical scenes specially commissioned by *National Geographic*." Further, readers learned that the book had been printed by presses working "a Biblical 40 days and 40 nights to produce 400,000 copies of *Everyday Life in Bible Times*—largest single book printing in the Society's 79 years."[31]

This kind of information about *National Geographic* helps to contextualize and interpret how the magazine represents the Arab world. In fact, if for no other reason than that *National Geographic* often communicates these connections to its readers, a critical analysis of the magazine cannot minimize or ignore them. We should take the magazine's connections as seriously as it does. *National Geographic* identified itself as an educational journal following the seven guiding principles mentioned earlier and, at the same time, publicized particular associations by way of introducing readers to its Board of Trustees, by advertising and publishing with a Christian focus, and by producing articles by and about people and places high in government and military offices. This was a strategy to legitimate what appeared in *National Geographic*.

However, a critical approach reads implication and vested interest instead of validation. Claims of non-partisan, objective, mirror reflections of the world run thin with a resistant reading that tracks, juxtaposes, and interrogates text and image. And a critical reading works with a memory: When I read about the Arab world, I remember *National Geographic*'s associations. It is faulty research that forgets or does not account for the context within which its subject is located—a context that *National Geographic* itself presents. This is information that the magazine wants readers to know for its own agenda, but how one understands and employs it cannot be finally determined by the magazine.

POPULAR ORIENTALISM

Speaking about Orientalism, Said's landmark study on the West's construction of the East says:

> Taking the late eighteenth century as a very roughly defined starting point Orientalism can be discussed and analyzed as the corporate institution for dealing with the Orient—dealing with it by making statements about it, authorizing views of it, describing it, by teaching it, settling it, ruling over it: in short, Orientalism as a Western style for dominating, restructuring, and having authority over the Orient.[32]

It is the discourse of Orientalism that I was reading for in *National Geographic*—looking at how it was delivered through this popular educational–cultural vehicle.

I tracked Orientalism in its popular incarnations through the textual and visual tropes signifying Arab women, Arab men, Arab culture, and Islam. What James Clifford refers to as a "process of representational essentializing . . . in which one part or aspect of peoples' lives come to epitomize them as a whole" was followed decade after decade in the magazine's representation of the Arab world.[33] (An example of this emblematizing process is the role of the veil in an Orientalist representation of women.) Further, structures employed by popular Orientalism such as oppositions of East/West and Muslim/Christian, and using the West as the standard measure against which the Arab world is compared, were collected and examined.

Uncovering popular Orientalism in *National Geographic* also entailed reading for what Said points to as the canonical authority of the discourse—that is, this study examines the "sense of self-sufficient, self-correcting, self-endorsing power [that] gave and still gives Orientalism its remarkably un-self-conscious rhetoric."[34] In relation to this, the assumption that "no Oriental can know himself the way an Orientalist can" is recognized in the patronizing treatment of the Arab people that can be identified and followed over a century of *National Geographic*'s history.

In this study I also read for the depersonalization of the Arab people established through a rhetorical device that both Albert Memmi and Mary Louise Pratt point out. Pratt speaks of the "initial ethnographic gesture"[35] that turns a people into a collective "they," and Memmi refers to "an anonymous collectivity"[37] produced by an abstracted "they." I read for this depersonalization, which often melts down to the single prototype: *the* Arab, *the* Arab mind, *the* Arab personality, *the* Arab woman. This systematic reading for popular Orientalism also exposes the long and unaltered history of male-dominant discourse in *National Geographic* magazine.

FEMINIST CRITIQUE OF ORIENTALISM AND *NATIONAL GEOGRAPHIC*

Because of *National Geographic*'s male-dominant character in terms of its institutional history and its gendered perspective of the world, and because Orientalism and the Orient have been so feminized, this study inherently calls for a feminist critique. Earlier, I discussed the ways in which my critique understands issues of identity, neutral perspectives, and innocent research. A feminist critique brings additional approaches and sensibilities to a study. In a way, using feminist criticism means that certain antennae are out when I look at *National Geographic* magazine and listen for Orientalist discourse.

Myra Jehlen describes feminist critique as "rethinking, an examination of the way certain assumptions about women and the female character enter into the fundamental assumptions that organize all our thinking."[37] Feminist criticism, understanding gender as a social–historical concept, explores and engages male-dominant systems of representations. And as Acker and Barry explain, feminist critique is "understanding gender as central in constructing all social relations." Among the principles of feminist research they identify are producing knowledge that women can use and continually developing a critical perspective that questions dominant intellectual traditions.[38] A feminist critique of *National Geographic* means analyzing its treatment of gender, revealing its patriarchal stance, and generating alternative readings of the magazine.

Gillian Rose's analysis of the academic discipline of geography also helps to develop a feminist critique of *National Geographic*. She contends that the discipline "has historically been dominated by men, perhaps more so than any other human science," and that this has had "serious consequences both for what counts as legitimate geographical knowledge and who can produce such knowledge."[39] Rose states that "geography is masculinist" and explains that "masculinist work claims to be exhaustive and it therefore assumes that no-one else can add to its knowledge; it is therefore reluctant to listen to anyone else." To explore what Rose calls "the gender of geography" in *National Geographic* magazine, we can draw on feminist conceptions about the "connections between masculinity, men, knowledge and power."[40]

The cover illustration of Rose's book *Feminism and Geography* is a meaningful picture of a photograph (untitled) by Barbara Kruger. It shows a head shot of a woman lying on grass with leaves covering her eyes. On the photograph are the words, "We won't play nature to your culture." This feminist critique of culture and nature and the construction of gender is one that informs my study. *National Geographic* frequently represents the Arab world in ways that naturalize what is clearly cultural. "Woman becomes Nature, Nature becomes Woman, and both can thus be burdened with men's meaning and invite interpretation by masculinist discourse," contends Rose. At the same time, she makes it clear that the "'naturalization' of some women is asserted more directly than that of others."[41] Rose also points out that "gender is not the only discourse through which geographers' claims to power and knowledge are mediated. Race, class, and sexuality are also central."[42] A feminist understanding of these connections and strategies can identify them in a popular geography magazine's representation of the Arab world.

I also bring a feminist approach to my critique of Orientalism in *National Geographic,* producing parallel lines of research. Anne McClintock argues that, in the colonial image, "the Orient was feminized in a number of ways: as mother, evil seducer, licentious aberration, life-giver."[44] A feminist critique of the representational process creating the Orient and Orientals reads for the construction of gender and hierarchies of male dominance. The distinctly different roles served by Arab men and Arab women in Orientalist discourse are unearthed and charted throughout the historical representation of Arabs in *National Geographic*. Combining feminist criticism and a critique of Orientalism means simultaneously unpacking gender, race, and national identity in *National Geographic*.

Along with gender, other social–historical concepts unfold in a critical reading of *National Geographic*'s Arab man and Arab woman. The binary oppositions at work in Western thought, such as man/woman, white/non-white, and Western/non-Western, all run through *National Geographic*'s system of representation. They are analyzed separately and as they interact to socially produce the Arab world in American popular education. Julia Clancy-Smith says that when colonial military domination was completed and civilian rule and moral subjugation put in place in Algeria, "the status of Muslim women became increasingly significant for judging the culturally different, subordinate other." She argues that dominant colonial discourse constructing "an active, masculine, seditious Islam" was "accompanied by a parallel discourse" about the oppression of women due to Islamic rules and customs. Establishing colonialism was as much the forging of a "spectrum of gazes fixed upon Muslim women as it was the assembling of mechanisms for political and economic control."[44] Clancy-Smith continues, in sum, that colonized Arab women became "the measure of all things . . . hidden and concealed yet on display."[45] Clearly, the subject of this book—the representation of the Arab world in *National Geographic* magazine—demands a feminist critique.

According to Yael Simpson Fletcher, "the widespread use of gendered rhetoric and images was crucial for the process of constructing difference between 'us' and 'them' and for naturalizing the colonial relationship."[46] Within this process occurred the eroticization of Arab women for Europeans, in which "representations of women played a crucial role in orientalizing" the Arab world, Fletcher says. "The veiled woman was thought to be ignorant, illiterate, and oppressed, and her image functioned as a marker of Muslim cultural inferiority." At the same time, says Fletcher, "in the male European imagination," the veiled woman also expressed "sexual availability in private, in the harem."[47] And both Clancy-Smith and Fletcher point out that within the discourse constructing the colonial relationship, gendered representations resulted in the feminization of the Arab world and the masculinization of Europe. This gendered rhetoric is something that a feminist critique can identify and analyze.

CULTURAL CRITICISM

One of the definitions of cultural studies, according to Patrick Brantlinger, is: "The exploration of the social production and circulation of meanings—that is, of culture."[48] John Fiske offers an almost identical definition: "Cultural studies is concerned with the generation and circulation of meanings in industrial societies."[49] Brantlinger argues, echoing Said's understanding of the "oppositional critic," that a major task of cultural criticism analyzes and alters the dominant culture's misrepresentation of others.

Social institutions such as the media, the educational system, organized religion, and the family present themselves as neutral, fair, and autonomous. Cultural criticism is concerned with understanding ideological foundations, practices, and relationships at work in sites and vehicles involved in the social production of reality. Mimi White explains that alternative readings—variously referred to as subversive readings, sub-cultural readings, and reading against the grain—emphasize a marginal position and turn a medium on its head.[50] This allows for its deconstruction (uncovering underlying assumptions) and the possibility of alternative thinking about that which was taken for granted or understood as a reliable reflection of reality.

My research in tracking, collecting, and coding consistent patterns and signs through a century of *National Geographic*'s travels to the Arab world is done from a perspective aligned with current critical thought, which understands knowledge as socially produced. Therefore, nothing is recognized as natural about the classifications and categories used by the magazine in its construction of the Arab as other; these classifications and categories are deliberate choices and inventions. Trinh T. Minh-Ha maintains that "the theorization of racial and sexual otherness has become not only recognized and accepted as a legitimate area of investigation; it is occupying a central position within the renewed terrain of cultural critique."[51] In addition, she argues that critical practice must not be reduced to "a matter of evaluation and judgment or, of declaring what is not right in the state of things." Rather, its importance lies in "its potential to set into relief the frame of thought within which operate the practices we accept."[52]

Trinh's position on the task of cultural criticism is shared by Chris Weedon, Robert Stam, Homi Bhabha, Stephen Greenblatt, Bill Nichols, Mimi White, and others. They all agree that, although useful, early work on representation that focused on identifying images as negative or positive does not take us far enough. It is reductionist and methodologically inadequate to understanding a system of representation.[53] Weedon points out that "feminist analysis of the representation of gender in texts has developed from these initial descriptive analyses of images of women to attempts to theorize the ways in which gender is constructed within texts and how representations of gender exercise power over readers."[54]

An example of this wider critique is Greenblatt's examination of the representations that Europeans of the late Middle Ages and early-modern period gave to non-European peoples whose possessions were being "discovered" and taken. My project proceeds as did Greenblatt's. He describes his project as "looking attentively" at the nature of representational practices rather than distinguishing between true and false images, notwithstanding the fact that he sees the authors of the travel accounts he is analyzing as "frequent and cunning liars."[55] This is the same sort of reading that Bhabha applies to colonialist discourse; it is aimed at "an understanding of the processes of subjectification made possible through stereotypical discourse," rather than putting its representations to "a normalising judgment."[56]

Similarly, White says that ideological criticism is not about finding the truth "beneath" or "behind" a text; rather, it is about understanding how a given system of representation "offers us a way of knowing or experiencing the world."[57] And Nichols explains that ideological criticism puts representations into conceptual frames that move us "away from factual accuracy to an entirely different level of engagement."[58] Finally, Trinh says: "Knowledge (a certain knowledge) cannot merely be rejected (in a contaminated world where every gesture reverberates endlessly on others). But it has to be exceeded."[59]

Thus, *National Geographic*'s system of representation is examined not for so-called positive or negative images of Arabs, but for the meanings its representations have in the construction of the Arab. My research, like Alloula's on the colonial representations of Algerian women, "map[s] out, from under the plethora of images, the obsessive scheme that regulates the totality . . . of this enterprise and endows it with meaning."[60] My critique of *National Geographic* analyzes one hundred years of a very large, diverse, and at times contradictory collection of signs standing for the Arab world.

The understanding of critical practice that shaped this project also determined that researching the treatment of Arabs in *National Geographic* not be based on comparing their portrayal with that of any other group in the magazine. The discussion concerning the inadequacy of studies identifying representations as negative or positive also applies to setting up comparisons: There is no meaning to be drawn from finding people who are represented "better" or "worse" than Arabs. This research documents the case of Arabs, which stands on its own and tells us much about the magazine's structure of representation, underlying assumptions, associations, and ideological interests.

Moreover, as Lata Mani cautions analysts of colonial discourse, we must adequately localize concepts rather than simply export and extend them, and we must avoid eliding historical and current differences in systems and relationships.[61] A serious loss of specificity would result if this research threw together various areas of the world represented in *National Geographic* for comparative analysis. Further, signs are erased or confused when a word or image is tracked by appearance as the same thing through the varied contexts holding for different peoples—that is, meaning is emptied when context is ignored. This is not to say that signs are never located across contexts, but different historical and social conditions and relationships must be taken into full account. Judith Williamson wrote: "A sign is quite simply a thing—whether object, word, or picture—which has a particular meaning to a person or group of people. It is neither the thing nor the meaning alone, but the two together."[62] Therefore, a sign in *National Geographic* has to be understood as consisting of both the signifier (the material object) and the signified (its meaning).

Not only must we be careful not to confuse signifiers with signs; we must also, according to Nichols, learn "to see signs where there appears to be only natural and obvious meaning." He explains that conceiving language semiotically, "as including all forms of communication based upon signs, whether they are words, clothes, gestures, or moving pictures," means that all human activity involving communication and exchange produces meaning. Elements of this production in the dominant group's interests are ideological elements. From here, the task of "identify[ing] these ideological elements, to discover the aspects of representation that embody them," is carried out against "a way of seeing invested with meanings that naturalize themselves as timeless, objective, obvious." Doing this requires an "act of interpretation" that can be from one or more points of view.[63] My research in identifying and interpreting signs in *National Geographic* that produce the Arab world in American popular education relies on adopting the critical reading perspectives of feminist and cultural criticism.

As discussed, the signs interpreted in this research include both words and images, but these are not neatly separated. In any sign system, there is play between signifiers that must be mapped, including play between words and images. This demands not only that we give attention to pictures, but that we interpret them with their related words in the body of the text and in captions that direct our viewing. Given the role of photography in *National Geographic,* examining visual images representing Arabs is crucial to critiquing the magazine.

CRITIQUING VISUAL REPRESENTATIONS

With three pages of pictures to every page of text, photographs have long been the hallmark of *National Geographic.* The significance of the magazine's "extraordinary pictorial records" was pointed out to its readership in a 1936 article by Gilbert H. Grosvenor, in which the editor reviews the magazine's history, goals, principles, and successes:

> Even more important than their esthetic appeal is the educational, scientific, and historical value of THE GEOGRAPHIC'S [*sic*] pictures, which contribute not only to current information but also to man's accumulated store of knowledge. For historians, ethnologists, and scientists of future generations, The Society's rich album. . . will constitute a priceless, not-to-be-duplicated record, authentic in proportion and tint, of the dress, scenery, architecture and daily life of the civilized nations and isolated tribal communities of the present age.[64]

Clearly, I must take visual representations as seriously as *National Geographic* does. And one must not evaluate these visual representations using purely technical or artistic criteria, which is how they are usually regarded. The pictures produce meaning and must be read that way. For example, in the *National Geographic Index, 1888–1988,* we read that with the early success of photographs in the magazine—they had become a basic feature by 1907—it was decided that *National Geographic* could not only adapt the pictures to the text, but adapt "the text to the pictures." It was understood that "the photograph could be turned into a narrative device that was, for journalistic purposes, more dramatic, more enticing, and more interesting than words."[65] However, concerning its overall use of photography, *National Geographic* represents itself as "a window on the world."[66] These conflicting statements—to be at once manipulating pictures and texts, and acting as a transparent window on reality—are examined against the actual body of photographs of the Arab world.

The claim that photographs are like windows is a fundamentally important one that often passes by us because, as Roland Barthes argues, "a photograph is always invisible: it is not it that we see. In short, the referent adheres."[67] Nichols explains that this sort of error—mistaking the image for its referent—

is "explicitly invited" by certain types of representations, such as documentaries. Although we do not "mistake a menu for a meal or a map for a territory,"[68] we do confuse the photographic image in *National Geographic* with its referent. The magazine explicitly invites us to do so when it describes itself as educational and as a "window on the world."

Along these same lines, Susanne Kappeler argues that "the aim of realism [in forms of representation] is to obliterate our awareness of the medium and its conventions and to make us take what is represented for a reflection of a natural reality." This is precisely what *National Geographic* intends when it declares that its purpose is to educate by portraying the world "mirrored in many striking pictures" and by presenting people in their "natural state." Critically examining the magazine's photographs of the Arab world entails asking questions about "who is holding the mirror, for whose benefit, and from what angle."[69]

Susan Sontag explains that while a painting or a prose description is always understood as an interpretation, a photograph can be treated as a transparency, even though it is "as much an interpretation of the world as paintings and drawings are." Unlike handmade visual representations such as drawings, she continues, photographs seem to be "miniatures of reality"; they "furnish evidence" and pass for "incontrovertible proof."[70] Analyzing *National Geographic* means understanding its images to be in need of interpretation. They are signs that communicate, and they represent concepts; they are not windows or mirrors. As Ellen Seiter points out, the often-used phrase "The camera never lies" tells a lot about how we understand—or misunderstand—the photographic image.[71]

My critical analysis of the photographs in *National Geographic* deals with the systematic representation of Arabs and does not treat each photograph as a singular case. Kappeler speaks to this approach in her feminist critique of pornography, explaining that attempts to construct "an argument of 'counter-examples,'" or tokenism, rely on particularizing, and are therefore unable to undertake an analysis recognizing structures in the typical.[72] My study interprets what I have determined to be the typical after examining thousands of pictures. This is an approach that allows us to map *National Geographic*'s underlying assumptions, to identify stereotypes, and to discern the links between text and visual image in its construction of the Arab world. In addition, this approach is important because, as Keith McElroy points out, geographic and ethnographic photography have yet to be systematically treated by historians of photography, although they are able to come "closest to revealing the essence" of a period and have played a significant role in the education of the masses.[73]

In Rene Magritte's painting *The Treachery of Images,* the words "This is not a pipe" appear beneath the pictorial image of a pipe. Magritte is pointing out that the image of something should not be confused with the tangible thing. Suzi Gablik explains this wonderfully by citing a Zen proverb: "You can point out the moon with your finger . . . but you must be careful not to mistake the finger for the moon."[74]

Representations stand for a thing but do not, in fact, have to resemble the thing itself. Anything can be used to represent anything else and worked into our coded systems of recognition. Gablik highlights this telling us, "To a complaint that his portrait of Gertrude Stein did not look like her, Picasso is said to have answered: 'No matter, it will.'"[75] Understanding that there is a world of difference between being and representing is central to reading and viewing *National Geographic*'s representations of the Arab world. Thinking of Magritte's painting, I might represent my study as writing across the pictures of Arabs produced by *National Geographic* the words: "This is not an Arab."

2

"THE ARAB IS AN ANACHRONISM"

NATIONAL GEOGRAPHIC, 1888 THROUGH THE 1920s

This first period, 1888–1920s, was the height of European empires and when Ottoman rule of the Arab world was challenged and displaced by Western colonialism. In 1800, Western powers held about 35 percent of the Earth's surface; by 1878, that proportion had risen to 67 percent; and by 1914, Europe held 85 percent of the Earth within various kinds of colonial relationships.[1] European scientific and technological advances were such that certain Western European countries became dominant military powers in the world, against which the Ottomans were no match. In this period, European expansion in search of resources, markets, and colonies culminated in the French and the English having developed the two greatest colonial systems in the world. Arabs witnessed and experienced this changing international balance of power firsthand.

In the nineteenth century, France completed the first major European conquest of an Arabic-speaking country, Algeria (1830–1847). In 1839, Britain occupied Aden, and in due course Egypt, Sudan, Tunisia, Morocco, and Libya fell under European domination. By the end of World War I, the Ottoman Empire was completely destroyed, and, except for parts of the Arabian Peninsula, the whole of the Arabic-speaking world (including Syria, Lebanon, Palestine, Iraq, and Transjordan) was divided among European powers, primarily England and France. The political structure under which most Arabs had lived for four centuries, the Ottoman Empire, came to an end, and European colonial systems were entrenched in all areas of life. Arab commerce, finance, raw materials, agricultural production, schooling, government, import and export markets, and more were in the hands of Europeans.

National Geographic's most recent portrayal of this historical period will usher us into an examination of the Arab world in the magazine's first thirty years. In January 1987, as it entered its one-hundredth year, and again in January 1988, in its anniversary issue, *National Geographic* shared with readers its reflections on the magazine's history and a description of the late nineteenth century, the era during which it was founded. Looking back a century, *National Geographic* sees a time "of action, and the relevant word was conquer—be it wilderness, disease, paganism, or ignorance."[2] This understanding of colonialism, what I refer to as the good-works theme, is one we shall encounter repeatedly. We will see how its various components are identified, employed, and "conquered." The heroes of the late nineteenth century are said to have been "daring explorers" who matched the industrial tycoons of the day "in initiative, and in go-getter spirit."[3] The magazine says of that historical period:

> The formation of societies like the National Geographic Society was just one expression of the demand for progress through organization and efficiency spawned by the experience of handling large numbers of men and machines during the Civil War. Indeed, the individual explorers became heroes, because they stood out as individuals— exotic examples of a new "can do" mentality that overtook Americans in the decades after the Civil War. As symbols, they represented those Darwinian, survival-of-the-fittest emerging "captains of industry."[4]

This period of "heroic exploration," or colonialism, is portrayed in the 1980s by *National Geographic* as having been a generally high-spirited, positive time. Against this interpretation we go back in time and examine "heroes," "the demand for progress," and social Darwinism at work.

But before we enter that era, another quotation from *National Geographic* in the 1980s further sets the historical scene:

> The youthful United States was coming of age—going through a sort of national puberty and maturing as a world force. . . . Missionaries and businessmen were scattering into Asia and Latin America. Our explorers were competing with Europeans to reach far recesses of the

world. . . . With equal vigor inventors and entrepreneurs were grabbing for shares in the industrial revolution. . . . Hand in glove with this ferment was the growth of national research and exploration societies.[5]

Characterizing becoming a world force during the era of colonialism as going through puberty presents that particular historical system of appropriation and exploitation as natural and as growth from boy to man (this gendering operation is a favorite that we encounter often in the magazine). Here, national puberty is marked along a masculinist growth chart, and the activities of American and European missionaries, explorers, and businessmen "in the far recesses of the world" are framed as manly competition. Made completely invisible in all of this, because of the particular interests being supported, are the peoples of those "far recesses," which allows *National Geographic* to offer readers a rather clean, nostalgic look back at the heroic era of colonialism.

THE MIDWAY

National Geographic's description of the heyday of colonialism, given in the late 1980s, speaks to a connection to, and pride in, the activities associated with America's so-called coming of age. This perspective was shared by other research and exploration organizations that developed at the same time as the National Geographic Society. In her examination of the American Museum of Natural History, Donna Haraway says that the museum's popular activities in the early 1900s were like those of *National Geographic* in that they "taught republican Americans their responsibilities in empire after 1888."[6] She notes that, in addition to dioramas exhibiting animals, the museum constructed "a Hall of the Age of Man to make the moral lessons of racial hierarchy and progress explicit, lest they be missed in gazing at elephants."[7] Agreeing with Philip Pauly, Haraway says that *National Geographic* "was, and is, a first cousin to the natural history diorama."[8]

In fact, the family tree has another branch: *National Geographic* is a close cousin to the world's fairs that also promoted the United States' world expansion. Curtis Hinsley describes the world's fairs as "carnivals of the industrial age . . . undergirded and directed by corporate boards and interests of state."[9] As mentioned earlier, *National Geographic* also boasts solid connections to business and government. Robert Rydell asserts that the fairs "performed a hegemonic function precisely because they propagated the ideas and values of the country's political, financial, corporate, and intellectual leaders and offered these ideas as the proper interpretation of social and political reality."[10] This assertion can be made about the role of *National Geographic,* in addition to other shared ground.

World's fairs, for example, were understood and promoted as a combination of entertainment and education. The Chicago World's Columbian Exposition of 1893 had a Department of Ethnology and Archeology headed by Frank Ward Putnam and Franz Boas, two major figures in the area of anthropology.[11] Under the auspices of this prestigious department was the midway, which, according to the *Chicago Tribune,* "afforded the American people an unequaled opportunity to compare themselves scientifically with others."[12] Through its human exhibits, the midway provided scientific sanction for the view of the non-white world as barbaric; introduced fairgoers to evolutionary ideas of race; and was the place where "evolution, ethnology, and popular amusements interlocked."[13]

The Louisiana Purchase Exposition in Saint Louis in 1904 was said by *Harper's Magazine* to leave visitors "full of pictures and of knowledge that keep coming up in his mind for years afterwards. It gives him new standards, new means of comparison, new insights into the conditions of life in the world he is living in."[14] The Saint Louis Exposition's Anthropology Department was directed by WJ McGee, a nationally prominent anthropologist whose exhibition aimed to display "particularly the barbarous and semi-barbarous peoples of the world, as nearly as possible in their ordinary and native environments."[15]

McGee's vision for the fair's anthropological exhibition was based on his theory of human progress. He had been delivering national lectures, including a series on national expansion sponsored by the National Geographic Society. One of those lectures for the Society, titled "National Growth and National Character," focused on the role of the Anglo-Saxon "to subjugate lower nature, to extirpate the bad and cultivate the good among living things ... and in all ways to enslave the world for the support of humanity and the increase of human intelligence."[16] According to Rydell, McGee's lectures tracked racial progress according to industrial development, "stretching humanity out on an anthropological rack that highlighted racial 'grades.'"[17]

A promotion for the Chicago fair that appeared before its opening, and was aimed at constructing rather than reporting on the experience, described the midway as "a jumble of foreigners ... gorgeous with color, pulsating with excitement, riotous ... and peculiar to the last degree." Hinsley calls such rhetoric "the language of the Midway," and this is the same language we shall hear throughout *National Geographic's* text.[18] So much of the world's fairs' aims and practices directly correspond to those of *National Geographic:* the links to industry and state, the impact of the visual, the combination of education and entertainment, people as spectacle, (re)creating "native environments," race and evolution, and endless means of comparison as part of the mass education of Americans to the new international situation.

THE GEOGRAPHIC LINES OF DIFFERENCE

National Geographic's 1894 annual address by the president was given by Gardiner G. Hubbard and titled, "Geographic Progress of Civilization." The address began:

> If parallels of latitude were drawn around the earth about fifteen degrees north and fifteen degrees south of Washington, the land within these parallels would include all the countries of the world that have been highly civilized and distinguished for art and science. No great people, except the Scandinavians and Scotch, who, from their climate, belong to the same region, ever existed outside these limits; no great men have ever lived, no great poems have ever been written, no literary or scientific work ever produced, in other parts of the globe.... The nearer man lives to the polar regions the greater his inferiority in intellect, the greater his barbarism.[19]

Hierarchical difference was geographically charted, with only a minor break necessary in the parallel of latitude to include Scandinavia and Scotland. Continuing the geography lesson, readers learned that changing the starting point and drawing two parallels fifteen degrees north and fifteen degrees south of the equator would delineate the region of the world with the richest lands and greatest varieties of vegetation and animal life. In these countries were found "both animal and vegetal life carried to the highest perfection, save only in the case of man, for whose development a different zone has been required."[20]

But Hubbard was optimistic that advanced man (read White man) and the world's richest environmental zone (read non-European countries) could successfully be united. This optimism was based on the power of Western industrial advances: "In the progress of civilization man with his inventions and discoveries, by the applied power of steam and electricity, has practically annihilated time and space. In the early history of man he was controlled by and subject to his environment, which shaped his life and formed his character; now he in turn controls his environment."[21] Thus, it would seem, the lands outside Hubbard's parallels of difference were assumed the property of those peoples inside the parallels of latitude. In fact, this period—with its relevant word being *conquer* and its "go-getter spirit," as characterized by *National Geographic* in the quotations from the 1980s—found the Western world taking over the non-Western world.

These two worlds are clearly distinguished as such by the magazine from its earliest days, and this difference is not without assigned value. Hubbard's address set up man/nature in a binary opposition in which the former dominates the latter—as with industrial/non-industrial and civilized/primitive. Subheadings in the text of the address signal these hierarchies for the readers: "The Changeless People of the Nile," "Slow Progress of the Dark Continent," "The Decadence of the Savage," and "Where Whites Fall Before Blacks."

Problematically, the Arab world falls within the geographic zones of both civilization and barbarism. Unlike European exceptions to latitudinal lines of difference, even those Arab countries in northern Africa and the Arab Gulf that were cut in two by the line drawn fifteen degrees south of Washington were not given exceptional status. (Actually, given the logic at work, with the Arab world straddling the zones one could explain what was seen as the area's great past civilizations and achievements, and its later backwardness and need of colonization.) The science that drew these lines of difference along parallels of latitude is what Edward Said would refer to as "imaginative geography."[22] What is presented as natural fact, including geographic information, is so often human invention. Hubbard's geographic zones of difference were so imaginary and arbitrary that he had to allow for great latitude in making exceptions to the rule. To make the geographic lines confirm the political realities of Western expansionist drives and the accompanying construction of race, breaks in the parallels of latitude to include or exclude a given country were acceptable.

GEOGRAPHY AND POSTCARDS

Another "fact" in *National Geographic* that is less of nature than human production is revealed in photographs that overlap a series of vulgar French postcards of Algerian women analyzed in Malek Alloula's *The Colonial Harem.* The range of the French postcards includes pornographic images of women that go beyond pictures found in *National Geographic,* but similarities do exist that raise some questions. One is hard put to understand *National Geographic*'s photographs as educational material offering reflections of natural reality when they are identical to or employ the same models and studio backdrops as girlie postcards. Where do the needs of crass postcard producers and *National Geographic*

coincide? And how is it that natural reality is located in the photographer's studio? An examination of common photographs and models found among Alloula's
collection of colonial postcards from 1900 to 1925 and pictures published in
National Geographic demonstrate an "unnatural reality."

The magazine's March 1906 issue contains a photogaph of "A Moorish
Belle" (Photo 3). This same model is found among those photographed for
French postcards—there captioned "Moorish Woman." In *National Geographic*'s picture, the model was posed leaning lazily against a window; in the
postcard, she is leaning lazily against an open doorway. In both pictures, the

PHOTO 3

"A Moorish Belle," March 1906

same idle posture and bored facial expression adopted by the model reveal the photographer's deliberate attempt to represent a standard Orientalist interpretation of Arab women's lives.

National Geographic's January 1914 issue contains a photograph that is identical to one of the French postcards (Photo 4). In both, the women are identified as "Ouled Nail." By the early 1900s, the designation "'daughter of the Ouled Nail' [tribe] had become a code word for prostitute" among Westerners.[23] The *National Geographic* caption further explained that the girls, who "resort to the city to earn money by dancing . . . , are outside the pale of respectable women."[24]

In the same issue of the magazine, the model to the right in Photo 4 appears again. In the second picture (Photo 5), she is photographed alone, but wearing the headdress of the model to her left in Photo 4 and holding a cigarette. The

PHOTO 4

"Two Ouled Nails in Characteristic Garb," January *1914*

PHOTO 5

*"A Dancing Girl of Tougourt, Algeria," January
1914*

caption to this picture tells readers that "these *ouled nail* girls are very dark in complexion. . . . They heighten their charms by a liberal application of grease paint
and rouge."[25] The postcards in Alloula's collection and in *National Geographic*
overlap again with another female model (Photo 6). The magazine's picture of
this woman was titled "A Moresque Beauty." In its caption, the term *Moresque*
was explained as referring to North African coast "Moslems of mixed blood" in
whose "veins flows the blood" of various peoples, often including Christian ances-
tors, and among whom were many "strikingly handsome" women.[26] In the French
postcard, titled "Beautiful Fatmah," the same model was posed leaning against
a balcony and holding a cigarette.[27] Both sources agreed on the model's beauty.

Arab women were usually presented "arranging their hair, lounging in doorways, and smoking."[28] The French postcards and the magazine's photographs
discussed earlier use the same props: cigarettes, excessive jewelry, and rich lay-

PHOTO 6

"A Moresque Beauty," January 1914

ers of clothing. Additionally, the women were posed in sexy attitudes and photographed outdoors to provide a sense of realism, in contrast to the studio portrait. Also in common, the images created stereotypes of Arab women: the dancing girl, the beauty (the French postcard's "Beautiful Fatmah" and *National Geographic*'s "A Moresque Beauty"), and national types (the Moorish type). As Yael Simpson Fletcher argues, "Orientalist stereotypes triumphed over determined images of actual women."[29]

On the operation of interpreting the colonial postcard, Alloula says that we must "admit that a kernel of truth, or rather, verisimilitude, survives beyond the conventionalism of the pose and of the stereotype. . . . The counterfeit realism of the postcard requires a minimum of truthfulness without which the whole thing would degenerate into gratuitous fantasy."[30] This, likewise, applies to the photographs in *National Geographic,* and not only those happening to overlap directly with French colonial postcards. All images in the magazine are facts of human production and need to be examined as such. If for no other reason than discovering that the same models and pictures were used for both colonial postcards and *National Geographic,* we must recognize visual images in the magazine as deliberate constructions, some complete with studios, models, and props. The magazine's claim to photograph people naturally, as they are, does not hold up against the commonalties shared with studio-constructed postcards appearing in 1906 and 1914.

According to Alloula, "Falsely naive, the postcard misleads in direct measure to the fact that it presents itself as having neither depth nor aesthetic pretensions. It is the 'degree zero' of photography."[31] *National Geographic* photographs occupy this same "falsely naive" position and, at the same time, reflect photographic sophistication. The magazine as educational journal produces postcard-quality pictures of women and retains its reputation for high-level photography because the picture is read within an educational context. It is approached differently from a postcard. In addition, like the colonial postcard—which Alloula asserts is supposed "to limit itself to a photographic survey of society and landscape" according to its "ethnographic alibi, its avowed purpose"—*National Geographic* works under its educational alibi.[32] And that is a very powerful alibi for both images and text.

PRESTIGE OF THE WHITE RACE

A good, bare-bones definition of racism is offered by Albert Memmi, who says it is "the generalized and final assigning of values to real or imaginary differences, to the accuser's benefit and at his victim's expense, in order to justify the former's own privileges or aggression."[33] How this plays itself out can be seen in reports about a visit to Sudan, one of the Arab countries that falls outside of the civilized region produced by drawing parallels fifteen degrees north and fifteen degrees south of Washington. In a 1929 *National Geographic* article, we read that since British rule "amazing change" has taken place in Sudan. It was previously a land of "war, famine, disease, and more war. Life was cheap." As the author listens to the stories of the British assistant district commissioner, a Scottish captain of the native Camel Corps, and a Scottish doctor, he wonders how it is that the millions of "wild men" who inhabit "savage Sudan" are ruled by so few such Englishmen, who manage to live unprotected and yet be "absolute masters and governors of all."[34] His explanation is: "Courage, unshaken belief in their race and their caste, and rigid, absolute, unswerving, impeccable justice have given to these administrators this mastery over the warlike and still fanatically religious tribes of the Sudan. It is because of this prestige of the white race that the British administrators have established [their authority]."[35] The arrogance and racism driving this account of Sudan are among those attitudes and assumptions basic to the colonizing project and its racist underpinnings.

This racism is also demonstrated in a *National Geographic* account of Arabia (present-day Saudi Arabia). There, an author found that "living this free open life, so remote from the law courts and police, through so many generations, has made the Arabs a bold defiant, headstrong people, not easily ruled and impatient of restraint. They are familiar with only one quick way to settle a dispute—to fight."[36] And in an article on Iraq, a visit to a holy city discovered the inhabitants to be "uncouth, swaggering desert men" with "long hair, faded dress and camel sticks, or oversupply of guns and side-arms, marking them as from the wild places."[37] The author's impression was of "a spirit of crude, barbaric primitiveness in the crowd." Against such descriptions of Arabs, it would not be difficult to justify colonial privilege or aggression.

WOOING WHITE MEN

National Geographic establishes difference through an intricate racial grid that creates and assigns value to physical and mental markers. And so it is, we read, that while traveling through Egypt and Sudan one finds: "In color these Arabs range from coalhole black to taffy yellow. From Luxor to Khartum the Arab and the Negro have become a blend."[38] In Morocco, the Berbers "looked and dressed alike. Their skin was swarthy, features rather flat, eyes small and brown."[39] In the Arab world one finds "unwashed children, with the limpid eyes of Arabs."[40] And Arabs are "often far lighter in color than a sunburned European. Their eyes, which are very beautiful, belie their jealous and deceitful natures."[41]

A visit to Sudan found old black women "as gentle as the 'mammies' of our own Southland" and "discovered the American Negro's love for watermelon is a hereditary influence. All these black people were excessively fond of melons."[42] Traveling past Khartoum, the author reported that "the characteristics of the natives changed. So far, we had seen only Arabs and mixed breeds. Here we met Negroes and Negro-and-Arab half-castes. The Negroes were genuine savages; they wore feathers in their hair and rings in their noses."[43]

How one was able to distinguish between these breeds was explained: "One finds it easy to recognize the Negroes with a mixture of Arab blood. The eyes betray them. The Arabs have eyes of a peculiar and distinctive luster, moist and luminous, and shaded by long eyelashes. The dirtiest little Arab girl can perform tricks with her eyes that are astonishing. It was amusing to see those half-caste girls attempt to woo the white men their eyes."[44] Not only eyes help sort out breeds, castes, and half-castes: "For all his sins, the Arab is one of the strongest and brainiest individuals the world ever produced. Show me a black boy . . . with one percent Arab blood in his veins and I will show you one who is smarter than his fellows."[45] This seeming compliment to Arab intelligence plays out much like the "beautiful eyes which belie deceitful natures" mentioned earlier.

Paralleling what Said calls a "'bad' sexuality" ascribed to Arabs, we also find that Arab intelligence is a "bad" intelligence of cunning and plotting.[46] Another twist on this is found in a description of Arabs that highly compliments their appearance as "singularly handsome" and their mental capacity as "second to none," but also points out a critical flaw: *National Geographic* tells its readers that Arabs, "like some other people of the East . . . seem to lack the powers of organized effort and combined action, a defect which may have tended to keep them so long a subject race."[47] With this reasoning, all sorts of colonial activity could be justified.

Still at the work of establishing race, we read in *National Geographic* that the Nuba are "one of the wildest tribes of the Sudan . . . dirty, savage, and suspicious." And their "woolly hair, thick lips, and dusky hues show how their race, though mixed in origin, remains essentially Negro."[48] Nile blacks are said to be "shiftless, vain, noisy, and warlike." And "no one yet has devised a plan for making the native Africans work. They seem to wish for nothing that is not free and under their hands. . . . Meanwhile, the land and civilization languish."[49] All of these examples work within Memmi's definition of race. It is by assigning and then continually pointing to the essentially negative physical and mental characteristics of others that race becomes a natural fact accounting for all manner of traits.

BECOMING GOOD MOORS

Clearly, establishing race is a very complicated matter; one has to see difference everywhere and keep seeing it or risk its falling apart. Throughout this study, *National Geographic*'s tireless search for difference is demonstrated. While an analysis of the advertisements in *National Geographic* is a study in itself and not something I can take up here, let me introduce just one. A 1924 advertisement for a Mediterranean excursion that included stays in Egypt and Palestine read: "Just imagine it! A vacation time . . . in a different world. The people of Mars are no further away from most of us than are those on the other side of our small planet. . . . See them with your own eyes!"[50] Sightings of difference surface in advertisements, photographs, captions, and articles. Constructing the other was constant work.

In an article on Morocco, reported French practices of not interfering with Muslim customs and architecture and of building French towns outside native villages were explained as the colonialists' understanding that "[t]he Moors are not an inferior, but a different, race from the French. We want them to become good Moors, not poor Frenchmen."[51] This is a good example of how "different but equal" worked—the French colonized Morocco, enforced segregation, and trained Moroccans in how to be good Moors. There can be no doubt that such difference is riddled with value judgments that allow—indeed require—one side to dominate the other. This is the very same racism, no milder, as that in preceding statements on Sudan. Helping Moroccans become good and doing something about the "languishing of land and civilization" were standard examples of colonialism's good works.

The same policy was practiced by the British in Egypt and Sudan. It was reported that they taught Arabs in Arabic and did not attempt to interfere with their religion. The colonial focus was somewhere else: "The chief effort at the present time is to train a body of young men who will be able to exercise among their own people the function of minor magistrates, according to European standards and ideas." And to this end, 150 young men had been selected and were "under instruction with most encouraging promise." In addition, there was a manual training school where forty Arabs were said to be showing such progress that "it would be difficult to believe that in two years so much could be made of the wild Arabs of the desert."[52]

ON THE FRINGE

Robert Stam says that "colonialist historians, speaking for the 'winners' of history, exalted the colonial enterprise, at bottom little more than a gigantic act of pillage . . . as a philanthropic 'civilizing mission' motivated by a desire to push back the frontiers of ignorance, disease and tyranny."[53] It is from this same perspective that *National Geographic* speaks of colonialism. The open, self-righteous way in which it does so reveals the pervasiveness of ideas regarding a West-to-non–West hierarchy.

In Algeria, a key region necessary to controlling the Sahara's important north-to-south caravan routes was described as "difficult to manage" because

"fanatical nomads of the interior long prevented fuller knowledge of the peoples and places of the center of the great desert."[54] To end this situation, the
French put together a trans-Saharan automobile expedition that included specially constructed Citroens mounted with rapid-fire guns. This expedition was
said to have added an important page to France's record of exploration in Africa
and to have helped it develop a political and commercial link between its northern and western African colonies. And with it, "civilization approached a bit
nearer to the heart of Africa's most mysterious domain."[55]

An amazing turn of logic blames people of an area for standing in the way
of others' acquiring knowledge about them and their area. The blame-the-victim
strategy works here because it is already understood that only the West can know.
Moreover, without the slightest degree of self-consciousness, the article reports
that machine guns were mounted on vehicles to clear the way of any Arabs
("fanatical nomads") resisting the French quest for knowledge and, incidentally,
caravan routes. In the end, learning that "civilization approached nearer" enabled
readers to make sense of the expedition; nothing more need be said.

With the same lack of self-consciousness, another *National Geographic*
article discussed similar colonial problems with Tunisia's fanatics: Once again,
the natives were in the way. Readers learned that, "owing to the fanaticism of
the inhabitants, it has not been possible to make any thorough study of the possible mineral wealth of the land. . . . The intense antipathy of the inhabitants to
foreigners and to foreign ideas has rendered the mineral and agricultural wealth
of the country practically useless."[56] This was especially troubling because the
author believed that under "proper conditions" Tunisia could be made into an
even richer agricultural country than Algeria and Morocco—France's other
colonies. And an article on Oman reported that the coast—which is referred to
as the "Pirate Coast"—"was noted for the savage ferocity and fanaticism of its
inhabitants," but, "thanks to English commerce and gunboats, these fanatic
Arabs have become tamed."[57]

It was, after all, as *National Geographic* reported, the "age of swelling
empires and shifting frontiers" that saw "Greater-France-in-Africa . . . 20 times
larger than France-in-Europe" and "Great Britain, with a territory 30 times
larger than the British Isles."[58] This European swelling from the right to know
and to own was colonialism in its heyday. Stam offers a basic definition of colonialism that suits the purposes of this study: Colonialism refers to "the process
by which the European powers (including the United States) reached a position of economic, military, political, and cultural domination in much of Asia,
Africa and Latin America." This process began with the "voyages of discov-

ery," reached its height between 1900 and the end of World War I (at which time
Europe had colonized about 85 percent of the Earth), and began to be seriously
altered with the disintegration of European empires after World War II.[59]

According to V. Y. Mudimbe, *colonialism* and *colonization* mean "organization, arrangement, . . . [and] derive from the latin word *colere,* meaning to cultivate or to design." Examining the colonial process, Mudimbe identifies three
main keys to colonial organization: "the procedures of acquiring, distributing,
and exploiting lands in colonies; the policies of domesticating natives; and the
manner of managing ancient organizations and implementing new modes of
production." Out of this emerge three complementary actions, Mudimbe continues: "the domination of physical space, the reformation of *natives'* minds,
and the integration of local economic histories into the Western perspective."
All of this constitutes the "colonizing structure, which completely embraces the
physical, human, and spiritual aspects of the colonizing experience."[60]

As we have seen, *National Geographic* magazine openly supported colonialist perspectives and projects—so much so that it clearly explained Western
designs on Iraq in an article that began: "Baghdad! What a magic word to conjure with! How it hints at romance, adventure, intrigue. . . . No tales can compare with the 'Arabian Nights', the old tales of Baghdad. . . . But how many
Americans know just where Baghdad is or how important it has become lately?"
The authors answered this question by saying that Baghdad was important "not
because of its romantic past . . . but because it has become the busy center of
a great field of action—the theater of international war for political and commercial supremacy in the Middle East."[61] The right of colonial powers to dominate the Arab world was not questioned.

EDUCATING MEN, TRAINING WOMEN

It is against Stam's and Mudimbe's understanding of colonialism that
we now continue to listen to *National Geographic* report on European colonial
activity in the Arab world. At the same time, we should keep in mind those very
different understandings of colonialism read earlier in Gardiner G. Hubbard's
1894 Annual Address and the nostalgic description of this era given by the magazine in the late 1980s, on the occasion of its one-hundredth anniversary.

National Geographic readers learned that because of Morocco's simple sameness, it was necessary for the French to work hard and spend much money. "All
Moroccan mosques, medersas, homes, shops, and cemeteries look more or less
alike, forming an incomparable setting for a people whose dress, regardless of

station, is alike in form and coloring." In all this Moroccan sameness, the French "had to build extensively"—administrative buildings, barracks, warehouses, railway stations, post offices, hotels, shops, and homes. They reforested the hills, tamed the rivers, and built irrigation ditches; archeologists unearthed Roman ruins; and France "spent a small fortune on the port of Casablanca ... home of most of the European residents."[62] This inventory is just what Said talks about as an appeal "to an imagined history of Western endowments and free hand-outs, followed by a reprehensible sequence of ungrateful bitings of that grandly giving 'Western' hand."[63]

National Geographic readers learned that not all Moroccans were grateful for French good works. There were still some "rebellious" tribes in "regions unsubdued." But "profiting by their mistakes in Algeria and Tunisia, the French have made a steady advance in pacification, unification, and progress." Moroc-can "aristocrats are being educated" for future military and municipal positions, and "women of the leading families are being trained." The fate of "warriors who have been thorns in the side" of European colonialism in Morocco has been sealed; they are surrounded by a "pacified zone" that spells their "ultimate sub-jugation, the fate that has overtaken equally brave aboriginal tribes blocking Civilization's path throughout the world."[64]

For those resisting civilization, there were pacification and unification pro-grams—to which the barracks mentioned earlier would no doubt have some relationship. For others, there were French programs to educate aristocratic Moroc-can men and train women of leading families—that is, produce good Moors of the upper class. Training Arab women was a colonizing strategy that was not particular to Morocco. For example, in a 1914 article, we read about "modern education" in Tunis in the form of an Arab girls' school headed by a French woman who "thoroughly understands Mohammedan ways." The woman explained the work in the following way: "No effort is made to proselytize or influence them in any way, the desire is simply to make these young girls intelligent and useful members of the community, so that when they marry they may have attractive homes and be intelligent companions to their husbands. They are taught plain, common-sense sewing, hygiene, common-sense cooking, how to set a table properly, to read and write; also arithmetic and bookkeeping."[65] It was with complete self-confidence in the colonizers' ability to know others and prescribe what they need that this French woman and *National Geographic* could so matter-of-factly report such efforts to uplift Arab women. One never gets a hint of self-doubt in descriptions of such unilaterally developed projects for the natives' betterment. It goes without saying, it would seem, that West-erners could identify problems and set solutions for the colonized population.

Arab women also needed serious training in motherhood. During a 1914 visit to Palestine, an author reported that "mortality among the babies is great and is not to be wondered at, for in view of the rough treatment they receive, it becomes a question of the survival of the fittest."[66] The evidence given of this rough treatment was: 1) babies were carried tied onto the backs of mothers; 2) while working in the fields mothers erected small hammocks from sticks and cloth to hold the babies; and 3) in some districts, babies were put in crude wooden cradles and carried on their mothers' heads.

The women, rather than economic and health conditions, were held responsible for infants' mortality. Given the evidence offered, this was due to their non-Western mothering practices. The logic behind training Arab women to use Western baby carriages was that it would cause the infant-mortality rate to drop. The Western model of motherhood, in all its detail, was to be adopted. If Arab mothers caused the high mortality rate among children, they clearly needed to be trained by colonial teachers in domesticity and motherhood.

The objectives of colonial programs to train Arab women were in essence the same as those discussed by Nancy Rose Hunt in her analysis of the Belgian *foyer* system in Africa. Citing Ester Boserup's work, Hunt points out that "colonial notions of development for women meant 'training for the home.'" She argues that the *foyer* project points to "important connections between Western family ideology, the colonial construction of womanhood and domesticity, and the emergence of a colonized African urban elite."[67]

The Belgian system, like the French system, intended to achieve support for the colonial state from upper-class natives who could, through education and training, learn to cooperate with the colonizer. These educational programs were an important part of colonial efforts to strengthen class structure and inscribe within it "colonial standards of prestige and status." And they "worked to establish, maintain, and enhance hierarchies" of gender, class, and race.[68]

Training Arab women in basic, common-sense activities of running the nuclear-family household held up Western womanhood and Western patriarchy as models to imitate. This carried with it the denigration of Arab women's culture and the Arab family unit, both of which became signs of backwardness in colonial training programs. It is also important to note that domesticating Arab women during this era did not speak to any economic role for them. They were being trained to keep house and be suitable companions for men — for Arab men, that is. The colonizer/colonized hierarchy was never lost in education and training programs that, as part of the racist context of colonialism, aimed not at assimilation or Westernization, but at "colonial mimicry."[69]

BORN OF THE DESERT

Some of the differences between Arabs and Westerners can be high-lighted by rearranging photograph captions from an article on Algeria that has forty-one illustrations in its twenty-seven pages.[70] Organizing two separate lists of phrases from the captions gives us on the Arab side:

- "Where centuries have seen no progress"
- "Living in primitive fashion"
- "Pure-food principles are not seriously regarded by the Arabs"
- "The Arab diner usually uses his fingers"
- "Domestic arrangements are often extremely squalid"
- "Algerian girls still weave 'magic carpets'"
- "Still suggest, in custom and in costume, the time and clime of the *Arabian Nights*"
- "A gaily bedecked daughter of the desert"
- "The fame of their dancing spreads afar"
- "An Algerian Bedouin type"
- "Color and picturesqueness of veiled, white-robed women and brown faced men"

And it gives us on the side of "civilization":

- "Until the French came to Algeria good water was a rare commodity"
- "The French have made the Botanical Gardens of Algiers the finest in North Africa"
- "Numerous French artists have helped to make the beauties of this oasis known to the world"
- "Pirates . . . finally subdued by the French"
- "The French Foreign Legion have penetrated the Algerian Desert with good roads"
- "The life of the Legionnaires seems romantic, but instead is the sternest reality"

These two very different lists speak for themselves. Arabs are constructed with familiar signs of cultural belatedness, and the French with a series of good works aimed at raising the level of Arab life.

Among the predictable markers in the first list—the Arab time warp, dancing girls, *Arabian Nights,* filth, and human categories—is being born of the desert.

Arabs are often identified in *National Geographic* as sons or daughters of the desert, an essentializing move that accomplishes quite a bit. "Of the desert" denies one's being part of a human community or nation as, for example, a son of France would be. Being a daughter of the desert places one too close to nature, producing a primitive woman who, because nature is understood as something to be conquered and controlled, needs to be pacified, trained, and subjugated. Further, because this particular piece of nature is a desert, and deserts in *National Geographic*'s Western gaze are empty wastes (except when economic or military significance can be spotted), the daughter of the desert, with sexual significance already located in her as "primitive woman," is like the land— there for the taking, with nothing in the way.

The whole Arab world seems to have been little more than an empty desert or worse until the good works of colonialism. One *National Geographic* author said that, while traveling through Tunisia, he passed "squalid villages, with their ever-present dung-heap, on top of which often sat the chief man of the village, as upon a throne, surrounded by his wives, slaves and others, all wrapped in oriental silence and eyeing us curiously." To avoid fevers while in Tunisia, the author and his companions were careful to boil their drinking water; they noted, however, that unlike themselves, "Arabs drop down by the first fetid puddle, little better than a hog wallow."[71] In an article on Egypt, another author wrote about stopping at a railway station "set in the waste" where "voluble Arabs made the usual din, apparently about nothing." He noticed that "the desert Arabs live in desperate squalor, on the fringe. On what they subsist is . . . a mystery. The hot sun burns up their filth; otherwise they must of necessity all die." And, of course, Arabs were found "covered with contented flies."[72]

Flies, usually contented, are a regular part of constructing the primitive. Flies perform several functions: Most obviously, they mean a lack of personal and public hygiene; they signal that Arabs are too lazy even to shoo flies away; they point to the animality of Arabs who, unbothered, are at one with the contented flies; and, finally, flies on Arabs create the image of the Arab world as a decaying corpse. This was an important image to hold against that of Western expansion. It explained so much.

In *National Geographic*, Sudan was described as "a country of calamities," where medical missionary work had doctors "literally giving their lives to save the black man from savagery and ignorance and disease." We read that only the lucky ones came out alive; nevertheless, "when one dies, another comes in."[73] This was not the only example of British sacrifice in Sudan. Passing Kitchener's camp, readers were reminded that "the great British soldier spent something like three years equipping an army with machine guns and artillery to go into the Sudan to subdue a religious zealot and his fanatical followers."[74] All this sacrifice was not for nothing: The author speculated that someday Sudan would be a great cotton producer, supplying Britain with all that it was then buying from the United States.

Readers learned from *National Geographic* that Italian fascists also had a colonization program full of good works. Tripoli, Libya, was said to be a "promising modern Italian colony" where "Italy is turning to good account the martial instincts of the restless sons of the desert."[75] The difference between the Arab world and Western civilization (including European fascism) was made clear throughout a 1925 *National Geographic* article: "Arabs and Negroes, wrapped in the universal dingy white woolen shroud . . . shuffle by groups of smart Italian officers in khaki and silver and Fascisti in black shirts and caps. Arab and Negro women, with only one eye peering from beneath an all-enveloping cloak, use that eye to stare at the short skirts and silk stockings of European ladies. Thus East and West meet."[76] Upon leaving this main street, the author wrote, "one plunges into the Arabian Nights," where the market sights include sellers who "recline silently at their ease, waiting, like true Easterners, for customers to come to them," and one shop owner "dozes among baskets of carrots and cabbages."

This is all familiar—creating the other as lazy and violent and using Western women's dress as a sign of freedom. What makes this example interesting is that even fascists were presented as more civilized and more advanced than Arabs. It was the martial instincts of the sons of the desert, not those of fascists, that needed to be controlled. In the zone where the Italians had established control, there was "peace, justice, order, freedom, and coming prosperity. Outside it lie[s] the stony desert . . . where lawlessness still exists." And although "Italian soldiers have pacified" most of the western province, for extra protection they built a wall around their area against "raids by bands of desert warriors."[77]

In another *National Geographic* article, readers learned not only that sons of the desert were violent, but also that Syrian bedouins were said to be "robbers by nature and tradition." But when shown an American tractor and plow, they "were as enthusiastic as children with a new toy."[78] This string of seemingly contradictory descriptors actually hangs together to produce the terrible child image that is so often employed to represent Arabs in need of Western parental authority, guidance, and discipline. As Johannes Fabian argues, "Talk about the childlike nature of the primitive has never been just a neutral classificatory act, but a powerful rhetorical figure and motive, informing colonial practice in every aspect."[79] The conception of the colonial relationship as parent and child is often repeated in *National Geographic*.

TIME

Another often encountered piece of colonialist rhetoric is that which constructs the primitive as existing outside time or in another time. (However, as my reading of a century of *National Geographic* suggests, there seems to be nothing so timeless as primitive discourse itself.) Fabian's discussion of the political and oppressive uses of time is useful here. He argues that time is not a natural resource, but an "ideologically construed instrument of power." The West's colonialist–imperialist expansion "required Time to accommodate the schemes of one-way history," a history that charts cultures according to select indicators of civilization, development, and modernization. According to Fabian's analysis, "geopolitics has its ideological foundations in chronopolitics," and "relations between the West and its Other . . . were conceived not only as difference, but as distance in space and Time."[80]

This same temporal discourse is used in *National Geographic*'s rearrangement of coeval cultures along an evolutionary scale based on a denial of shared time. Arabs are usually found stuck in past centuries, and the colonial relationship is portrayed as helping to pull such backward cultures into more advanced time.

Traveling from Syria to Baghdad, one *National Geographic* author found the area to be "the dust heap of the world," where "*Arabian Nights*' splendor has departed." His disappointment in Baghdad was due to its having "existed in the minds of most people only as a mythical city, for in childhood they had read the fascinating *Arabian Nights' Entertainments*." However, the British presence in Baghdad brought about "miraculous change," making the city almost unrecognizable from ten years earlier. Roads, bridges, motor vehicles, a taxicab service of luxurious cars, an efficient police force, a new town for Europeans, electric fans, ice factories, and heat-resisting architecture were listed as examples of "civilization's conveniences" brought by the British to Iraq. In addition, there was a club with polo, tennis, and golf facilities, and there was a racetrack, because "wherever the Briton has penetrated, he has taken his sport with him."

Alongside this world of Western progress, the author described another world: "Baghdad is still the real East"; once you enter the bazaar gates, you will find, "civilization has halted."[81] In a different article on Iraq, an author explained: "Time seemed to turn back 20 centuries when I stepped off the Tigris steamer at Baghdad. Old Testament men in turbans, sandals, and quaint flowing robes (abbas) crowded about calling each other 'Yusuf' and 'Musa'— Joseph and Moses."[82] While in Tunisia, an author observed farmers using "primitive agricultural methods" and the same implements as those used "a thousand years ago." He also claimed to have seen "a horse, a donkey, and the plowman's wife or female slave (the distinction in the country is often fine) hitched before the plow." The author commented that this and other "scenes too numerous to mention carry the mind back to nearly two thousand years to a succession of biblical pictures."[83] This time warp also existed in Morocco, where, we read, "shadowy figures . . . hooded, shrouded in ghostly white . . . seemed to belong to an age long past. . . . Little changed since prehistoric days." But with the entry of France, Morocco was brought "face to face with civilization in its most advanced stage—the railroad, the automobile, the airplane."[84] Centuries were thrown about so easily that almost anything in the Arab world seemed to send Westerners time-traveling into prehistory.

In a 1914 article, readers learned that "Palestine, often called the Holy Land, is in a general way familiar to all of us from our study of the Bible [notice the assumed audience]. Few, however, realize that the manners and customs which prevailed there in Biblical days are still unchanged, even after an interval of 3,000 years."[85] This is quite a time warp, but biblical times were a *National Geographic* favorite for the Western, Christian traveler to imagine while in the Arab world. And even though the successful "secularization of Judeo-Christian Time by generalizing and universalizing it" had created a universal history, the Arab world was often found occupying a parallel universe.[86]

TYPES

National Geographic's other favorite time period within which to locate (freeze) the Arab world were the eighth and ninth centuries—the time of the *Arabian Nights*. In fact, even in the twentieth century there were "*Arabian Nights* Type[s]" to be seen, as the caption to a picture of a Moroccan woman informed readers (Photo 7). The woman in this photo is wearing a turban heavy with gold jewelry, large gold earrings and necklace, and a gold belt. The excess jewelry is part of the general excess imagined to exist behind doors in the Arab world. This "*Arabian Nights* Type" woman was positioned to the side of an open door and standing in a very unguarded, submissive pose with her hands behind her back—she welcomes you into the harem.

The dream of entering harem space was a recurring one in *National Geographic*. While this photo displayed an open door to the harem, any image or idea of trespassing the harem—getting into this forbidden women's territory— was about opening closed and mysterious doors. This one was opened for magazine readers by the photographer, who produced, with the image of a woman

PHOTO 7

"An Arabian Nights *Type," March 1925*
(Photo: National Geographic Society Image Collection)

welcoming strangers into the harem, the common Western representation of
harem as brothel. Claude Gandelman, in a discussion of the meaning of doors
in paintings, says that they are "explicit signs of passage," "signs of the possibility of seeing, of penetrating directly the mystery."[87] This speaks as well to
doors in photographs, and particularly well to the open door of the harem.

The relationship between the door and gaining access to Arab women also
unfolded within text in *National Geographic.* The following is what an author
watching the doors to a public bath in Morocco reported:

> Out of a dark alley come two white-robed figures, veiled to the dark eyes
> that, lustrous and beautiful, shine under the black eyebrows and fair

foreheads. Massive silver and gold necklaces hang on their bosoms, broad silver bracelets adorn their wrists, and heavy anklets surround the silk-stockinged ankles thrust into dainty slippers. Their henna-tipped fingers are loaded with rings. With a lingering backward glance, these two enter slowly a carved marble portal leading . . . to the Moorish baths.[88]

One is immediately struck by all the physical detail the author was able to glean from "two white-robed figures" who were passing by. Once again, the description of massive and excessive jewelry is used to signal excessive sex, as do the stockings and the colored fingertips.

And what were readers to make of the reported "lingering backward glance" from eyes that had already been described so sensually? Were the Arab women flirting with the author? Were they sending an invitation to the observer (who also becomes the reader–viewer of *National Geographic*) into the women's bath? This is an Orientalist fantasy. We hear it also in another author's imaginative thoughts on his stay as a guest in a Tunisian home. He says, "I have never been quite certain if there were not peep-holes from some of the harem rooms and that the fair dames of the various households had not watched me dressing! Who knows!"[89] Indeed.

Another author found her visit to a harem a rude surprise. She reported a sight contrary to her expectations of "marble baths wherein olive-skinned beauties lolled, as in the soap advertisements." She had imagined the harem to be a place with "precious perfumes and beveled mirrors 30 feet high, of priceless jewels blazing on the beautiful breasts, and of bronze eunuchs waving peacock fans, while sinuous serving-maids gently brushed the soft tresses of some harem favorite." Instead, she reported that the fourteen women she met "were not beautiful—at least they were not to be compared with any type of feminine face and figure commonly thought attractive in our Western world." She declared the women of the harem to be "absolutely commonplace, some of them even stupid-looking."[90] The author expected to find the harem as created within Orientalism; reality fell short. And, of course, Arab women always fell short when compared with Western women.

Notwithstanding this woman's disappointment, there was enough of a general "air of enchantment and mystery" about the Arab world that even the cover to a sewer could be intriguing in *National Geographic*. While in Fez, Morocco, an author noticed the city's drainage system, said to have been built by a renegade Frenchman in the late eighteenth century. This stirred her imagination:

"Dark tales of other days are whispered—a lid in the conduit lifted, a thrust—who knows!"[91] Even sewers helped Westerners conjure up Orientalist fantasies.

In fact, one need not even be on the ground in the Arab world to work up an *Arabian Nights* fantasy. While flying over Baghdad, one author said that, if not for keeping to his schedule, he would have liked to land "where storytellers in turbans drone the racy, unexpurgated tales of *Arabian Nights;* or to sample that seductive arrack drink and hear the East's oldest flute tune played while a lithe-limbed girl dances."[92] In another article, this whole sense of Arabs out of step with time was put most succinctly. Upon seeing some "old Arabs in doorways," the author remarked: "Here, as elsewhere, the Arab is an anachronism."[93]

ARABIAN DAYS

Through text and photographs, *National Geographic* created not only Western fantasies of *Arabian Nights* and harem dreaming; just as deliberately, it also created the mundane. "Forced realism"—when signs are deliberately put into a picture to suggest that the scene is natural or truthful—is one of the ways through which this is done.[94] An example of this is the photo "A Daughter of the Libyan Desert" (Photo 8). In this picture, a rock wall forms the background; the subject is wearing cotton clothing, as opposed to silks and brocades; the subject is posed as fixing her head covering, which is meant to suggest that she is acting naturally, although the actual effect is rigid and awkward; and finally, the caption informs readers that "[h]er elaborate jewelry includes a commonplace key, a safety pin and a piece of a comb."

Pointing out these everyday items hanging off the necklace helps produce the desired realism in contrast to the shock produced by a great deal of heavy gold jewelry. The items noted in the caption are commonplace Western objects that help create a sense of the mundane—noting commonplace Arab objects could not perform the same function for a Westerner. In addition, the Arab woman is making inappropriate use of a key, safety pin, and comb—an example of what Marianna Torgovnick calls "culture contact" photographs, or "indigenous peoples incorporat[ing] Western materials into their dress, rituals, and art."[95] In *National Geographic* this image is regular fare used more to designate culture clash than contact as such. Arabs' inappropriate use or misinterpretation of Western culture is always the point being made; it never seemed to occur the other way around.

In addition to the arrangement of details for forced realism, desired pictures were also produced by staging events to photograph. We read in a *National*

PHOTO 8

"A Daughter of the Libyan Desert," August 1925
(Photo: Luigi Pellerano/National Geographic Society
Image Collection)

Geographic article that during a visit to Sudan the author tried to set up a sham
battle between two tribes, thinking that it "might make an interesting picture
to stage." The chiefs of the tribes had their enthusiasm for the idea "aroused by
a promise . . . of much sugar and cloth." However, the followers were not equally
enthusiastic, fearing the danger of even a mock battle between two tribes that
have been "deadly enemies for generations." The author assured them, "no one
will be hurt. This will not be real, only a game. You . . . will only play together."
The requested performance did not take place, but later the author did get a tribe
to perform a battle with no opposing side.[96]

The author could not convince the tribes' members that the battle would not
be real—that it would be only a game; nor would the magazine's reader–viewers

be easily convinced of this. That is to say, even after reading about how a photograph representing the Sudanese as violent and warring was constructed by *National Geographic,* it would still be a struggle not to see the photo as reflecting reality because so much about Arab violence was already in place. The stereotype of the angry, violent Arab man was already known; therefore, pictures corresponding to that image became real enough. The magazine's credibility was perfectly safe, despite the declared artificiality of its pictures.

According to Irvin Schick, throughout the late nineteenth and early twentieth centuries "photographers scoured the Middle East and North Africa in a relentless quest to classify and catalog their ruins, markets, monuments, holy places, and especially their many 'exotic' peoples." Of the taxonomies they created, Schick asserts: "Any taxonomy fundamentally relies on the classifier's perspective; type, after all, lies in the eyes of the beholder."[97] And with *National Geographic,* the beholder's eyes were fixed on Orientalism.

The magazine produced and taught its types through visual images and text. For example, readers learned about types of Arab women: the difference between Berber and Moor women is that the former are "taller and leaner than their harem-bred sisters . . . in the cities where Moorish beauty runs to avoirdupois."[98] A picture of a Libyan woman identified her as "A Town-Bred Arab Woman" and noted that her brocaded clothing would be out of place among women dwelling in the desert (Photo 9). Because identifying women as city- and town-bred also meant *harem-bred,* according to *National Geographic*'s categories, the Libyan woman was dressed in heavy silks and brocades and too much jewelry, and posed seductively in front of open curtains on a balcony.

Sharing some of the tropes of the harem-bred type of women, but with her own distinct characteristics, was the dancer type who often appeared in the magazine. In a 1917 picture of an Algerian dancer (wearing the familiar ten pounds of jewelry), she was posed as though the camera had caught her daydreaming (Photo 10). The lengthy caption read:

A Desert Flower

"Somewhere in the Sahara" lived this child of the Desert until she came to Biskra, the "Garden of Allah," to earn her dowry as a dancer. One would imagine that she is dreaming of some turbaned knight left behind and counting the days until she may return to her natal tent.[99]

The reader–viewer has to participate in creating this woman as a dancer. First, you have to accept that this is a candid shot, not a studio portrait; and second, you have to agree to imagine along with *National Geographic* about her dreaming.

PHOTO 9

"A Town-Bred Arab Woman," August 1925
(Photo: Luigi Pellerano/National Geographic Society
Image Collection)

Incidentally, this picture, along with several other photos of Algerian dancing girls, first appeared in *National Geographic* in its January 1914 issue illustrating an article on North Africa. The second time readers saw these pictures
(1917), they were hand-tinted and within a mixed collection of fourteen pictures unconnected to any particular article. Leaps of imagination were often
required from readers who were not only called upon to contextualize and con-
ceptualize pictures as suggested by the magazine, but also, at times, to recon-
textualize them.

Another instance establishing types was an imaginative explanation of veiling that had to be believed in order to accept other *National Geographic* categories of Arab women. Readers were informed that "in Cairo all Mohammedan
women cover their faces—the ugly ones with black knitted veils and the pretty

PHOTO 10

"A Desert Flower," March 1917

ones with sheer white chiffon, which reveals the face clearly and endows it with a glorified complexion."[100] Assuming that this information was correct, which I would not suggest one do, readers were left to imagine how, when, and by whom these "Mohammedan women" were declared ugly or pretty and assigned their appropriate veil colors.

THE MOHAMMEDAN MIND

In this quotation from *National Geographic,* the term "Mohammedan" is used. What does it mean? The word *Mohammedan* is not used in Arabic; how does it come to be employed in the West in place of or synonymously with the word *Muslim?* Discussing how Christian thinkers interpreted Islam, Said says, "since Christ is the basis of Christian faith, it was assumed—quite incorrectly—that Mohammed was to Islam as Christ was to Christianity."[101] With this assumption at work, Mohammed was therefore understood by Christians as an impostor, because only Christ was the Son of God. How Muslims themselves understand the Prophet Mohammed and his role is neither here nor there. Christians who employ the term *Mohammedan* do so from an analysis of Islam that ignores Muslims' interpretations of their own religion. This arrogant way of knowing others sets Christians up with the one true God, leaving Mohammedans with Allah—not God. Thus, we do not find the Arabic word *Allah* translated to English (God) in *National Geographic*—it does not translate within the context of a Christianity/Islam hierarchy.

This religious hierarchy is apparent in an author's report that Baghdad "has been slow to yield to Europe's influence," and that in its bazaar's one finds "such a mob as Christ drove from the temple—a vortex of usury."[102] Another author, reporting on Oman, informed *National Geographic* readers that, except for the Pirate Coast, the Arabs of Oman are "remarkably free from fanaticism. . . . Most of them belong to the Abadhi sect which has beliefs in common with Christianity, and the experience of our missionaries has been that people are not only accessible, but willing to learn."[103] What made some "fanatics" and others "accessible" was clearly tied to religious bias. One female author stated, "Between us—women of the West—and these daughters of the desert is a gulf, impassable and not of our own making; it is a barrier of religion."[104] The difference being constructed was indeed impassable.

The Christian ability to know "Mohammedans" and the knowledge produced from that vantage point enabled readers to make sense out of what would otherwise be confusing information. For instance, readers could understand that dismantlement of a Muslim religious shrine helped establish colonial control, because "holy places are very dear to the Mohammedan mind," and one might eventually "develop into a disturbance center."[105] This same knowledge secured meaning in another *National Geographic* article, in which readers learned that one should gauge conversation with Muslims because "all Mohammedans hate the Christians and . . . they dislike being seen talking to them."[106] This would make sense to readers given what was already known about Mohammed as an impostor and Islam as a competing religion to Christianity.

In a 1909 article, the author shared with readers an anti-Christian incident he encountered while traveling through the Arabian Peninsula. It happened during a stop at an oasis in northern Arabia and was the author's "first real experience of Arabian superstition and hatred of the Christian." The author said that he was not allowed to occupy a guestroom but was, rather, told to sleep with the cattle in the stables. He did so, but was then ordered to move away from the animals because his presence might cause their deaths. He was then given a place alone in the palm grove, but once again he was forced to move because it was thought that close contact with the palms might harm their fruit-bearing. Finally, he was "confined in a tent to keep company with one afflicted with a disease not unlike leprosy."[107]

This Christian/Muslim opposition framed the colonizer/colonized opposition in religious terms that, in turn, used religion to legitimate colonial activity. As Rana Kabbani notes, a Christian sense of religious superiority was founded upon seeing Christianity as "the only system of belief that was correct and could enlighten ... those less fortunate."[108] That the less fortunate were non-Christians was clearly established in *National Geographic*.

For example, in a 1909 article that followed the route of Moses out of the desert, the author's religious journey came to an end at the town of Aqaba, Jordan, where he found "wretchedness and filth personified. . . . The people are despicably poor in their persons and characteristics, having lived like leeches on the Egyptian caravans to Mecca for centuries."[109] This description packed quite a bit in it. It represented Arabs as so morally poor as to rob religious pilgrims, and because these pilgrims were Muslims, *National Geographic* readers could wonder what these Arabs would do to Christians. And the author's use of the image of leeches reproduced familiar Orientalist stereotypes of the thieving Arab and the unproductive Arab.

This same representation of Arabs was found in a 1914 anecdote from a French officer in Tunis. The anecdote, said to illustrate "the Arab character," told of an Arab who had sown his fields with wheat, but at harvest time a swarm of locusts devoured it all. During the destruction of the crop, the Arab just looked on, impressed with Allah's having created such a small but powerful insect and "improvised a poem, without trying to drive them away."[110] This Muslim Arab was an obvious contrast to the stereotypical Western, Christian character–hero who, with an endless supply of energy and industriousness, would have saved the crop.

Another example of the magazine's Christian bias appeared in the report of the British district commissioner of a Muslim province in Sudan. He explained to readers that when called upon to settle an argument over responsibility for the death of a bull, he carried his Bible into court, having found a "suitable judgment" in the twenty-first chapter of Exodus, thirty-fifth verse.[111] The colonial commissioner's open use of the Christian Bible as the authoritative voice over colonized Muslims spoke to both the link between colonialism and Christianity and the Christian/Muslim hierarchy in place.

The Christian colonial disrespect for Islamic beliefs and practices that is revealed in *National Geographic* was indicative of the level of religious discrimination practiced and the sense of Christian superiority so taken for granted that attempts to cover it were unnecessary. Another example of this appeared in a 1925 description of Muslims dancing in religious celebration during the holy month of Ramadan:

> Off across the square, tom-toms beat perpetually and white figures of dervishes danced to the wild music. . . . Three musicians shuffled backward in a perpetual circle. . . . From time to time figures broke away from the tightly packed mob . . . and danced furiously. . . . Around and around they went, barefooted fanatics, leaping and gyrating in their long white robes and odd white turbans. One minute they struck a self-appreciative pose and held it; the next, they were in a frenzy again. They resembled nothing so much as chickens with their heads cut off, fluttering in the purposeless dance of death.[112]

Muslims were made hideous and out of control in this description of their religious celebration. Everything in the account served to distance readers from weird and wild Muslims. *National Geographic* established a strange, incomprehensible non-Christian religion with these reports, and here it portrayed Islamic holidays as meaningless.

DANCING GIRLS

This description of what sounds like nothing short of Muslim insanity was framed as a Christian watching Muslims dance. However, there was another dance spectacle more integral to *National Geographic*'s representations of the Arab world—Western men watching Arab women dance. Sarah Graham-Brown says that the "'Middle Eastern 'dancing girl' is an indispensable part of the Orientalist repertoire of images . . . used to suggest lasciviousness and sensuality, exciting both enjoyment and disapproval in Western viewers."[113] Brown also points out that the Western association between public dancing and prostitution runs through images of the "dancing girl."

This tension between enjoyment and disapproval produced reports on the dance in *National Geographic* that created an erotic moment suddenly punctured with denial. Listen to two different, yet same, accounts of Arab women dancing:

> We could see five graceful young girls facing one man. The girls were alternately advancing and retreating as they danced—at first slowly, rhythmically, and then, still keeping the rhythm, with an ever-increasing speed. Suddenly, before Schoedsack and I realized what was happening, the women, still unsmiling, not changing their rhythm at all, turned and danced right up to us, . . . the five of them stopped as one, shook their braided curls in our faces, and then hastily retreated—as we did.[114]

And:

> Her dancing! She moves on her toes, but barely raises them from the platform. In her hands she holds a silk handkerchief behind her head or waves it occasionally in the air. But feet and hands, legs and arms, do not enter much into the dance; she performs chiefly with the muscles of her neck, breast, abdomen, and hips. . . . The eyes of the interested spectators sparkle as they gloat on the dancer's charms and movements. To them she is the poetry of motion, but to a European she is almost repugnant.[115]

This sudden coming to one's Victorian senses after such an intense gaze corresponds with Kabbani's assertion: "The Orient of the western imagination provided respite from Victorian sexual repressiveness. It was used to express for the age the erotic longings that would have otherwise remained suppressed."[116] The focused and lengthy descriptions given to women dancing were not likewise written about women weaving, caring for children, working in fields, performing other activities. Only Arab women dancing received such concentrated treatment in *National Geographic*.

While watching dancing girls was integral to Orientalism, the "blame" was put on Arab women. In these descriptions, the women seemed to offend their Western observers. This operation brings to mind John Berger's discussion of the painting, *Vanity*, by Memling. He calls the moralizing in it hypocritical: "You painted a naked woman because you enjoyed looking at her, you put a mirror in her hand and you called the painting *Vanity*, thus morally

condemning the woman whose nakedness you had depicted for your own pleasure."[117] This same sort of hypocritical treatment went on in *National Geographic* when detailed observations of dancing ended with authors' disgust in
the women's behavior.

The representation of Arab women within sexual terms was common. A
1917 picture of a dancing girl, one of the photos mentioned earlier as having
twice appeared in the magazine, carried a caption shot with sexuality (Photo
11). Readers learned that the woman in the picture was "An Arab Shod with
Fire: She is a dancer of Algeria and the slow, throbbing music of the Orient
is just as necessary . . . as the jewels and coins with which she adorns herself."[118] The erotic, sexual desires of the Western man were put on the Arab
woman he portrayed as an essentially throbbing, burning dancing girl. His

PHOTO 11

"An Arab Shod with Fire," March 1917

needs were hidden through the invention of hers—his sexual motives were displaced onto her.

In this operation, signifiers now familiar to us were employed: the rock wall as background, excessive jewelry, the seductive pose, and a cigarette. The cigarette prop not only signified the loose woman, but also functioned as a pun. In this picture of the dancing girl who was holding a cigarette and "shod with fire," the cheap word and visual puns drove home the message that the woman was even cheaper than the pun. The fire, throbbing music, and gold said to be necessary turned the Arab woman into a whore and a prostitute. *National Geographic,* in search of the Orient, created the hot dancing girl through costumes, props, and poses, then proceeded to "find," categorize, explain, and display her for U.S. popular education.

While each fragment of this picture may on its own have been "authentic," in total design the fragments were the Westerner's image of an Arab woman and unconnected to "authenticity." No doubt the rock wall behind the dancer "shod with fire" was truly rock; no doubt the jewelry was from the Arab world; no doubt the outfit was made by Arab hands; and no doubt that it was a real cigarette she held. But when I try to take in the excess, make sense of the pose, and think about why, from all possible backgrounds, a rock wall was chosen, the picture's authentic pieces collect into a lie. Alloula speaks to this very issue saying, "Truthfulness in details may very well not constitute the truthfulness of the whole, however. The elements of dress and the jewels, viewed separately, are factual, but their arrangement on the model fails to produce an impression of veracity."[119] No matter how painstakingly constructed, this "realism" fails. It does not manage to "rise above trivial reductiveness."[120]

In looking at photographs of Arab women in *National Geographic,* something is learned about the relationship between those on either side of the camera. Norman Denzin calls the anthropologist's and tourist's camera an "instrument of power."[121] And Berger argues that "men act and women appear. Men look at women."[122] In the activity of constructing the Arab dancing girl, we can see both of these claims come to life. More insidiously, such pictures take on a life of their own in that the more often they appear, the more real the image. The power of the West to represent the non-West, and the power of men to represent women, come together on the body of the Arab woman with such force that she became the fake and representations of her, the truth. Susan Sontag summarizes this process, saying: "Photographs do not simply render reality   realistically. It is reality which is scrutinized, and evaluated, for its fidelity to photographs."[123] Arab women could not remove the Western image of the Arab woman from them. As Anne McClintock states, "With photography, Western knowledge and Western authority became synonymous with the real."[124]

But there is more than gender going on in photographs of Arab women. Berger's argument that men act and women appear, men look at women, becomes more complex when the relationship is also one of West to non-West. Working from Berger's words, we can characterize what went on in *National Geographic* as: Western men act and non-Westerners appear, or more specifically to this study, Western men act and Arabs appear. Arab men, as well as Arab women, were made into objects to look at. In addition, another hypocritical operation took place when Western men looked at the women but used Arab men as an excuse to do so. This fits within what Said calls a "'bad' sexuality" given to Arabs. Thus, when *National Geographic* wanted to peek inside a harem or watch dancing girls, it was framed as examining what Arab men and Arab culture did to Arab women.

BREASTS

When I take up the subject of *National Geographic* looking at women, it is from a perspective of the female body that agrees with Susan Rubin Suleiman's: "The cultural significance of the female body is not only (not even first and foremost) that of a flesh-and-blood entity, but that of a symbolic construct. Everything we know about the body ... exists for us in some form of discourse; and discourse, whether verbal or visual, fictive or historical or speculative, is never unmediated, never free of interpretation, never innocent."[125] From here, a fundamental question needs to be addressed: How did, and does, *National Geographic* get away with producing pictures of bare-breasted women that even currently are not to be seen in other popular magazines, except pornographic publications?

But first, let's be clear about what the magazine gets away with. Samuel Delany says that for *National Geographic's* first seventy years, it "survived and functioned as scientifically legitimated softcore pornography ... eagerly thumbed through by generation after generation of Americans, males mostly." Delany declares that he himself read it that way in the 1950s and 1960s, and that discussions with older men show that the same went on in the 1930s and 1940s. What he calls "marginally sexual publications," such as *National Geographic,* keep discussions of representations of nudity in the margins through the general "closure of the scientific discourse around them" and by covering pictures with explanatory rhetoric that excludes the sexual. Thus, explains

Delany, sexual content is left in the margins to be joked over or for masturba-
tory purposes.[126]

I agree with his overall analysis of *National Geographic* as a marginally
sexual publication, but some aspects of Delany's interpretation are confusing.
He says that American males looked forward to viewing the "parsimoniously
doled out photographs of uncovered black and brown breasts—and, once the
sixties got underway, of uncovered black and brown male genitals." Unlike
Delany, I consider the pictures of bare-breasted women anything but "parsimoniously doled out," and aside from some air-brushed shadows, there were
no pictures of male genitalia in *National Geographic*—I have seen only one such
photo, and that was published in the late 1980s. Catherine Lutz and Jane Collins
also note that pictures of male genitalia do not appear, and that the magazine
has "relied on lengthening loincloths, drawing in shorts, or simply air-brush-
ing offending body parts."[127]

I suppose what makes for "parsimoniously doled out" is an arbitrary number, so I won't get into a counting game, but given the magazine's long-stand-
ing popular reputation linked to its photographs of bare-breasted women,
Delany would seem off the mark. Moreover, his incorrect claim that *National
Geographic* publishes pictures of male genitalia produces a serious misrepresentation of the magazine's construction of gender. Women and men did not
get the same treatment in the magazine. Indeed, how could they?

At the same time that Delany fails to see how gender plays out in *National
Geographic,* he critiques Donna Haraway's *Primate Visions,* citing what he sees
as her failure to account correctly for the coding of race in her discussion of
National Geographic's treatment of women scientists. Delany notes that in Haraway's analysis of *National Geographic*'s portrayal of the white woman sci-
entist, she speculates that the inclusion of black women scientists would have
upset the magazine's pattern of excluding blacks from such roles. Regarding
this, Delany says Haraway fails to recognize that for *National Geographic,*
"there are no black women in the West [and] by the magazine's schema, black
women are all natives." And he goes on to say: "Certainly this oversight (a failure to see the pattern? a repression? an avoidance of problematic material?)
weakens the feminist aspect of Haraway's argument."[128] While Delany's criticism of Haraway may have some merit, I would turn Delany's questions back
to him regarding his confusion about gender in *National Geographic.* If you
don't read for gender (or race) in the magazine, you have a hopelessly flawed
analysis—a failure to see the pattern? a repression? an avoidance of problematic material?

Understanding the use of women as central to the sexual thread running through *National Geographic* does not ignore how the subject of black men's sexuality was and is a major part of the construction of race. As Sander Gilman points out, "by the eighteenth century, the sexuality of the black, both male and female, becomes an icon for deviant sexuality in general." But while both were portrayed as "possessing not only a 'primitive' sexual appetite but also the external signs of this temperament—'primitive' genitalia"—it was women, not men, who were exhibited for audiences to view buttocks and fantasize about the genitalia.[129] Gilman says that the same arguments about oversize genitalia were applied to black men, but it was around women's genitalia that most of the discussions, writing, and exhibitions were concerned. Even the autopsies of black males in the nineteenth century made no mention of genitalia, whereas autopsies of females did. So both men and women of color were represented as having a "bad" sexuality, but it is upon the bodies of females that this was examined, demonstrated, and displayed.

Frantz Fanon, writing on the European image of "the Negro," asserts: "He is turned into a penis. He *is* a penis." Fanon notes that while studies showed the average penis length to be the same for Africans and Europeans, facts did not interfere with the image of the black man as a sexual beast. He continues: "For the majority of white men the Negro represents the sexual instinct (in its raw state). The Negro is the incarnation of a genital potency beyond all moralities and prohibitions. . . . The Negro is taken as a terrifying penis."[130]

This is an integral part of racism, a racism that has depended on establishing the sexual animality of black men. At the same time that all this is true, attention must be paid to how women are specially employed in the sex/race fantasy's most practical, physical, and visual forms. Gender thrusts into the fantasy and works the women over differently from the men. The sexual exploitation of women of color must be highlighted, and that includes what *National Geographic* does to women between its covers.

Berger defines mystification as "the process of explaining away what otherwise might be evident."[131] It is through mystification that bare-breasted women were displayed in *National Geographic*. Discussing French postcards of Algerian women, Alloula says that in the quest for the harem, the obsession has produced an exhibition of breasts that amounts to "an anthology of breasts."[132] This also describes what *National Geographic* produced. So how do you explain away pictures of bare-breasted women—what McElroy identifies as the "stock-in-trade for ethnographic photographers" and "titillating in their photographic objectification of non-European women"?[133]

In her discussion of nudity in religious painting, Margaret Miles points out that images of nudity "must be carefully balanced with other visual content so that an erotic response does not dominate, causing the viewer's engagement with the painting to collapse into 'mere' sensuality." *National Geographic*'s photographs of nudity strike a balance between the erotic and the educational. In educational photographs, as in religious paintings, "nudity must be depicted naturalistically enough to evoke the viewers' erotic interest: on the other hand, it must not be dominant enough to render this erotic attraction primary."[134]

For example, a *National Geographic* photograph of four women positioned something akin to a police lineup and with breasts exposed was merely captioned: "From left to right, mother, daughter, grandmother, and great-grandmother in Darfur."[135] Thus, the breasts were ignored, and readers looked at different generations of women as they naturally appeared. With this "innocent" presentation, the generations were visually tracked through general physical variations and not "just," or even necessarily, by looking at the differences in the women's breasts. Meanwhile, this particular photograph concentrated within one frame an "anthology of breasts," as mentioned by Alloula.

George Mosse's examination of nudism within the German life-reform movement that gained momentum in the late nineteenth century explains how the Germans' nudes were presented as different from pornography. Among the primary means employed were calling up the Greek tradition of idealized beauty and framing nudity in a natural setting, such as the sea or meadows. In addition, to secure further a distinction from the nudes of pornography, the movement "advised the use of glossy paper, which would heighten the artistic merit of the female nude without arousing lust."[136] All three of these conventions are used in *National Geographic*. Clearly, there are established ways of getting away with producing images of nudity.

These, by the way, also apply to displaying the male body. Analyzing some nude photographs taken in the 1920s–1930s of the African American actor Paul Robeson, Richard Dyer asserts that Robeson was put into "a position of 'feminine' subordination within the dynamics of looking that are built into any portrait-image of a human being in this culture."[137] Dyer explains that while one would assume nude photos to be heavily coded as erotic, those of Robeson are able to produce a "double articulation" through poses similar to statues of classical antiquity. By referring to classical nudes, an erotic image can carry its own denial of eroticism and insist that it celebrates the human form on a higher level.

This double articulation is identical to that produced in photos of women in *National Geographic* that also appeal to classical nude images. In one such picture (Photo 12), mentioned earlier among those having appeared in the magazine in 1914 and in 1917, the woman was displayed wearing a toga-style robe exposing her right breast. She stood against a rock wall to inject naturalness and, at the same time, was distanced from real nudity by looking off to the heavens in a statuesque pose. For additional security, the photograph was captioned solely by a few lines of poetry from Byron:

PHOTO 12

"A Daughter of Araby," March 1917

A Daughter of Araby

"Full many a flower is born to blush unseen,
And waste its sweetness on the desert air."[138]

It is noteworthy, as Kabbani points out, that Byron, who traveled to the Arab world in the first half of the 1800s, was an avid consumer of Orientalist travel accounts.[139]

With a rock wall, toga, statuesque pose, and poetry, *National Geographic* could cover its erotic photograph with appeals to naturalness, classical images of the body, and high literature. (It also managed to slip in the idea that Arab women are wasted on Arab men.) This double articulation corresponds to what Barbara Kirshenblatt-Gimblett found in her study of the exhibition of humans beginning in the first half of the nineteenth century in Europe and America. She says that "reframing of performance in terms of nature, science and education rendered it respectable."[140] The "Daughter of Araby" picture also brings up an issue mentioned by Susanne Kappeler concerning women viewers of these photographs. She says that "what women find objectionable in pornography, they have learnt to accept in products of 'high' art and literature."[141] And so it is that the systematic objectification of women for men's interests by *National Geographic* can pass by women viewers with appeals to high culture and, of course, education. It is also within this framing that the magazine was to be understood as useful for children.

All these different readings exist because, as Miles echoing Barthes, reminds us: "All images are polysemous, they imply, underlying their signifiers, a floating chain of signifieds" and the viewer can "choose some and ignore others."[142] It is this looseness that enables *National Geographic* to supply "voyeuristic eroticism . . . under the guise of scientific curiosity and self-improvement."[143] Different reader–viewers take what they need and walk by other meanings that are simultaneously available. The magazine is always innocent because you cannot "prove" an erotic reading was meant. The erotic photograph, distinct from the pornographic, as Barthes understands it, does not have to show sexual organs (let alone, as with the pornographic, have them at the center) but "takes the spectator outside its frame," letting the viewer complete the picture.[144] Eroticism can be there and not there when *National Geographic,* an educational magazine, represents women.

In another picture of a toga-clad Arab woman with a breast exposed, the subject was positioned near, actually in, a vine to signify naturalness and was carrying a water jug (Photo 13). This added prop served as a visual and verbal pun—jug meaning breast, a slang term in use since the early 1900s.[145] This is

PHOTO 13

"A Bedouin Beauty," March 1917

a device, as Torgovnick points out, "exploiting the visual image's power to say things by juxtaposition that would be unacceptable to put into words."[146] The caption to the photograph—once again, poetry from Byron—further enhances sexual meaning while simultaneously offering a high-culture connection:

A Bedouin Beauty

"Around her shone
The nameless charms unmarked by her alone,
The light of love, the purity of grace."[147]

Jugs would seem so cheap a pun that it would almost clash with the injection of high culture, but the correlation made by the viewer between objects in a picture not directly linked by narrative is a connection, as Judith Williamson argues, "not on a rational basis but by a leap made on the basis of appearance, juxtaposition and connotation."[148] This transference of significance carried out by the viewer can seemingly leave *National Geographic* out of the meaning-making process, and this is how it gets away with it—the reader–viewer has to make, or not make, possible connections. If the peep show, as understood by Kappeler, is essentially a place where men observe women but do not encounter them, then *National Geographic,* which identifies itself as a "window on the world," may instead be something of a peep show on the world.[149]

NAMING

National Geographic not only created the visual images; it also named them. For example, a picture of a man and woman (her breasts exposed) standing side by side and looking straight into the camera was captioned: "Brother and sister of Darfur carrying a leather bucket. Although the inhabitants of Eastern Darfur call themselves Arabs and speak that tongue, they are negroids."[150] Readers learned that negroids were "negroes with a small admixture of Arab blood which has come down through the ages."[151]

This picture and its caption made moves that we have already become acquainted with, in addition to some new ones. Was the photo's central interest a leather water bucket? Was the woman's being bare-breasted just an incidental and natural fact? In the 1920s, many Western men were still wearing bathing suits that covered the chest—not to mention women's modest bathing suits. And generally, in the West, one did not find adult male and female relatives in company unless clothed according to the standards of the day. Against this, a picture of an adult man and woman, identified as brother and sister and standing together naked to the waist, must surely have suggested incest to the Western viewer. Why pose these two people together in this manner? Why identify them as brother and sister? The idea of incest reinforced the trope of sexual excess and depravity. Certain meanings were suggested for the Western viewer by this photograph, but because they were left for the viewers themselves to make, *National Geographic* remained "innocent."

But seeing with your own eyes does not mean that you are seeing "correctly." It was often necessary for *National Geographic* to supply additional or correcting information. This was a unilateral practice of naming that discredited how people identified themselves and named them otherwise. People called themselves Arabs, spoke Arabic, and lived in the Arab world—yet *National Geographic* decided who they really were. Complete and correct identification and representation went on without any input from those being tagged. The magazine's assumed power to see and know others—what Said refers to as treating the whole world "as viewable by a kind of Western super-subject"—meant that readers were offered what *National Geographic,* not others, saw.[152]

Another example of naming is found in an article that referred to people from three Sudanese tribes as "Fuzzy Wuzzies." Readers learned that the name was given to them by the British because of their "enormous heads of hair." Not once were the tribespeople called anything except Fuzzies or Fuzzy Wuzzies. Hair, in the text and photographs, occupied a major focus of the article. Readers learned, for instance, that the hair of Fuzzy Wuzzies "would be the pride and despair of any wigmaker for private theatricals," and that a long bone pin kept in the hair was "used to scratch at the numerous tiny residents of the big head-dresses."[153] It was with a great deal of Western arrogance, not to mention a poor sense of humor, that people were so named in a popular educational journal.

Another naming practice deserves attention. This has to do with actually identifying persons photographed and reported on (other than rulers of countries) by their chosen names. Although occurring infrequently in *National Geographic,* one of these rare occasions was the case of a man named Hamoudi.

The director of a 1928 expedition to Iraq said that because he was often asked whether he did the actual digging at an archeological site, he decided to write an article concerning "the characters and foibles of the Arabs who . . . have done the spadework of archeology . . . [and] deserve at least these few pages."[154] The author informed readers that one of the first tasks in training a gang of workers was "to waken their intelligence and to inspire them with a certain degree of interest in the work itself." Readers also learned that "the Arab [is] so much better a digger than the Egyptian."[155] (In this article, the author classified Egyptians as Negro, not Arab. These particular categories of being weren't stable in *National Geographic,* and at other times Egyptians were presented as Arabs. Here, as in earlier examples, the magazine did not combine race and ethnicity, but chose between the two according to its own criteria and classificatory needs.)

The author reported that the expedition found in Hamoudi, the Arab foreman chosen after a few days of watching the men at work, a man who not only met all their criteria as a laborer, but who also possessed an "almost unique virtue" for men of the East. He was "an honest man in a land honeycombed with corruption." Hamoudi has "never taken a penny from anyone which . . . has given him a moral ascendancy over the men . . . [he is] in a class by himself."

Hamoudi was the exception to the Arab rule, for as we have learned by now from *National Geographic:* "No man on earth . . . is capable of such utter detachment from the world as the ordinary Arab."[156] Here, once again, we are reminded of the magazine's cousin, the world's fair. The Arabs on exhibit in the midway at the Chicago World's Fair were said to be "lounging in oriental indifference."[157] It is no wonder that men like Hamoudi seldom came along, and when he did, he certainly deserved to be identified by name and photographed for Westerners.

Not only did the one-of-a-kind Hamoudi get special mention, but this rare specimen of an Arab was even photographed for *National Geographic* readers (Photo 14). Notwithstanding his being the declared subject of this article, Hamoudi was represented as just a speck in the photograph and remained faceless. But Hamoudi also had a voice. The author overheard him telling the work gang: "You can thank the British for this. You were wild beasts, and now you are men."[158] This was the Arab who was named (first names were adequate for non-Western laborers), and these were the Arab words that were quoted.

PHOTO 14

"Hamoudi at Carchemish Stands by the Great Stone Which He Replaced in Its Position," August 1928

(Photo: Maynard Williams/National Geographic Society Image Collection)

3

"THE FURY AND EXCESS"

NATIONAL GEOGRAPHIC,
1930s THROUGH THE 1940s

This chapter's historical frame, the 1930s–1940s, has as its center World War II and its consequences for the area. In the early part of these two decades, England and France were further consolidating their respective colonial positions in the Arab world, but by the late 1930s Italian and German challenges to their hegemony in the area were in earnest. The mid-1930s witnessed the coming to power and steady growth of the Nazis in Germany and of world fascism in general, which directly affected the area and its European power brokers as all fought for control over Arab territory.

In 1939, Italy occupied all of Libya and Ethiopia (the latter is not an Arab country), forming a serious threat to French colonies in the Arab countries of northern Africa, as well as to the British in Egypt. This time period is also characterized by the British producing oil in large quantities in Iraq by 1939; the vital importance of this resource was being set and secured on the Arab stage. In the Arab world, this historical period was most defined politically by the establishment of the State of Israel in 1948. This event, at that time and beyond, would rival all other political issues for center stage in the Arab world. National liberation movements in the area that characterize the preceding chapter's time frame continue to influence the Arab world scene radically, and will remain as important a factor as oil and Israel.

When the French pulled out of the war in 1940, their colonies of Morocco, Tunisia, and Algeria became theaters of war between the Anglo-American armies and the Germans and Italians. The former European colonial networks were disintegrating and, throughout the course of the war, the United States and the Soviet Union took up positions as the two major world powers. The 1940s saw Lebanon and Syria gain independence from France, while Britain added Libya to its rule. In 1947, Britain withdrew from India, making its Arab holdings all the more crucial, particularly in light of the increasingly important oil-producing capabilities of the area. Britain's general policy at this time was directed toward trying to establish "friendly" agreements (such as trusteeships) to secure its strategic interests. As we will see later, France set another course in dealing with its remaining colonies. It seems, however, that despite Europeans' different strategies and policies for the Arab world, they all in the end had to figure out how to "manage" Arabs.

And for all these Westerners, directing work in the Arab world was no easy business, especially since laborers of Hamoudi's caliber were rare—in fact, we won't meet another as exceptional as he in *National Geographic*. A 1930 article on an excavation site at Ur, Iraq, explained something of the work situation: "The men's vitality is remarkable, for after a hard day's work of excavating they will run home singing and dancing. By nature they are far from industrious, but under intelligent supervision they become both keen and efficient."[1] This is racist discourse at its most familiar and predictable, but beyond registering it as part of *National Geographic*'s record, its direct, material consequences must also be clear.

The textual strategy of describing Arab workers in need of training said, of course, that the Western worker was superior. This, Mary Louise Pratt explains in a similar example, means: "Forgotten already, or never recognized at all, are the intense processes of indoctrination and coercion required to create the . . . working class and compel it to embrace upward mobility and the work ethic."[2] And as Albert Memmi points out, within the mythical portraits of the colonizer and the colonized the lazy native meets the industrious, active European who is justified in harshly supervising and giving low wages to indolents. Similarly, the colonized is portrayed as thievish and having violent instincts, which justifies the colonial regime's police and army.[3]

Basic, one-size-fits-all racism, such as *National Geographic*'s comments on Arab workers, takes a specifically Orientalist direction when we read: "A neat hand with a dagger is often a neat hand with a pick. The workman in the Near East cannot always be selected according to European standards of reliability."[4] The image of a violent, dagger-wielding man gave this racism its Arab world color, as constructed within Orientalism. It was only a matter of hues and fine lines that distinguished one brand of racism from another.

Excavating in the Arab world also had to work around other problems regarding Arabs. We read that certain ruins were lost to archeologists because Arabs pillaged the bricks for their homes. And a legendary spot identified as a prophet's tomb and a Muslim shrine had not yet entered the archeologist's notebook because "native fanaticism has made excavation impossible."[5]

In another article, an author detailed measures taken at an excavation site to help guard against stealing by their Arab diggers: "As a rule, I left the natives in uncertainty as to what I was looking for. Often I gave baksheesh for quite insignificant pieces of clay which they had found, whereas valuable bronze objects I sometimes laid aside casually, after lightly praising the finders. A workman who put any object in his wide, baggy trousers was severely punished and dismissed."[6] The author informed readers that when the work was completed at this site, the collected find was carefully packed and shipped to France.

If one lets go of a Western right to know while reading these accounts, all sorts of questions arise: Whose ruins were these? Why should tombs and religious shrines be turned into Western archeologists' objects of study? Why was it wrong for Arabs to construct dwellings with bricks from Babylon? Why should an Arab be "severely punished" by Westerners for taking treasures located in the Arab world? Why should treasures found in the Arab world be sent to France? James Clifford asks the same question: "Why has it seemed obvious until recently that non–Western objects should be preserved in European museums, even when this means that no fine specimens are visible in their country of origin?"[7] Further, we must ask, why was a Western desire to collect and exhibit more legitimate than an Arab need to use materials from ruins in the Arab world to build homes?

The term "cultural property" refers to "archeological or ethnological objects of cultural or historic significance" and "cultural heritage" to "the mass of these objects, which as a whole are considered to be of importance to the identity of a nation or cultural group."[8] While these definitions seem straightforward enough, within the hierarchical relationship between the West and the Arab world they became complicated. The West's understanding of Arab cultural property and cultural heritage was based on assumptions of Western guardianship of world history. But, as Warren asks, "Who, if anyone, owns the past?" And, "Who has the right or responsibility to preserve cultural remains of the past?"[9]

It was Western arrogance and power that claimed ownership of everything and transferred Arab property to the West. It was colonial power that enabled the West to train, supervise, and punish Arab workers at excavation sites in the

Arab world. It was this same power that developed the control methods used in 1933 at a site in Syria, where we read that diggers were hired from two different religious groups, with the idea that they would report "any theft made by their religious enemies," and where, from a tall tower referred to as the "eye," the site's director "supervised his native diggers" and expended "constant diligence . . . to prevent careless handling of precious ancient objects."[10] The assumed righteousness and universality of the goals of the excavation project and the lines of control structuring the relationship among Arabs, Westerners, and artifacts located in the Arab world combined to create a site of European cultural and material imposition.

If there was a relationship of respect between the West and the Arab world, genuine concern about the preservation of the world's cultural heritage could have been met in other ways. As David Sassoon recommends, "Instead of removing antiquities from their place of origin, could we not contribute to preserving them *in situ?* Could we not share our expertise and wealth to build museums large and small, and of still unimagined originality, all over the world?"[11] Without getting into a detailed discussion of these kinds of recommendations, suffice it to say that there were ethical ways to protect rather than pillage what was seen as humankind's heritage.

These examples from *National Geographic* support Aime Cesaire's argument that under colonization there is "no human contact, but relations of domination and submission which turn the colonizing man into a classroom monitor, an army sergeant, a prison guard, a slave driver, and the indigenous man into an instrument of production."[12] Within the racist relationship there could not be human contact because the subordinate group was represented as less than human. Serving this relationship were colonialist images of Arabs based on their essential characteristics, which were so well known through popular Orientalism that they did not need proof.

For example, *National Geographic*'s audience could read "all these Arabs are warlike" and not have to stop to question the statement because it had already been reported, ad nauseam, that Arabs were violent and fanatical. Readers knew this about Arabs—it was why colonialist powers had been forced to take military measures to subdue Arabs. With such knowledge in place, one could even make sense of reading that "all these Arabs are warlike" in a 1941 article about Europeans fighting one another for Arab land and resources. The context did not matter—Arabs were always warlike, Europeans were not. The article reported on European nations battling one another for strategically important Arab territory and oil reserves; nevertheless, it was Arabs who were said to be warlike. The essential nature of Arabs was already well established; there-fore, readers could follow the article's "logic" without problem. The piece con-cluded once again with *National Geographic* pointing to the natural relation-ship between Arabs and war: "From today's rising battle smoke, Baghdad lifts its battered head, and licks its wounds. . . . Let Allah's will be done. War is no disaster; its a man's game, like falconry and horse racing. They always fight in Iraq."[13]

Another article reported that in 1942, with Egypt in a theater of war between the Allies and the Axis powers, the battles raging on land and sea had turned the country into an armed camp. The author noted that the war among European nations had spilled all around and that Egypt was economically, socially, and politically affected by it; however, he said, "she remains essentially Egypt" and "she has weathered invasion after invasion and retained her identity. Small won-der if this war fails to arouse her citizens, as it does the sons of the West. . . . Peace-ful, drowsy, pleasant Egypt must be for many men a land of blood and sand. . . . Egypt will remain a land of British victory if strength and fortitude and courage can keep her so."[14]

In an amazing combination of Arab laziness and warlike nature, Egyptians were too drowsy even to be bothered by the same old business of war. It would seem that Arabs either engaged in violent activities or were so lethargic that even large-scale war did not stir them. European colonialists seized Arab land and resources by subduing violent Arabs or by taking, without resistance, what sleepy Arabs let languish. This made Orientalist sense because Arabs, also already constructed through primitivist discourse, were naturally irrational and contradictory.

The arrogance of these discourses was such that a missionary–educator who had spent forty years in Iraq and the surrounding region, and wrote two stan-dard Arabic grammar books, could openly insult Arabs. He declared in *National Geographic:* "How that amazing tongue was developed by a primitive people living in a barren land, and was embodied in a rich and varied literature, is one of the enigmas of history."[15] With such little respect, Arabs and Arabic were separated—their language was too good for them.

Memmi points out that the traits of the colonized are a series of negations, and even those characteristics one would otherwise consider positive are twisted by the colonizer. And so it is that if Arabic is a rich language, worthy of study, it must be separated—or, at least, distanced—from Arabs. Memmi gives the example of this negating operation turning famous Arab hospitality into an indication of "the colonized's irresponsibility and extravagance, since he has no notion of foresight or economy."[16] The racism basic to Orientalism and primitivism never needs proof because it creates and relies on essential characteristics that are proved against one another within, not outside, the discourses. However, the power of essentialism for racist discourse is also its problem.

BLOOD, BONES, AND BRANDS

If Arabs were, and always have been, so essentially violent that a world war was like falconry in Iraq, that land and sea battles did not stir drowsy Egypt, and that in Yemen Arabs were "predatory, and quarrel with all and sundry over a few muddy waterholes," certainly this trait could be scientifically established.[17] Whatever was identified as Arab nature had to be in the blood—any racism must eventually, or initially, try to locate itself in blood.

National Geographic's audience learned that in certain regions of Egypt one could "see the people of ancient Egypt, alive and in the flesh," who through isolation have "kept their blood pure." The existence of this "sturdy race" made it evident that the physical effects of inmarriage had not been "disastrous." The mental effect of keeping the blood pure through such inmarriage left intact "much of the mold of character and the habits of thought and action of five thousand years ago." However, it seems that isolation and inmarriage were unnecessary, given the powerful Egyptian genes. (In the following, as we have seen before in *National Geographic,* Egyptians were classified as Negroes, not Arabs.) The author reported that in towns where "Arabs, Turks, and Greeks have mixed their blood with the old stock [Egyptians], the final result is not composite but Egyptian. There is something about this land ruled by the river, the sun, and the desert that stamps all men with the same brand."[18] This is not dissimilar to standard racist understandings of what is produced by mixing white and black blood.

Characteristics that the colonialist hung on the native were presented as permanent, unchanging—in the blood. Thus, as Abdul JanMohamed explains, all specificity and difference is changed into a "magical essence."[19] In this operation, there is no sense of anything being socially determined; only natural categories explain the native. Henry Louis Gates, Jr., is correct when he says: "Race is the ultimate trope of difference because it is so arbitrary in its application."[20] But the power to be so arbitrary lies in race being traced to the blood; it has to be in the blood to be race. And once in the blood, this "magical essence" builds a scientific case and presents evidence. Race always tries to do what it cannot do (does not have to do): prove itself and its categories.

This was part of the drive behind endless testing and measuring to establish racial difference. *National Geographic* informed readers that, with the task of tracking the historical chain of inhabitants in the Sinai, a 1948 expedition dug up tombs and measured skulls. Grave digging in the interest of science needed no further justification or explanation. A picture of the renowned anthropologist Dr. Henry Field and another expedition member busy at work on remains removed from Arab graves (Photo 15) carried a tongue-in-cheek caption: "Little did the owner think that scientists would study his skull. Dr. Field, the author, measures with his calipers one of the 19 skulls from an old 'beehive' tomb. . . . [Thirteen] measurements and many other observations [were] made on each skull by the anthropologist. Head shapes proved similar to those of modern Bedouins—long and narrow."[21]

The right of Westerners to dig up and examine bodies from Arab graves was assumed. The magazine could even be humorous about it. The power and domination that produced such events is clear if we try to imagine Arabs having same right to know about the West: A reversal of roles seems absolutely ludicrous, a joke. Not only who has the right to rob graves, but whose graves are understood as available for such desecration is limited. Richard Drinnon tells us

PHOTO 15

"Little Did the Owner Think that Scientists Would Study His Skull,"
December 1948

(Photo: National Geographic Society Image Collection)

that Thomas Jefferson dug up, collected, and published findings on Indian remains excavated from a mound near his home in Virginia. The sacredness of Indian burial grounds was of little concern to Jefferson, who, as Drinnon points out, would have been guilty of grave robbing had he done the same in a Charlottesville cemetery.[22]

This same right to know was still in place in 1948 in Sinai, where the American expedition also took the calipers to the heads of current inhabitants. Another picture showed Field measuring a living Arab specimen (Photo 16). In all, he measured the heads of 223 bedouins, writing: "On each individual, 40 measurements and observations were recorded in about eight minutes. Results, being tabulated at Harvard, indicate that the modern Bedouin is a descendant of the early Mediterranean race, which dwelt beside that sea."[23]

This information was presented as though its importance was self-evident. The photographs of measuring skulls (of the dead and alive) in *National Geographic* are visual confirmation of Said's contention that "As a cultural apparatus

PHOTO 16

"Puzzle—How to Measure the Head Without Removing the Headcloth," December 1948

(Photo: National Geographic Society Image Collection)

Orientalism is all aggression, activity, judgment, will-to-truth, and knowledge. The Orient existed for the West, or so it seemed to countless Orientalists, whose attitude to what they worked on was either paternalistic or candidly condescending."[24] And these pictures directly mirror what Anne McClintock explains about the role of photography in racial science. She says it was expected "to provide mechanical and therefore objectively sound 'factual' knowledge about racial 'types,' 'specimens,' and 'tribes.'"[25]

Forty measurements on each bedouin. This activity and the tabulated results had purpose within the need to identify what Rana Kabbani refers to as "the savage body."[26] Establishing otherness was the goal of Westerners taking measurements of non-European bodies. The drive to build a racial hierarchy led to countless skull and genital measurements and comparisons. This relentless search for difference took place because, as George Mosse says, "Stereotyping through looks was basic to racism, a visually centered ideology."[27]

The "savage body" was built on ideas of animality, and for *National Geographic* one of the signifiers of this in the Arab world was eating. Earlier we read how the negating operation turned famous Arab hospitality into an indication of irresponsibility. Arab hospitality (much of which has to do with food) received another negative twist in the construction of the savage body.

The caption to a 1932 picture of Arabs sitting on the ground eating (Photo 17) read: "Using no knife or fork, the Arab takes rice in his right hand, squeezes it into a ball, and bolts it. If fowl or mutton is served, the leader of the party tears it to pieces and tosses a portion to each diner, who deftly catches it in mid-air."[28] A 1935 article carried a very similar photograph, with a caption that explained: "All guests plunge their hands into the food and eat with their fingers. Large chunks of meat are torn off and swallowed between handfuls of cereal."[29] In another example, in 1940, the magazine's readers learned, from the dinner guest of an Iraqi sheikh, that even after eating until ready to burst, there was still a mountain of food left. But, he continued, there was no need to worry about the food's going to waste, because "it disappeared 'like snow upon the desert's dusty face' when the sheikh's followers were turned loose on it with their fingers."[30]

While the textual images linking Arabs eating and animality were delivered with blunt force, the visual ones needed help. Without reading the explanatory captions, it would have been impossible for the viewer to know what was going on in the photos of Arabs eating—one saw little more than a group of men huddled in a circle. So why look at seemingly dull photographs? Why publish such nondescript pictures in a magazine with an already well-established reputation for photography?

PHOTO 17

"Bedouins of the Author's Escort Enjoy a Meal of Rice and Dried Shark," October 1932
(Photo: National Geographic Society Image Collection)

Barbara Kirshenblatt-Gimblett explains this as the process of exhibiting the quotidian and relates it to what John MacAloon calls "a genre error: one man's life is another man's spectacle." She explains that framing what would otherwise be of no interest as something worth looking at can be achieved through comparisons that call the taken for granted into question. This is, of course, all the easier to produce in images of the non-West because "the exotic is the place where nothing is utterly ordinary."[31]

That is why and how *National Geographic* readers looked at photos of Arabs eating. These were not pictures of men sitting in a huddle on the ground; these were pictures of non-Europeans eating, and more specifically, Arabs who ate like animals. This framing changed everything. Viewers looked for and at difference; the photographs, therefore, became interesting and could reveal much more than they did at first glance.

In a 1946 article titled "Ali Goes to Clinic," an American doctor prescribed medicine with a dosage of three spoonfuls daily for a Syrian patient named Ali. The patient replied that he did not have a spoon, to which the doctor exclaimed, "What! No Spoon?" Ali answered, "We Arabs are wild beasts. We eat with our hands; we know not spoons."[32] The animality of Arabs that was marked by eating with one's hands would never have been confused with Americans eating ribs or fried chicken with their hands. It looked so different when Arabs did it because in their case it was indicative of an overall backwardness, a primitive culture. And the words of an Arab man (in remarkably stilted English) substantiated these ideas for Western readers.

In *National Geographic,* Islam was an important element responsible for Arab backwardness and the savage body. Western representations of Muslims branded them with their religion. For example, it was reported that "religious fanatics with bloodshot eyes and wild mien collect curious and morbid crowds when they mutilate themselves in the market places of Morocco. Sometimes in their frenzy the zealots put burning torches in their mouths."[33] And about a particular road in Morocco, readers learned it was where "Puritans of Islam have come up like locusts ... to seize at the points of their swords all that desert hearts can covet."[34] In another article, an author, explaining the muezzin, included a few lines of translated Muslim prayer, about which he said: "Whether it is recorded accurately or not, no words can fully and adequately convey the elemental weirdness of the cry."[35] And, of course, Muslim women wearing veils were always the sign of the ultimate savage body.

These images of the Muslim body in its essential primitiveness and animality were clearly linked to racial hierarchy and colonialism. *National Geographic* readers learned that for Western powers in the Arab world there was "the problem of religion," as an author characterized the tense situation in 1932 faced by France in its Arab colonies.[36] Regarding "the problem of religion," Said makes an important point on Islam and Orientalism: "Insofar as Islam has always been seen as belonging to the Orient, its particular fate within the general structure of Orientalism has been to be looked at first of all as if it were one monolithic thing, and then with a very special hostility and fear."[37] This understanding runs through *National Geographic* and accounts for the magazine's representations of the "Mohammedan" mind and Muslim fanaticism.

Among statements concerning Islam in *National Geographic,* one that stands out as fantastical thinking is: "There is a real possibility that if Mohammed had not been born, the Arabs would today be Christians."[38] Well, he was, and they are not. But Islam's presence did not prevent Westerners from conjuring up visions of biblical times while in the Arab world. A donkey, a robe, a dirt road—most anything could whisk *National Geographic* back to imagining the Arab world in a time before Mohammed was born. As Sarah Graham-Brown notes, biblical image-making was popular for the tourist and pilgrim market, and for publishing illustrated Bibles and biblical histories in Europe. Brown says that Europeans and Americans were so "steeped in the imagery of the Bible" that travelers could see biblical significance in scenes even outside Palestine.[39]

BIBLICAL TIMES IN THE 20TH CENTURY

As mentioned earlier, not only did the Arab time warp call up visions of the time of the *Arabian Nights,* but everyday Arab sights could instantly take one back to earlier periods of Christianity. This usually took place within articles devoted to retracing the steps of Christian saints and the Crusaders, visiting holy sites and churches, reporting on the latest work of biblical archeology, and taking pilgrimages to the Holy Land. Visual links to the past made through the faces, clothing, work, or housing, of current Arab inhabitants provided religious appeal to the magazine's Christian audience.

This also performed the function of setting up a Christian/Muslim comparison. After religious time-traveling to days gone by, readers were rudely brought back to the present with the magazine's representations of Muslim Arabs. For example, typically framed under the subtitle "Biblical Scenes in the 20th Century," a traveler in Syria noted that the "primitive conditions" included women making up beds of straw for their newborns, "just as women used to at the dawn of the Christian Era." Biblical images were created just that easily and directly in the magazine, and they were employed comparatively just as directly.

After conjuring an image of the Virgin Mary from the sight of Syrian women, the author described how the women delivered their offspring: "It often happens that she returns from the fields in the forenoon to give birth to her child at home . . . and in the afternoon she is back in the fields toiling under the hot sun." So much for the nativity scene. Alongside a Christian/Muslim comparison, others were set up: Western/non-Western men and Arab men/Arab women. Readers learned that while Arab women work in the noonday heat, "the man, muffled in white garments or even shaded with an umbrella, sits nearby and looks on." And during his travels through Syria, the author noted that he frequently encountered a man riding a donkey while his wife walked alongside carrying heavy loads, including a child tied onto her back.[40]

This was often the point made in *National Geographic.* Orientalism was so much about cruel Arab men and subjugated Arab women, who were further divided into categories of oppression. Brown notes two common photographic images of Middle Eastern women: indolent harem life depicting women in listless poses, eyes staring into space, and the life of drudgery led by women enslaved by lazy husbands.[41] These are the same images, produced visually and textually, that constitute *National Geographic*'s representations of Arab women.

During a visit to Morocco, an author said, the men "take color from their surroundings. They are treacherous and arrogant, the strong bullying the weak. They are cruel and oppressive and full of guile . . . a community of men seething with life and passion." Of the women, he said they were "veiled faces secreted behind high walls; women who toil like beasts of burden in the sun; and women, 'the daughters of joy,' who sing and adorn themselves for the warrior fresh from his fight and the trader with his new-gotten wealth."[42]

As we have seen, these Orientalist caricatures were common fare in *National Geographic* and completely predictable in words and pictures. This repetition of images is related to Homi Bhabha's discussion of the stereotype as a major discursive strategy in colonial discourse that "vacillates between what is always 'in place,' already known, and something that must be anxiously repeated . . . as if the essential . . . that needs no proof, can never really, in discourse, be proved."[43] The stereotypes of Arab men as idle, cruel, and violent and having a 'bad' intelligence and a 'bad' sexuality, and stereotypes of Arab women as dancing girls, harem sex slaves, and beasts of burden were, throughout *National Geographic,* "anxiously repeated." Not only did these stereotypes work into systems of racial and cultural hierarchies, but by the way they were gendered they allowed European men to be represented in the supreme patriarchal image of protector. As Gayatri Spivak puts it: "brown women saved by white men from brown men."[44] This is a favorite image for the colonialist project as a whole, and one that corresponds to what Said calls "male Orientalism."[45]

A SOFTNESS ALMOST FEMININE

A 1932 description of Morocco in *National Geographic* read:

Morocco, long an empire guarded from the coveting eyes of Europe by the will of a proud and exclusive people, remains in her subjection a land tempting to the traveler in search of new and even rude experiences. She is a country up-to-date, accessible, civilized; yet barbarous, antique, and forbidden. . . . She is an Eastern land in the marrow of her bones, though placed in Africa; and she has been penetrated through centuries by European influences, which lie deep under the surface of her oriental life. . . . Cities and peoples passionate with the fury and excess of Africa.[46]

Not only is this quotation a fine example of male Orientalism and what Cynthia Enloe calls "empire-building masculinity," but there is a logic of contraries woven within it.[47]

As we saw earlier, knowing the primitive as irrational enabled one to make sense of a string of contradictions, and those contradictions themselves proved that the primitive was irrational. The authority of Orientalist and primitivist discourses produced what Said discusses as a circularity in which "the perfect closure of the whole thing" made it unassailable; a powerful system where alternative interpretations were eliminated, made unthinkable.[48] It was a system in which Morocco could be civilized yet barbarous; in which Arab men could be lazy, yet sing and dance after a hard day's labor; and in which Arab women could be secluded and veiled behind walls yet photographed bare-breasted. Somehow everything, anything, said about Arabs hung together in a logic of contraries that needed no validation outside its own circle of meaning.

On a visit with nomads in Morocco, the author said it was impossible for him to convey the feeling "of having fallen upon a strange and other world; Africa, violent, and barbaric, yet of a singular refinement and of a romantic beauty."[49] This was clearly a gendered description—it was Arab men who supplied the violence and barbarism, and Arab women, the refinement and romance. Another description spoke of Morocco as a land in which "'the last enchantments of the Middle Ages' mingle with a primitive barbaric violence, and the mechanical paraphernalia of our current civilization."[50] These three elements were supplied by Arab women, Arab men, and European colonialism, respectively.

Marianna Torgovnick says that the ensemble of tropes, those ideas and images that construct and control our perceptions of primitives, "however miscellaneous and contradictory—forms the basic grammar and vocabulary of . . . primitivist discourse, a discourse fundamental to the Western sense of self and Other."[51] In *National Geographic,* we see the miscellaneous and contradictory makeup of this discourse and how gender runs through it. Further, we see how primitivism joined with male Orientalism to produce Western images of Arab men and Arab women.

And so it was that a river was described, "like all else in Morocco . . . a creature of strange and violent contrasts."[52] And after a desert drive from Damascus, "the air beside the Euphrates had a softness almost feminine."[53] Clearly, these discourses were, to borrow from Laura Donaldson, "gender-saturated"[54]— so much so that we read: "To one who lives in dreams, modern Baghdad, in spite of all twentieth-century improvements, spells disillusion. My body enjoyed my private bath; but my thoughts squatted with story-book characters [*The Arabian Nights*] around a marble pool."[55] Gender was spilling all over the place.

REMINDERS AND RECEPTACLES

But just as Orientalism and primitivism were gender-saturated discourses, this gender was race-saturated. In an article about Allied soldiers stationed in Egypt, *National Geographic* offered some glimpses into the role of Arab women in their lives. The caption to a photo of soldiers dancing with Arab women at a local club said that the Cairo girls "brighten the lives of lonely soldiers in from the desert for a few days' leave." This half-page photo was juxtaposed with a picture of British women in uniform who were members of the Women's Auxiliary Air Force. The photo was titled, "Tired but Smiling WAAFS Arrive at Cairo from Britain."[56] In the text of the article, readers were told that when the women of the British services appeared "neatly togged in full military uniform, Cairo's sheltered hyperfeminine girls hardly knew what to make of it."[57] When Western and Arab women were put side by side in this context, difference was easily established. The "hyperfemininity" of Arab women made them useful for providing entertainment for the soldiers; the European women had other services to offer. Different women performed different functions for these Western men, who had a variety of needs.

In another set of half-page pictures included in this article, juxtaposition again offered comparison between types of women (Photos 18 and 19). The picture of the Arab dancer was titled: "Rhythm of the Nile Retains Its Witchery," and the caption said that this "Cairo night club beauty" entertained soldiers by "gliding through voluptuous routines such as delighted Mark Antony at the court of Cleopatra." The caption to the picture of the Arab woman in Western dress told readers that "The intelligence and comeliness of the Levantine are a revelation to many Englishmen."[58] The Arab woman sitting with the British soldier was Westernized enough to accompany him publicly, while others served as pure spectacle. Dancers and traditionally dressed Arab women never appeared in *National Geographic* "with" Western men. The visual suggestion of a heterosexual couple did not occur with an Arab woman who was not recognizably Westernized. And even when such outward appearances were adopted, Arab women were merely imitations and temporary substitutes for the women back home—Western men made due.

In this 1942 article, *National Geographic* explained that military recreation committees and the YMCA provided various services and entertainment for

PHOTO 18

"Don't You Just Love to Watch People Dance?"
April 1942
(Photo: National Geographic Society Image Collection)

enlisted men, and that they provided "something more important—feminine companionship." Readers learned that daughters of wealthy Arab families given some European education in mission or convent schools were acquiring Western ideas about social life. The author saw the time as a "somewhat delicate period of social transition" that found some Arab girls allowed to date the Western men stationed in Egypt.

But this transition wasn't occurring fast enough. The author reported it was still "numerically inescapable that there are not enough girls to go around." However, he continued, the YMCA was trying to help out, because men who had been out in the desert for months had "an entirely legitimate yearning for feminine company." To this end, the YMCA hosted dances twice weekly and invited "local girls of good family" to dance with the men.[59] Here, Westernized Arab women were seen as a source of enjoyment for Western men living

PHOTO 19

"Rhythm of the Nile Retains Its Witchery," April 1942

(Photo: National Geographic Society Image Collection)

in Arab countries. This perspective fell within a patriarchal understanding of the needs of men and the uses of women. At the same time, Arab women were never confused with Western women in *National Geographic*.

In a 1944 article about the work of Red Cross women, written by one of that organization's members, gender and race unfolded. The author's assignment was said to be located "in the middle of some nowhere with an Arabic name." She told readers that her duties in Egypt included more than just serving coffee and doughnuts to combat men or merely dancing with GIs: "We served as a reminder of everything these soldiers had left at home" and "receptacles for the outpourings of all their troubles, problems, joys and sorrows." While both had very gendered roles, Western women served functions different from those of Westernized Arab women, who could not be reminders of home.

The author shared an anecdote that also revealed gender and race at work. While sunbathing outside her tent one day, she noticed a group of GIs nearby who were heavy in discussion. She found this curious and eventually understood what was going on when a spokesman for the GIs said, "'Look, sister, for heaven's sake don't do that! White skin is too scarce in this part of the world to roast.'"[60] There were women, and there were women.

White skin mattered, and this came through in *National Geographic* in a perfect example of what Pratt calls "the courtly encounter," a characteristic scene found within the "sentimental" branch of travel writing. These scenes are built on a European arriving in a village and presenting himself to the local leaders. Pratt illustrates this with a passage from Park's *Travels in the Interior Districts of Africa* (1799), which she identifies as one of the most popular travel books of the 19th century. In the passage, a European entered the tent of an Arab king where, he reported, the attendants and "especially the ladies ... searched my pockets and obliged me to unbutton my waistcoat, and display the whiteness of my skin; they even counted my toes and fingers."[61]

In what could be called a textbook example of "the courtly encounter," in a 1932 *National Geographic* article, under the subtitle "Wild Bedouin Women Laugh at Our Gold Teeth," the author gave the following account of his visit to a bedouin camp:

> The boldest ventured to rub my bare arm with her hard, black fingers to see if she could remove some of the white. . . . The examination was continued to my throat and breast, and before I knew what was happening the tail of my shirt was pulled out and a black hand was passed admiringly over that part of my anatomy which is usually decorously covered. . . . my investigator would have proceeded further, but I laughingly assured her that I was the same color all over.

The author informed readers that he was invited to spend the night at the bedouin camp and offered the gift of a wife. He "glanced about the circle of far from beautiful women" and made a facial expression understood by his hosts as a refusal. They responded by clarifying the offer: "Oh, no, not these! The young maidens are with the flocks, but they will come back at sunset."[62] The author ended the anecdote here—whether he actually accepted the invitation was never stated. I suppose readers were to assume that he would not treat women as Arab men did, but then again, even the YMCA acknowledged that men had "an entirely legitimate yearning for feminine company."

What meanings about the Arab world were readers expected to take from this story of bedouin "hospitality" in *National Geographic?* The images of Arab men and Arab women produced in this nearly sexual adventure were embedded in a lascivious Orient constructed within Orientalism. I am not arguing that Westerners would not have had plenty of opportunities for sex with Arab women: As in the rest of the world, there was a readily available market of women for sale or favor. However, the author was saying much more than this with his Orientalist tale of Arab hospitality. I do not believe his story, but its veracity aside, what were readers supposed to learn from it? *National Geographic* employed all-too-familiar exotic, erotic signifiers, and the images conjured up were about Western male sexual fantasies of the East.

A strategy within Western patriarchy used Arab patriarchy as a cover for its own gender-saturated practices and images. Often, representations of Arab women that were framed as looking at what Islam and Arab men did to women were actually what *National Geographic* did to women. This critique neither denies nor mitigates the oppression of women throughout the Arab world, but it does insist on also recognizing the West's very real patriarchal structures and operations.

WOMEN SHROUDED IN MISERY

A picture taken from the waist up of a bare-breasted young woman standing with her hands on her hips carried the following caption:

> This Sudanese slave girl belongs to a rich Arab merchant of Mocha. Treaties among Christian nations to suppress the slave trade are without effect on human behavior in remote nooks of the Moslem world. When a traveler visits a sheik and admires a slave, his host—true to desert hospitality—may make him a present of his human chattel![63]

Several important things were going on with this picture and its caption. The caption employed the familiar stereotype of the rich Arab slaver, represented Arab men as oppressors of women, set up a Christian/Muslim hierarchy, and perverted Arab hospitality. All of this served as a cover in order to exhibit a bare-breasted slave in the magazine.

But even more was going on: *National Geographic* was participating in the exploitation of this Sudanese woman by borrowing her from the Arab slaver to take one of its bare-breasted photographs. Norman Denzin argues that with the practice of photographing the Third World, "the entire social body of these nations becomes a commodified picture that can be bought and sold; just as the bodies of the natives were previously bought and sold within the colonizing classes."[64] The magazine directly participated in the woman's exploitation and oppression while presenting and selling its activity as educational.

There was no innocent way to produce this picture, which was driven largely by a Western male fascination with Orientalism's harem and female slaves. There were two possible ways that this picture came into being, both damning. Either the photograph was the result of dealing with a slave owner and temporarily sharing his property for *National Geographic*'s particular needs, or the woman was not actually a slave and the Orientalist's slave fantasy was constructed on film with a real Arab body. Whichever method was used, there is no way out of this picture's violence. Neither the alibi of education about the Arab world nor the alibi of Arab men oppressing Arab woman can cover *National Geographic*'s complicity.

This photograph was additionally insidious in its power to beautify slavery. Susan Sontag discusses the ability of photographs to beautify and cites Walter Benjamin's observation on the camera given in an address delivered in Paris at the Institute for the Study of Fascism in 1934. Benjamin said that in front of a tenement or a rubbish heap, "photography can only say, 'How beautiful'. . . . It has succeeded in turning abject poverty itself, by handling it in a modish, technically perfect way, into an object of enjoyment."[65] *National Geographic* did exactly the same thing by photographing the oppression of women.

The bare-breasted slave on loan from her Arab owner became an aesthetically pleasing object—a fine, nude body accented by the play of technical lighting. Such photographs of the domination of Arab women are part of that domination. Sontag says, "Gazing on other people's reality with curiosity, with detachment, with professionalism, the ubiquitous photographer operates as if that activity transcends class interests, as if its perspective is universal."[66] *National Geographic*'s professional gaze did not transcend gender and race interests.

This fact was clearer to those who were the objects of the magazine's gaze than it was to its consumers. An author told readers that upon sighting women washing their brightly colored laundry at a stream, he rushed to set up his camera, but the women retreated behind mud walls. He said, "They thought my camera had an evil and immodest eye."[67] *National Geographic*'s audience would be expected to read this remembering that primitives were superstitious and forgetting pictures of bare-breasted women.

National Geographic's "evil eye" not only photographed slaves, it hallucinated them. In an article on Tunisia, a country geographically within "honeymoon distance" of Europe, readers followed the author through the *souk,* where he sought out "the slave market." He wrote, "For every beautiful slave, her blond hair spread wide on brown fingers whose real delight was in firmer gold, there were hordes of pitiful creatures, so shrouded in misery that it is a wonder they could be sold." This description was set up in a way that led one to think it was actually what the author saw as he walked through the Tunisian market. But then the author said, "In the former slave market of Tunis, I watched American visitors buying jewelry."[68]

This was a journey into the Orientalist's ultimate sexual fantasy—"honeymooning" with slave women. Readers would not have known that the slave-market scene was invented until they read the last sentence, in which "the slave market" became "the former slave market." The vision of white slaves being traded with Arab gold turned out to be a blond American woman buying gold jewelry. The whole slavery scene was created in the eye of *National Geographic*—an eye that saw what it wanted and, with or without the camera, saw the Arab world through the lens of Orientalism.

HEROES AND THEIR GOOD WORKS

The Arab world offered more than harems and slave women. According to *National Geographic,* it offered Westerners "opportunities of advancement and adventure," with colonialist armies fighting Arab "die-hards," and the attraction of a different life "for a man grown tired of his boulevards and the charms of an overripe civilization."[69] For others, the Arab world was a place where people were "so restful and free from ambition"—a contrast to the West, where there are "restless ones, with great and unsatisfied longings."[70] After having lived "among these primitive peoples," some find themselves "incapable of resuming European life." One author explained, "Among these simple men . . . I felt I had not aged, for their mentality was exactly the same as that of their fathers. . . . There is a softness and sweetness in forgetting our troubled humanity in this forgotten corner where live ageless men as unchanging as the rocks."[71]

The magazine's romantic views of life among Arabs, which offered Westerners the choice of adventure or simplicity, were not unique, but they were typical of colonialist rhetoric in its wider incarnations.

Beyond the economic drive of the colonial project, Laura Rice points out the
contradictory desires to escape Western society's trappings and repressive codes
of behavior by entering primitive space, and "the desire to civilize the wilderness by making 'them' resemble 'us.'"[72] As we have seen, contradictions were the
stuff of primitivist discourse; it will come as no surprise that the softness and
sweetness of living among primitive peoples had its other side. And so it was
that a *National Geographic* article explained, under the subtitle "The Problem
of Primitive Peoples," that:

> It must be recognized that there are many peoples who are not yet ready
> for independence on the lines of Western democracy. . . . In fact, many
> primitive peoples, when found by the white man, were living in con-
> ditions of indescribable horror. . . . To overcome all this, thousands of
> heroic white men and women—officials, soldiers, missionaries, and
> doctors—have given their lives. . . . Democratic government is the high-
> est achievement of great intellects. . . . It is not a natural state to which
> primitive people spontaneously revert. It demands a high standard of
> civilization and advanced education.[73]

So much for the simple life. This quotation mirrors Said's words on the
colonial perspective, "Independence was for whites and Europeans, the lesser
or subject peoples were to be ruled; science, learning, history emanated from the
West."[74] *National Geographic*'s 1943 description of colonialism relied on the
familiar parent/child metaphor and presented primitives (children), after more
than a half-century of colonial rule, as still unable to govern themselves. This must
certainly have left *National Geographic* readers suspicious of these people's
ability ever to meet the standards set by the West (parent).

According to Said, the Orientalist saw himself as "a hero rescuing the Orient
from the obscurity, alienation, and strangeness which he himself had properly
distinguished."[75] This assertion corresponds to the grand role of the colonialist portrayed earlier and also rings true in the following quotation on colonialism's good works:

> The British colonial system has been marked by the peopling of empty
> lands by industrious colonists, and the production in those lands, often

formerly waste areas, of goods which have helped to raise the standard of living of the whole world; the advance of backward populations from poverty and hardship to prosperity and self-reliance; the overthrow of cruel tyrants in many regions and their replacement by the rule of law and the abolition of slavery.[76]

These statements made in the mid-1940s on the merits of colonialism echoed many of the ideas already encountered in this study (including the 1988 description of the historical era in which *National Geographic* was founded). As we will continue to see, they have remained timeless.

Cesaire's understanding of colonialism is very much different from that of *National Geographic*. He works through a list of what colonialism was not: "neither evangelization, nor a philanthropic enterprise, nor a desire to push back the frontiers of ignorance, disease, and tyranny, nor a project undertaken for the greater glory of God, nor an attempt to extend the rule of law." Cesaire also says that the education offered within a colonial system was "a parody of education, the hasty manufacture of a few thousand subordinate functionaries, 'boys,' artisans, office clerks, and interpreters necessary for the smooth operation of business."[77] This is at odds with colonialism's education-and-training record as presented in *National Geographic*. Although written with no relationship to the magazine, Cesaire's words read like a point-by-point rejection of *National Geographic*'s descriptions of colonialism. The reason for this correspondence is the magazine's use of classic colonialist discourse. One need not be familiar with *National Geographic* to produce anti-colonialist arguments that stand in word-for-word opposition to the magazine's representation of colonialism. One need only know colonialist discourse to do this.

And what of those heroic missionaries mentioned along with officials, soldiers, and doctors? V. Y. Mudimbe's contrasting view to the magazine's maintains that the programs of missions were "more complex than the simple transmission of the Christian faith" and were identified with colonial "cultural propaganda, patriotic motivations, and commercial interests."[78] The overall Christian/Muslim hierarchy and the relentlessly negative portrayal of Islam cannot be read separately from the role of religious missions in the Arab world. It was no coincidence or mistake that missionaries were always included in *National Geographic*'s lists of colonial players.

In every account, the colonial record in the Arab world was lauded by the magazine. Readers learned that, in Jordan, "Petra at last [was] open to serious travelers" after the British cleared the way for modern transportation through what was "country infested with lawless Bedouins."[79] In another article on Jordan, an author said that Great Britain "gave them [the Jordanians] and the rest of the Arab world the first taste of freedom they have experienced in many centuries."[80] We read that, in Aden, an author was "astonished at the presence of this little white civilized colony" in the middle of a wilderness where beyond British areas of control was little law and order.[81] It was pointed out that, in Syria in 1918, travel guides described Latakia as dirty and unhealthy. In 1933, thanks to the French, Latakia boasted a casino, boulevards, hotels, running water, a public library, and hospitals. The author remarked that while the French tried to better conditions, "here, as in most other parts of the Orient, social reform comes slowly."[82] In Palestine, it was said, the inhabitants had not much experience in handling money, but under British rule "money is now universal, and the Arab, while learning its use, must be trained in thrift." The author also informed readers that effecting change was easier done by explaining new ideas to a group of Arabs together rather than "by arguing singly with each man," because "initiative by the individual is rare."[83] In Morocco, an author saw a sign of "French dominion" in his presence as a Christian stranger "alone, unarmed but safe" in the place where, "two dozen years ago, France's sons—officers, soldiers, and civilians—were cruelly massacred." Moreover, "this change has been achieved without harshness or injustice to the native inhabitants."[84] Again and again, *National Geographic* pointed out the pure and unselfish motives behind colonialism, and Europeans always occupied the high moral ground while building empires.

SEEING AND KNOWING

The colonialist record of improvement through good works was especially impressive given the Arab's nature and the Arab wasteland. A 1942 article on Iraq shared an anecdote told to the author by a Turk ridding himself of "his anti-Arab rancor." The story was built around the idea of Allah deciding to visit the world he created. Allah goes to Germany and does not recognize it for all the improvements made by the Germans. Allah then visits America and, again, is unable to recognize his creation because of the wonderful changes. He continues his visits, finding each place greatly changed and unrecognizable, until he comes to Iraq. Allah immediately recognizes Iraq—everything is exactly as he left it. He says, "The Arabs have done nothing with the treasures I put there, nor used the secrets I cunningly laid there." The author responded to this anecdote by reminding the Turk of "the civilizations that had risen and flourished and gone again." But the Turk was given the last word, saying, "But you only prove my point . . . The Arabs, the heirs of the ages—and today naked as a newborn babe."[85]

With this story, *National Geographic* readers were once again taught the West–non-West hierarchy through a lesson in the Arab world's time warp and in Arab backwardness, idleness, limited intellectual capacity, wasted resources, and lack of progressive history. Past civilizations of the area were represented as unrelated accidents of place, unlike Western civilization's grand history.

The story of Allah and Iraq was also an example of the uneasy humor that was sometimes used in representations of the Arab world. As Curtis Hinsley points out in his work on the world's fairs, this rhetorical device is "intended to encourage sympathy with the exotic and simultaneously to keep a certain ironic distance."[86] The amusing and deadly negative portrayal of Arabs established the desired distance between colonizer and colonized—close enough to accept the idea of the West being involved in the Arab world, and far enough away to support the means necessary for establishing Western domination.

According to Hinsley, this uneasy humor was produced at the world's fairs in "lighthearted" captions used on ethnographic images, a popular-selling item at the expositions. We find the same vehicle for uneasy humor in *National Geographic*. For example, a photograph of an Arab woman carrying a large basket on her head was captioned: "Down will come baby, cradle and all—if mamma trips!" Additional information explained that the Palestinian woman was carrying a sleeping child in the basket while she "[went] her way with apparent indifference." Readers were asked to "Fancy a fond young American mother facing traffic with her first-born balanced on her head!"[87] Of course, Western readers of *National Geographic* could not imagine this, and the difference was driven home. Yet they could still imagine the possibility of training the Palestinian mother.

Although it was through the content of the Allah and Iraq story that an uneasy humor and the lessons of hierarchy were produced, the text also operated on a visual level. The text was placed in the middle of a two-page layout, with pictures on either side that repeated and reinforced the text's messages. On the left was a picture of a beggar who was said to have placed a curse on the author for refusing to give him money. On the right of the text was a photo of several Arab men eating. The caption read: "Not polite to use the fingers? But it is in Iraq! Spoons go unnoticed as these town Arabs plunge into the big pan of rice and lamb."[88]

The pictures, though not directly connected to the text, visually signified the same ideas carried in the Allah and Iraq story. In addition to the beggar signifying miserable conditions, he also carried ideas about Arab revenge, superstition, and powerless curses. The picture of Arabs eating, as we have already seen, was a favorite image, but further identifying the men as "town Arabs" gave added confirmation of their essential animality. These pictures performed another function: They upheld the text through their physical location on the page, creating what Claude Gandelman explores as reading pictures and viewing texts.[89] All the words and images created by the text and photographs, including the captions, work together textually and visually, and again in the image created by their relationship as one integrated picture. They spill into one another, asking us to read the pictures and view the text.

The uneasy humor in *National Geographic*'s "lighthearted" anecdotes and captions cannot be anything but uneasy. At the heart of these representations of Arabs was serious colonialism and Orientalism. But while an Arab eating with his hands (these images always used men; male Orientalism's sexual fantasy did not portray Arab women acting in ways understood as too unfeminine), or a woman carrying a child on her head (as no responsible Western mother would do), were among those predictable images of Arabs in the magazine, there were also predictable images of Western men.

One of these images originates in what Pratt calls the "monarch-of-all-I-survey" genre in travel writing. As a rule, she says, European discovery of sights involved asking local inhabitants about the surrounding areas, then hiring them to take you to one of them, "whereupon with their guidance and support, you proceeded to discover what they already knew." Discovery of this sort meant "converting local knowledges (discourses) into European national and continental knowledges associated with European forms and relations of power."[90] Here Pratt consciously puts aside the heroic dimension of discovery, insisting that, danger and hardship notwithstanding, in the end the act of discovery is in the experience of seeing. According to Pratt, the monarch-of-all-I-survey scene not only is enacted in the early explorers' landscape panoramas but, more recently, takes place from the balconies of hotels in big Third World cities. These different sites speak to different periods—from building the great empire to improving the underdeveloped.

In *National Geographic,* the monarch-of-all-I-survey scene was enacted in contexts of past and present. In one example (Photo 20), a Western archeologist was portrayed as monarch of past civilizations. In another photo (Photo 21), the Western soldier was portrayed as monarch of the current Arab world. Both

PHOTO 20

"From this Tall Tower the Author Supervised His Native Diggers," July 1933

(Photo: Claude Francis A. Schaeffer/National Geographic Society Image Collection)

pictures, with the men on top, are good visual representations of—borrowing Enloe's phrase—the "empire-building masculinity" of colonialism.[91]

The dominant position that Western men held over ruins and capitals in the Arab world enabled them to see (or discover) and lay claim to all below and to construct knowledge. The tower upon which the archeologist was perched was called the "eye," and his position ensured seeing (discovering) treasures and supervising Arab diggers. The caption explained that "constant diligence was needed to prevent careless handling of precious ancient objects" by the native workers.[92]

The caption to the picture of the British soldier (see Photo 21) informed readers that he was atop the Ibn Tulun Mosque overlooking Cairo. It was significant that he stood on a mosque and struck a pose that signified both his position as a conquerer and total irreverence toward Islam. This was a very powerful photograph—the Christian/Muslim and West/non-West hierarchies could not be lost on the dullest *National Geographic* reader.

PHOTO 21

*"British Tank Corps Men on the Ibn Tulun Mosque
View Cairo and Its Citadel," April 1942*
(Photo: National Geographic Society Image Collection)

In addition to images of Arabs and Western men, *National Geographic* also carried pictures of Westerners dressed like Arabs (Photo 22). This colonialist cross-dressing produced an interesting, if not ridiculous, image. Kabbani reports that "shedding European clothes for Oriental garb became a pleasant pastime for the traveller . . . making a journey East more exotic, and it seemed to allow the traveler a deeper access to a cloistered world."[93]

The notion of being able to gain deeper access by dressing as an Arab treated Arab clothing as costume much the same way that an actor would see a character's costume. Discussing film-costuming development, Jane Gaines calls attention to the practice of actors' putting on costumes as a way to learn about a character. She says that this "aided an actress in the realization of the character. . . . in the discourse on costume . . . close association with the body

FIGURE 22

*"An American Envoy and His Wife Put on Arab
Dress and Welcome Smiles," April 1948*

(Photo: Maynard Williams/National Geographic Society
Image Collection)

helped to construct costume as behavior."[94] Putting aside the fun of masquerade, publishing pictures in *National Geographic* of Westerners dressed in Arab clothing had to do with knowing the character, imagining and demonstrating Western access to the Arab mind. And, as we will see in the next chapter, even putting on the veil was revealing.

4

"THE ARABIAN NIGHTMARES"

NATIONAL GEOGRAPHIC, 1950S THROUGH THE 1960S

The Arab world in the 1950s and 1960s was most character-ized by resistance to British and French control. Additionally, the changing inter-national balance of power was reflected on the Arab scene by the United States' developing financial and military strongholds there. For example, in this period, large U.S. investments in Saudi Arabian oil production led to its replacing Britain as the main Western influence. In Egypt, a popular movement mounted serious opposition to the British presence in the country, and the powerful Arab nation-alist leader Gamal Abdel Nasser began to take up his historic role. At the same time, demands for independence from French domination in Tunisia, Morocco, and Algeria gained momentum.

By the middle of the 1950s, most Arab countries that had been under Euro-pean rule (with the important exception of Algeria) achieved formal indepen-dence, although differing terms were negotiated. A major Arab move at this time was Egyptian nationalization of the Suez Canal. This, and the subsequent mil-itary invasion by Britain and France—later ended because of pressure from the two new superpowers, whose own interests were now primary—created a boost to Arab nationalist forces throughout the area.

The Cold War (between the United States and what was then the Soviet Union) was in full force in this period and playing itself out in the Arab world, with countries and political movements generally divided into Western- and Eastern-bloc alignments. This period was also marked by the long and bloody war of independence fought in Algeria against the French. Finally ending in 1962, this war was one of history's most brutal examples of colonialist military power. And critical to this period was the birth of the Palestine Liberation Organization (PLO) in 1964 and the Arab defeat in the June 1967 War.

Against this general backdrop of the 1950s and 1960s, in an almost surreal juxtaposition, *National Geographic* continued to present the Arab world in much the same way that we have already seen. Continuing the previous chapter's discussion about understanding costume as behavior, some 1955 photographs of veiled women will prove instructive and of additional interest, given the veil's role in Orientalist discourse.

Among pictures of Westerners dressed like Arabs were those of an American woman in traditional Arab clothing. *National Geographic* readers were given a picture that showed Mrs. Shor being helped into Arab clothes by two (unnamed) Arab women—one was arranging Mrs. Shor head scarf, and the other was arranging her dress. The second photograph (Photo 23) presented the American dressed in the finished costume. Its caption read: "Mrs. Shor conceded that her veil established an aura of mystery but found that it made breathing a little difficult."[1] Mrs. Shor confused what Orientalism had constructed around the form of the veiled woman with the actual Arab woman under the veil. The "aura of mystery," in fact, was always established on the other side of the veil. A veiled Arab woman would not feel herself in an aura of mystery; rather, that was how she was perceived by the West. Mrs. Shor obviously knew about this Oriental aura before she put on the veil. The veil did not, could not, give it.

Moreover, reporting that the veil made breathing difficult enhanced the image of Arab women's total oppression—subjugated Arab women could not even breathe as well as American women. Without the Arab costume, Mrs. Shor was an emancipated woman wearing the clothes of freedom. Putting a veil on a Westerner set up a clear comparison between American women and Arab women, because readers saw the American woman metamorphosed into an oppressed Arab.

Orientalism was a very gendered discourse, as demonstrated by *National Geographic*'s treatment of another picture of a veiled woman. The magazine presented readers with an image of a veiled Moroccan woman (Photo 24) that was captioned: "With eyes like this . . . a veil need not be a disadvantage."[2] The Arab woman's aura of mystery—that is, her sexual aura—was different from Mrs. Shor's, because here both race and gender were at work. When serving in

PHOTO 23

"Jean Shor Tries Moorish Garb," February 1955
(Photo: Franc Shor/National Geographic Society image Collection)

a West-to-non-West comparison, the American woman's sexuality was displaced onto the Arab woman. Mrs. Shor temporarily "lost," or had suspended, something of her gendered being to make room for race. Within a racial hierarchy, the American was more white than woman, and therefore, unlike for Arabs, a veil was a disadvantage to her. And as we have learned from *National Geographic,* Arab women were "hyperfeminine."

VEILS AND HIGH HEELS

Western women's dress signified, among other things, emancipation and modernity. Arab women's dress signified domination and backwardness. For example, in a 1960 article, readers learned that "emancipated women of

PHOTO 24

"Fez Beauty Prefers a Veil," February 1955
(Photo: Franc Shor/National Geographic Society Image
Collection)

Morocco drop the veil at will." The author also said that he "sensed their grad-
ual independence in the variety of styles. . . . Their personalities are changing,
too. Veil-less women are outgoing and positive, while those clinging to tradition
are shy."[3] In other articles, women were seen as: "Black-robed women with filmy
scarlet veils. The romance is still there. But now high heels click beneath the
robes"; and "[l]ike passing shadows, Syrian women in dark robes and veils slip
by."[4] About Tunisian women, an author wrote: "Dressed in white lehfas, these
statuesque women look like sheeted ghosts."[5] And in Sudan, "the dark blue and

white worn by Moslems here . . . seemed depressing. Even more so, to me, was the sight of dark-robed women tilling fields under the broiling sun."[6] In Saudi Arabia, a veiled bedouin woman looked "like a black ghost at Halloween."[7]

These "depressing" images of veiled Arab women correspond to Vron Wares' argument that discussions in the West of the Muslim woman's head scarf or veil are used to make modes of femininity speak for wider cultural values. She says, "representations of white femininity articulate powerful, if subtle, racist messages that confirm not only cultural difference but also cultural superiority." The image of the Western woman's freedom to dress as she likes is held next to the image of the Muslim woman's complete submission and veiling. Different styles of femininity are compared, and levels of civilization are determined, by evaluating the position of women against a "specifically white femininity."[8]

Signs of this white femininity in the Arab world were directly linked to progress and modernity by *National Geographic*. A photograph of an Egyptian woman holding a compact mirror and applying lipstick carried the caption: "Emancipated Cairo girl reddens her lips. Egyptian women may vote, attend college, and hold jobs."[9] In Algeria, it was noted that "nylons add [a] modern touch" with veiled women wearing high heels.[10] This linkage demonstrates what Irvin Schick points out in her critique of Sarah Graham-Brown's research on photographs of Middle Eastern women. Schick says that photographs of unveiled professional women or women in athletic competitions are not so much a comment on the changing roles of men and women as they are "a symbolic evocation of a 'modernizing' country.'" As such, these photographs are not different from pictures of tractors or new railroads—they merely symbolize another achievement of men. Therefore, Schick continues, "once again reduced to mere objects, women were, in these images, at the service of a political discourse conducted by and for men."[11]

In addition to pointing to lipstick and nylons or women in professional careers as signs of modernization, *National Geographic* located modernization in shampoo. In a 1969 article, readers learned that "Kuwait, on the surface, remains a man's world. Women do not yet have the vote, but things are not all as they were; modernity has begun to creep into the Kuwaiti woman's outlook."[12] The single example given of this modernity and women was that they no longer use sidr leaves pounded into a cleanser to wash their hair—they used shampoo. And in an article on Lebanon the caption to a picture of bikini-clad women exclaimed: "Veils are 'out,' bikinis 'in.'"[13] Once again, white, Western femininity was the measure.

RIFLES AND WIVES

Within male Orientalism, white femininity always remained in view as the model, but it never replaced or overwhelmed the sexual fantasies about Arab women. So while the oppression of Arab females was pointed out in *National Geographic,* it never reached a level that would destroy Orientalist fantasies. Thus, on a visit to Yemen, the author of a 1952 article found the children "exceptionally gay and playful. . . . Girls in families with whom we visited were invariably pretty, bright-eyed, lovable little people, and we pitied them their later life of veiled seclusion."[14] Yet, in a 1966 article on Syria, an author met an eight-year-old girl who was "surprisingly unafraid of the male strangers" and who greeted him with an old-fashioned Arab salutation. The girl kissed his hand, pressed it to her forehead, and kissed it again. Regarding this, the author said, "Syria would do well to think carefully before abolishing all its ancient ways."[15]

So although white, Western femininity was the supreme model, there was also the relentless sexual fantasy tied to Orientalism and primitivism that needed submissive women, women with an "aura of mystery," and dancers who performed "pulsating to the beat of drums."[16] Even while authors were looking at little girls, never far behind were the Orientalist fantasies of Arab women, figures who, as Malek Alloula puts it, "define the essence of the harem more than they describe its inner life."[17]

But, of course, creating the harem also meant creating the Arab man who ruled it. The Arab world was, as a 1964 subscription ad for the magazine described Yemen, a "medieval land where veiled women and dagger-bearing men reckon distances by days and time by sun and moon."[18] And the Arab world was, according to a *National Geographic* article, a place where—as druggists in Iraq and Kuwait reported—among the three most demanded products were "stimulants to make old men virile."[19]

And whom did Arab men want? Under the subtitle "Fair-skinned Beauty Worth 45 Camels," readers heard about the author's and his wife's visit to a bedouin camp in Saudi Arabia:

> The Arab loves his coffee break. It's the sum total of his social life. It often lasts all day, . . .
>
> We talked about rising prices of rifles and wives. The emir had three of each.
>
> "Wa-llaah, but this fair-skinned one is a jewel," said the old emir with a nod toward Lynn. "Worth thirty camels at least."

"Fifty," I countered, defending Lynn's market value.

"Possibly thirty-five."

"Forty-five (may you live long), forty-five!"

It was Lynn's first time on the auction block. She began to fidget—until all broke into laughter.[20]

This now-familiar slice of Orientalism—an Arab world in which women were bought and sold, the most sought-after being white women—was about gender and race. In *National Geographic,* images of slavery were never constructed around male slaves, and Arabs usually desired white women. In fact, it seems that even Arab women wanted white skin. Another married couple traveling in the Arab world reported that the wife's suntanned arm caught the attention of bedouins in Jordan, who said the word *sun* in Arabic to her. The reason for this was that, "to these bronzed women, who must always live out of doors, any woman not a Bedouin has enviable lily-white skin."[21]

Clearly, certain understandings about racial hierarchy, women's work, and standards of beauty had to be held, or willing to be held, by readers in order to believe that Bedouin women envied something called "lily-white skin." To accept this anecdote in *National Geographic,* one had to know, or newly learn, that people of color wished they were white, that women resented working outdoors, and that lily-white skin (as if there were such a skin tone) was universally acknowledged as the most beautiful. In addition, one had to assume that race within the Arab world was constructed the same way as race in America. It was not. The Arab world has never known anything similar to the social, political, and economic consequences of skin color experienced in America.

THE PRIMITIVE BODY

Race and gender were always on the surface in *National Geographic,* and because they were themselves discourses that clung to body surfaces, physical descriptions of peoples persisted. A visit to Yemen found that "The lowland people are darker than highlanders. They show considerably more Somali and other African mixture." And the mountain people reminded the author of "storybook pirates, with their wild hair and beards, sharp features, dark skins, and jackets open in the middle revealing often huge and hairy chests."[22]

In addition, as seen throughout this study, primitivism and racial hierarchy produced the Arab man as essentially violent. The cover of a 1966 issue of *National Geographic* relied on and reinforced this characterization with a photo of an Arab on horseback with raised sword. The stereotypical image was constructed from the completely familiar—raised weapon, Arabian steed, and older Arab man with a somber facial expression. (So often in Orientalist representations, the men are old and the women young.) The magazine's inside cover explained that the photo was from a horse show in Saudi Arabia, but that really did not matter; readers would have already recognized and registered the familiar image of the violent body.

Gender and race worked with a vengeance to produce the primitive body found in the report of a research group in Sudan. What Alloula refers to as the "ethnographic alibi" best describes the stated project and the actual activity of the group studying Sudan.[23] The group's declared objective was to make documentary films recording primitive cultures in Sudan before they disappeared. The group was composed entirely of men; a father, son, son-in-law and two family friends.

The group leader and *National Geographic* author told of an incident that happened while the group's small expedition caravan was traveling over mountain roads. The lead vehicle suddenly came to an abrupt halt, almost causing an accident with the vehicle behind it. Those in the following vehicle shouted to the driver, "Are you crazy? We almost rammed you!" But, the author continued, "Horst [the driver] just stared. I followed his gaze to a graceful young girl standing in the breeze on a rock outcropping. Unencumbered except for bead strings around neck and waist, she was a black nymph on a pedestal." This story speaks for itself.

The group's ethnographic research (alibi) also led them to photograph a woman showering. The caption to the full-page picture read: "Running water in every compound amazed the author. Still wearing her finery [some strings of beads], a young Nuba woman takes her daily shower between two turrets of her home." A description of how the shower worked followed, and the decorations on the shower walls were pointed out to "reveal Islamic influence."[24] The group's interest in Sudanese plumbing is suspicious.

Norman Denzin says that all tourist performances "occur within discursive sites wherein a particular subjectivity is produced."[25] A woman showering—rather than a man or a child—as a tourist performance exposed the gender and West-to-non-West power relationship in place. If one tries to imagine switching the players, as we did earlier with the 1948 photo of anthropologists measuring skulls, the violence of this ethnographic research becomes clear. The idea of Sudanese men photographing Western women showering in their private homes is nothing short of absurd—the power relationship makes it so.

The research group also studied women's manual labor in a Sudanese mountain tribe. They reported testing these "Goddesses in ebony" who carried heavy loads of millet in baskets on their heads. Their results showed that "these human work horses endure burdens and heat that would fell a European." The group's work also included other familiar activities. They reported that: "Anthropological measurements were taken from more than 200 people . . . including five photographs of each one's physique."

This 1966 activity was firmly lodged within the tradition of nineteenth-century physical anthropology that, as Brown explains, employed photography in a major way to document and classify people "according to the 'evolution' of their physical features."[26] The ethnographic alibi used to document "black nymphs," women showering, "Goddesses in ebony," physical characteristics, and Sudanese women's endurance compared with Europeans' served in operations establishing difference. The information gathered by the group—in the form of written reports, 1,000 photographs, fifteen films, and eighty tape recordings—was turned over to research institutions to produce studies on anthropology, education, and agriculture. This group's ethnographic activities were the same as those examined earlier in the 1948 article on the Harvard anthropologists' Sinai expedition. Again, we see the timeless nature of primitivism.

THE DISCOURSE OF DEVELOPMENT

This Western activity of collecting, sorting, and analyzing information went on within the process of development. According to Marc DuBois, "trainer–judges" enter into the development process that calls for an "accurate diagnosis" based on investigations and information gathered on all aspects of the lives and lifestyles of the beneficiaries. Experts then analyze this knowledge against what they already know through "established scientific discourse and Western methodologies." Following this, there is "the introduction of 'safer,' 'more efficient,' 'healthier,' 'better,' 'newer,' and 'proven' ways of doing things." This process produces a power relationship that governs future contact—or, as DuBois puts it, "the statements of anybody wearing French shoes and carrying a clipboard . . . are imbued with a certain meaning and importance."[27]

It was this power relationship that gave Western men with cameras entry into the lives and bathrooms of non-Westerners and allowed them to represent natives to themselves and the world. There was a hierarchization of cultures in place that was produced and reproduced through the discourse of development. Different ways of doing X were assigned value-creating categories of developed and developing nations as a result of "the sum (effect) of a multiplicity of local-ized hierarchizations or judgments regarding economic, political, social, and cul-tural aspects." This is not to deny the existence of economic, political, and social conditions that demanded change, but as DuBois insists, "'underdevelopment,' one interpretation of these conditions, is a construction." Whether or not a cer-tain fertilizer would increase crop yield or some medical treatment would improve health is not the issue here; rather, the issue is the framing of such information within the discourse of development. It entails a great deal of "destruction or, at the least, discrediting and subordination of local techniques, knowledges, prac-tices, and lifestyles."[28]

Said makes the same argument, noting that following World War II, when the United States took over the role played by Britain and France in the Arab world, the United States came up with modernization plans for what it saw as the "underdeveloped" Third World "in the grip of unnecessary archaic and sta-tic 'traditional' modes of life." Modernization theory applied to the Arab world understood Islam to have "existed in a kind of timeless childhood, shielded from true development by an archaic set of superstitions, prevented by its strange priests and scribes from moving out of the Middle Ages into the modern world."[29] It was from such perspectives that Yemen was applauded in a *National Geographic* article titled "Yemen Opens the Door to Progress." The country was described as having long lived in isolation and excluding foreigners. Yemen, readers learned, an exporter of grain, hides, and world-class coffee from Mocha, was now "ready to import foreign experts and see what [could] be done for the improvement of the country."[30]

These development research projects constructed and reconstructed an over-all West-to-non-West hierarchy that not only ran through Western institutions such as *National Geographic* but that appeared in the non-West, as well. Accord-ing to DuBois, the discourse of development has, among other things, allowed the First World to strengthen its presence in the Third World and has created individuals who perceive themselves as "lacking, and part of an inferior cul-ture."[31] We have already heard examples of Arabs echoing Western criticism of Arab society. Arab voices that mimicked insulting colonialist discourse were very different from Arab voices offering progressive social, political, and eco-nomic critiques of their society and foreign domination. The magazine's use of native voices mimicking Western judgment was a validating tactic.

The magazine's readership heard Arabs themselves declare that "some Arab leaders, they must to have too big bellies, they must to have too many womans"[32]; that domed housing in Aleppo was "a sign of backwardness"[33]; that orthodox Muslims "are holding Syria back. It's one of our big problems"[34]; and that "Arabs are awakening. We have to catch up with the centuries."[35] So when *National Geographic* authors said, "Kuwait, the former sleepy village, has awakened with the coming of oil and is stretching its strong new limbs,"[36] or that Amman, until recently, "a dusty, desert-edge village" was now "in the momentary chaos of a city coming of age,"[37] such general images were verified by Arabs who had learned the lessons of advanced Western civilization.

Said speaks to this process, explaining that because global media and data networks are concentrated in the "so-called metropolitan societies," those in the peripheral societies are to a great degree made "reliant upon this system for information about themselves. We're talking now about *self*-knowledge, not only knowledge about other societies."[38]

THE PARENT/CHILD IMAGE

In *National Geographic,* we often find the Arab world represented as a child in need of parenting from the West. In a 1960 article titled "Algeria: France's Stepchild, Problem and Promise," readers learned that "France directs twin efforts to crush revolt and to lift Algeria into the 20th century."[39] The familiar Arab time warp helped produce the image of a child, and the familiar parent/child metaphor allowed France to discipline and raise its troublesome stepchild.

A more-than-fifty-page article covering a 1960 tour of Africa (which included trips to Egypt, Libya, and Tunisia) was framed at the outset for readers within the discourses of primitivism, colonialism, and development. A lengthy quotation from the article's introduction will enable us to hear how *National Geographic* ran these discourses together in a concentrated dose intended to position readers:

> At a time in the long ago, while Europe plodded forward, Mother Africa lay down to sleep in her incomparable sunshine.
>
> She sighed in her sleep; the wind of her breath buried the works of the Pharaohs in sand. She stirred, making the earth shake, and the Roman temples of Tunisia fell.
>
> For thousands of years ships brought slavers to her coasts. Finding Mother Africa drugged with sleep, they seized her children and hurried them away.
>
> In 1800 Africa on maps was a narrow coastline encircling a great white blank. Intrepid explorers filled it; . . .

Hosts of missionaries, traders, engineers, doctors, and teachers followed them. Devoted scientists came. . . .

Mother Africa awakened.

Many things had changed, she saw, while she lay sleeping. Guns mocked the spears of her sons. A thing called a wheel carried the white man's loads.

[Freedom] carries with it responsibility as well as privilege. New Africa has had freedom pressed shining into her eager hands. Now the world asks the question: What will she do with it?[40]

Within this space, *National Geographic* managed to pack a good number of themes: advanced Western civilization and the non-Western time warp; the energetic West and the drowsy non-West; the portrayal of the non-West as a woman and the West, therefore, as a man; the heroic Western explorer, devoted white missionaries, and experts of all sorts; colonialism's civilizing mission; and the West (the parent) giving freedom and responsibility to the non-West (the child).

Here, as we have seen before in *National Geographic,* missionaries traveled with colonialists. This connection is one that V. Y. Mudimbe also recognizes, although from a conflicting interpretation. Mudimbe argues that "the missionary's objectives had to be co-extensive with his country's political and cultural perspectives on colonization, as well as with the Christian view of his mission." Missionary speech, Mudimbe explains, is established within a framework of the authority of the truth. If the Western missionary is doing God's work according to God's word, then he does not, cannot, "enter into dialogue with pagans and 'savages' but must impose the law of God that he incarnates."[41] And, of course, missions sustained by God are entitled to use all means necessary to achieve God's objectives on Earth. As both Mudimbe and *National Geographic* note, missionaries and colonialists walked together, sharing the tasks of the West's civilizing mission—or, as Marx referred to it, the "Christian colonial system."[42]

WAR ON MISERY

By the magazine's portrayal, colonialism would seem to be a series of altruistic projects aimed at improving the living standards of the non-Western world. The litany of colonialist good works recorded in the 1950s and 1960s in *National Geographic* did not vary from previous periods. This persistently positive spin on colonialism sharply contrasts with Albert Memmi's critique.

To those who would say that the colonized benefited from colonization through the building of roads, schools, and hospitals, Memmi asks why we should suppose no changes in the countries would have occurred without the colonizers. He says that we might just as well suggest that, "If colonization had not taken place, there would have been more schools and more hospitals."[43] Memmi states that after shutting the colonized out of history and forbidding development, the colonizer asserts the colonized's essential immobility. Memmi rejects the romantic picture of the colonizer as a noble adventurer or pioneer doing battle against nature, serving mankind, and spreading culture. Writing in the 1960s, he declared: "The economic motives of colonial undertakings are revealed by every historian of colonialism. The cultural and moral mission of a colonizer, even in the beginning, is no longer tenable."[44]

In *National Geographic*, on the other hand, Elsie May Bell Grosvenor's account of her African tour from Cairo to Cape Town informed readers that "Invariably we were impressed by the work British colonial governments are doing. . . . Most of this work in modern times is devoted to improving the status, not of the English settlers but of the Africans; to eradicating disease, improving agriculture, and introducing new industries. . . . And there is great consciousness that the long-range objective is to teach Africans to govern themselves."[45]

This portrayal of colonialism, the absolute reverse of Memmi's, employed what Mary Louise Pratt calls the rhetoric of the "anti-conquest." This refers to "the strategies of representation whereby European bourgeois subjects seek to secure their innocence in the same moment as they assert European hegemony."

These strategies of innocence found in *National Geographic* were in keeping with the terms of the anti-conquest as Pratt defines them: What is seen in the colonized territories is encoded as "unimproved," meaning that it is in need of capitalist "improvement," and that which is encoded as "available for improvement" represents the objective as uncontested. Moreover, as Pratt explains, "It is not only habitats that must be produced as empty and unimproved, but inhabitants as well."[46] In classic anti-conquest form, we read earlier that all through Africa, the British were busy improving agriculture and industry and improving the status of natives who happened, still, to be unable to govern themselves.

In an article on Algeria, readers learned that when French colonists first arrived, many died from malaria before the French were finally able to drain the marshes and turn the area into rich farmland. In addition, the French "mounted a massive campaign to lift Algeria's nine million Moslems from the poverty that has ground them for centuries." Under the subtitle "Death Is Always Close at Hand," *National Geographic* explained and applauded the bravery involved in France's "war upon misery." In a given area, the army gathered the families into a "regroupment village," where volunteers carried on "the risky business of nursing and teaching the Moslem population." These villages were established inside "rebel-infested territory," which explained why with this work "the danger is great" and "death lurks."

More of the same anti-conquest rhetoric appeared under the subtitle "French Risk Lives for a Better Land," in which the magazine told of the daily danger faced by the colonists in building "the new Algeria." Nevertheless, readers were assured that "in schools all across Algeria, an entire generation is discovering the 20th century." And "in a drive to westernize family life, educators stress learning for once-neglected girls. The curriculum excludes Arabic and Berber in favor of French."[47]

Brown states that colonial rule created "new images to be superimposed on the old stereotypes: 'backward' people were shown to be reaping the benefits of Western rule in the form of schools and hospitals, while those who resisted were portrayed as gangs of criminals and wreckers."[48] We just read *National Geographic*'s writing about the good works that France carried out in spite of rebel spoilers. In addition, with the alibi of better treatment for girls, the magazine applauded an educational program of Westernization that excluded native languages.

National Geographic articles were laden with examples of "points of contact," which Alison Devine Nordstrom says are where exposure to white civilization has improved natives through, for example, schooling and medical care. Citing points of contact functions to emphasize "the moral correctness and practical necessity of the West's responsibility to restructure the rest of the world in its own image."[49]

Points of contact fill an article that described Sudan as "undergoing a relatively painless transition to 20th-century progress." This transition was said to be due to the British administration, which, since the 1920s, had been working on eliminating tribal fighting, designating chiefs to regulate communities, ending sorcery and witchcraft, establishing schools, maintaining hospitals, interesting the natives in the use and value of money, and setting an annual tax for governmental services. In the area of law, tribal chiefs took care of certain cases, but "English experts try the more difficult ones," and Western laws were applied to nontribal matters. In addition, British district commissioners were directing local government until "the people [had] enough experience to govern themselves."[50]

And how was this sustained history of colonialist good works explained by *National Geographic?* "The Briton who works in the Sudan looks upon the country with missionary fervor and feels it his personal obligation to guide it gently on the road to good government."[51] The points-of-contact list, the link to Christianity, and the parent/child metaphor were examples of what Schick understands as visions used by the West to define "the white man's burden" and "cast the colonial enterprise in a benign and paternalistic, rather than subjugating and exploitative light."[52]

In Morocco, authors of a *National Geographic* article arrived at a time when the French were using "stern military measures [to] put down the rioting" of the nationalist movement. A French official explained that his country was "willing to give the Moors every bit of self-government they can exercise, but ... won't yield to terrorism." During the authors' visit to a French agricultural-modernization project, a tribal council member told them that the French teams responsible for the "farming revolution" were "sent by Allah." Readers also learned that the energy and hard work of French colonists "created magnificent vineyards, orchards, grain fields, and dairy farms where only goats grazed 40 years ago."[53]

To those who would justify colonialism by pointing out certain material progress achieved in the colonial regime, Aime Cesaire contends that "no one knows at what stage of material development these same countries would have been if Europe had not intervened." In fact, he argues, the colonizer has distorted and slowed progress by disrupting natural economies, destroying food crops, orienting agriculture only to the needs of the metropolitan countries, and looting products and raw materials.[54]

DOMINANCE AND HEGEMONY

In the *National Geographic* article on Morocco mentioned earlier, quick work was made of resistance to the French presence. It was pushed aside as the usual sort of "trouble" the colonialists had to deal with to get on with the business of improving the country and its people. The nationalists had to be controlled because Moroccans were not ready for self-government; it was for their own good that the French military disciplined them.

It is important to realize that throughout *National Geographic* little attention was given to the very bloody battles fought to secure Western domination. When fighting was mentioned, it was either to establish the heroism of white men—who carried out the civilizing mission against all odds, human and environmental—or to create the essentially violent Arab. In all the *National Geographic* accounts of colonialism in the Arab world, readers would never have sensed the brutality and exploitation brought down on colonized peoples, or the mass resistance to it. There were no hints that colonialism was a system of domination in which, for example, "one Algerian in six would die before independence was won."[55]

Instead of this sort of information, an article told readers that the role of the French Foreign Legion in Algeria was similar to the rolel that it played in Indochina, where the legion also suffered high numbers of casualties and wounded. The author speculated that the reason recruits continued to enter the legion's ranks in Algeria was because the "Foreign Legionnaires are the world's last romantics—men wholly in love with war and half in love with death."[56] As Richard Drinnon puts it: Bringing countries out of the dark Ages into the twentieth century through Westernization, Americanization, Europeanization, civilization, modernization, or progress "was never a burden to be shouldered by those with no stomach for bloodshed."[57]

Borrowing a great phrase from Ranajit Guha's analysis of the colonial state in India, Lata Mani says that it achieved not hegemony but dominance, and that a disregard of specificity can "endow dominance with hegemony."[58] Likewise, an analysis of *National Geographic* must not lose sight of the fact that a great deal of physical violence accompanied colonialism in the Arab world. *National Geographic* ignored the military dimension of colonialism and that places it in direct support of those activities. Western colonial power was achieved in the Arab world as a result of dominance, not hegemony. This needs to be stated against the magazine's overall image of colonialists basically encountering only sleeping or grateful Arabs, or resistance in the form of of desert bandits or religious fanatics.

I rely here on Abdul JanMohamed's distinction between dominant and hegemonic phases of colonialism, and between its material and discursive ideological practices. The dominant phase goes on from the first moment of colonization until a colony is granted "independence." During this time, "European colonizers exercise direct and continuous control and military coercion of the natives." Colonialist discursive practices are not yet of much use. In the hegemonic phase, which is neocolonialism, "the natives accept a version of the colonizers' entire system of values, attitudes, morality, institutions, and more important, mode of production." JanMohamed points to the moment of "independence" as the formal transition to hegemonic colonialism—the stage when "the active and direct 'consent' of the dominated" has developed, though the possibility of military action always remains known.[59] Simply put, there is a clear distinction to be made between shooting and jailing a native population into submission and teaching them their inferiority through colonialist schooling.

While the material and discursive practices of colonialism and neocolonialism are profoundly related, it is necessary to sort out their different features and strategies in order that we not "endow dominance with hegemony." *National Geographic* had its readers imagine the story of colonialism as one in which white heroes with missionary fervor encountered either Arabs in awe of Western civilization or crazed Muslim fanatics, not organized nationalist movements or mass resistance.

The "romantic" Legionnaires mentioned earlier were reported to do most of their fighting in eastern Algeria, "where the European population is submerged in a sea of hostile Moslems" and where "the police, bedeviled by a terrorism that has killed or wounded thousands since 1954, had completely barricaded certain sections of the Moslem quarter."[60] The Europeans (read Christians) needed protection from a "sea of hostile Moslems," not Algerians or Arabs. The dominating force becomes the victim in an equation that puts Muslim terrorists in opposition to the good works of a Christian colonial system.

And what was a "Moslem quarter" in an Arab country where most of the native inhabitants were Muslim? There were actually Arab quarters and European quarters; an area became a "Moslem quarter" when barricaded by the French military to secure colonial domination. *National Geographic* said that thousands were killed or wounded by these "hostile Moslems"; once again, there was no hint of a colonial power that would leave one in six Algerians dead before the country could win its independence.

Framing any resistance to European domination as "Muslim" was a frequently used strategy in the magazine. Of course, Islam was the predominant religion in the Arab world, but, as discussed earlier, the West constructed it as a violent, backward, anti-Christian religion. To do this, Islam had to be defined by its most orthodox interpretation, become monolithic, and be located within Orientalism and primitivism. To call up an image of a "sea of hostile Moslems," therefore, gave the colonial state the right to take all measures necessary to enforce its authority. In fact, within such a framework "hostile Moslems" was redundant. How could they be otherwise?

PHOTOGRAPHING NON-WESTERNNESS

This Orientalist representation of Muslims was so pervasive in *National Geographic* that the magazine could show a picture of Arabs milling about to point out religious frenzy to its readers. In a nondescript picture of approximately twenty-five Arabs (men, women, and children) gathered outdoors at a religious shrine, one sees several people sitting on the ground and others walking around or standing. Other than one man playing a small hand drum, no one is doing anything noteworthy. However, the photograph's caption informed readers that: "Moors chant and wail to throbbing drums at the shrine of a patron saint. . . . Worshipers of all ages lay bare their emotions in frenzied religious rites."[61] The photograph does not even include a shot of the religious shrine, because the people, not the shrine, are the focus. In a completely boring image of a group of Moroccans milling about, readers were to imagine wailing Muslims, throbbing drums (drums were usually throbbing, not beating, in the Arab world), and bare emotions and frenzy. Viewers could recognize what the caption identified as present in the photo because the Muslim was already known in those terms, and Islam was frenzy and fanaticism. Arab Muslims already signified all of that; what they were actually doing in the picture really did not matter.

Any *National Geographic* photograph of Arabs was part of the magazine's overall construction of Arabs. Otherwise, it would hardly make sense to look at a picture of Arabs milling about, some not even facing the camera. The magazine's camera not only has the power to photograph what is not there; it also has the power to force itself on unwilling subjects. An example of this is a picture of a Syrian woman running away from the *National Geographic* camera (Photo 25). This photograph is a harsh reflection of Sontag's argument that there is "something predatory in the act of taking a picture. To photograph people is to violate them . . . it turns people into objects that can be symbolically possessed."[62]

The photograph's caption explained that the woman was hurrying down the street, "since decorum demands that she keep her distance from men, especially strangers."[63] Knowing this and yet taking the picture makes it a violent act. It is a picture of a Western male stranger chasing an Arab woman. Because of his zoom lens, he had the power to follow her down the street and capture her just at the moment she turned to see whether she had escaped him. Why take a picture of a woman who does not want to be photographed and publish it, complete with explanation? It was a deliberate display of Western power, patriarchy, and cultural elitism. These were the lessons to be learned from *National Geographic*'s camera chasing Arab women.

As discussed earlier, the people targeted by the cameras often had a clearer understanding of its power and intention than those viewing its pictures in the magazine. While photographing in an Iraqi village, an author and a photographer from the *National Geographic* staff were asked by an Iraqi teacher, "Why

PHOTO 25

"A Woman Hurries Her Donkey Down the Street," December 1966
(Photo: Dean Conger/National Geographic Society Image Collection)

do you take pictures here? This is only a village of poor people living in the old way. In the towns you can see cement buildings with many glass windows and modern furniture, as in your country. All that is much more interesting! Do not show old ways." The author told readers, "The theme was to become a familiar one." And he replied to the teacher, "But the old ways interest people in our country."[64]

The "old ways" were those that best served Orientalism and primitivism. The "old ways" showed Arabs in their most non-Westernness to establish difference. The "old ways" attested to an Arab time warp, backwardness, and need of development. Additionally, in this particular instance, the "old ways" also reflected biblical times. The stated objective of the visit to Iraq was to follow the "epic journey" of Abraham from his birthplace in Ur, Iraq, to Egypt. The article opened with words from Genesis 11:27, 28, and a dozen other quotations from various passages in the Bible were scattered throughout the text. The journey itself and the religious framing of the article's text produced a *National Geographic* and Christian connection—as did seeing images of biblical times in the Arab world mentioned earlier.

The matter of photographing the "old ways" appeared in another article in which, again, local resistance to *National Geographic*'s camera was discredited. We read that when the authors (both of whom were also staff members) were setting up to photograph a Baghdad pottery shop with its great water jars, a crowd gathered objecting to the picture, saying that it would indicate a lack of plumbing in the country. The authors were asked to take pictures of the city's modern buildings instead. They replied that they had done that and wanted to show all sides of Iraq, but the crowd continued to protest, and the authors eventually gave up the photo.

A similar incident took place in the countryside when they attempted to take a picture of a water buffalo pulling a plow. When asked why they did not, instead, photograph a tractor, they answered that there were a thousand draft animals for every one tractor, and "*National Geographic* readers want to see the country as it is, not as it hopes to be." However, the authors reported they were never able to get their point across on this matter. They encountered an "intense" Arab nationalism and "a distrust of the Western World's approach to the Arab people." The authors stated that they were uninterested in "such political shadings"; rather, they "wanted to know how Iraq looked, what its people did, and how they lived."[65]

Said says that while "the Orientalist has traditionally been affiliated with colonial offices . . . books and articles continue to pour forth extolling the nonpolitical nature of Western scholarship."[66] *National Geographic*'s ethnographic alibi rang hollow to Arabs who did not understand Western representations of Arabs as neutral, benign, or non-political. When the magazine claimed to show "the country as it is" to its readers, it presented itself as an objective, disinterested observer of Arab society. This was an impossible position, a nonexistent perspective that, according to Said, assumed objectivity "to inhere in learned discourse about other societies, despite the long history of political, moral, and religious concern felt in all societies."[67] We have already seen that *National Geographic* did indeed have a particular perspective from which it operated. It could not show an Arab country "as it is."

What Denzin says of an anthropologist's work representing the Masai experience applies, as well, to how *National Geographic* observed and represented others. Denzin says that the anthropologist allows us to see through his eyes: "[H]is anthropological theory has structured what his camera sees. His theory structures an aesthetic of performance; unfortunately he does not analyze that aesthetic, or the performance it structures."[68]

National Geographic did not show a country as it is, but as the magazine saw it. And when readers found the representation, in text or visual image, to be portraying reality accurately, then *National Geographic,* according to Denzin's analysis, had "succeeded in matching [its] theory of the 'real' with the viewer's theory of the same experience."[69] Thus, if the magazine's images of the Arab world made sense, were recognized as corresponding to reality, then *National Geographic* had produced a good reflection of the reader's interpretation of the Arab world. That interpretation was, at the same time, produced and reproduced by *National Geographic*—its readers recognized what the magazine had already put there as the Arab world.

Intense Nationalism

In the earlier example of *National Geographic* staff members confronted with Arab protests when they attempted to take photographs, the authors attributed this attitude to an "intense nationalism" and "distrust of the Western world's approach to the Arab people." This nationalism and distrust was, in other words, anti-colonialism and, as such, threatened Western interests in the area. For authors to state that the magazine was not interested in such political matters contradicted its long history of colonial support. In addition, describing Arab nationalism as "intense" employed one of the tropes of Orientalism. Similarly, in another article, it was said that "nationalism, with its strong emotional appeal, promises primarily a political solution to the Arab's difficulties. But his most pressing problems—illiteracy, disease, and low living standards—cannot be solved with slogans or votes. . . . Realistic Arabs know the road ahead has many pitfalls and offers not only a challenge to the spirit but a call to hard labor."[70]

Arab nationalism was belittled by *National Geographic,* yet readers were asked to understand the magazine's photographs and text as non-political reflections of a "country as it is." The magazine's interpretation must be read against the fact that this Arab nationalism, with its so-called emotional appeal, was driven by anti-colonialism and anti-imperialism. One should ask why the pressing problems noted earlier existed after so many decades of colonial rule and good works. Why were programs of Arab nationalist movements portrayed as consisting only of slogans and votes? And why weren't Arab votes important? Why were nationalists—that is, anti-colonialists and anti-imperialists—not "realistic Arabs"? And why claim that there was a need for a call to hard labor?

Why did *National Geographic* take a paternalistic attitude toward Arabs in this quotation?

Ross Gibson offers an analysis of colonialism that notes the strategically useful role of Western countries' nationalism in establishing a colonial state. He cites the powerful "nationalist contention that a region and a nation are destined for one another." Continuing, Gibson says that nationalism is the "cultural strategy which most effectively disenfranchises the indecorous and dissatisfied communities" that it encounters.[71] Clearly, *National Geographic* represented Arab nationalism differently from the nationalism of colonial powers: There were conflicting interests, and, despite its claims, we have seen that the magazine was not a disinterested observer.

One of the most important of these interests was oil. As early as the 1920s, the West was drilling for Arab oil. By the 1940s, more than 4,000 Americans were living in Hasa, Saudi Arabia, connected to its immense oil deposits and refinery. However, oil received little mention in *National Geographic* until the late 1950s—the period when oil began to be pumped into Orientalism. A 1969 article on Kuwait told readers that when the first oil well gushed in Kuwait in 1938, it "hurled a pastoral Bedouin society into the whirlwind of the 20th century." Examining how oil money changed Kuwait and how the country modernized as a result of it, the author said, "Its overwhelming problem is not how to get money but how to spend it wisely." He asked, "How are such huge sums being spent? What is little Kuwait doing with it all?"[72]

An article on Iraq reported that "prosperity came to the nation on the magic carpet of black gold," and that "in the city of *The Arabian Nights,* Chevrolets outnumbered camels." However, the authors reported, "the city of the *Arabian Nights* has growing pains which have turned into Arabian nightmares."[73]

And so the image of the oil-rich Arab entered Orientalist discourse. This was a slick addition that did not disrupt Orientalism at all. The excess already in place now included oil and oil money. The time warp remained, but now oil helped move the Arab world a few centuries closer to the twentieth. The child metaphor was still used, but it was oil money causing growing pains. And because the Arab world had never lived up to the West's *Arabian Nights* fantasies, there really was nothing new about finding images of Arabian nightmares instead.

5

"ANONYMOUS WOMEN"

NATIONAL GEOGRAPHIC,
1970s THROUGH THE 1980s

The last period covered in this study—the 1970s and 1980s—was one in which the United States solidified its role as the predominant foreign power in the Arab world. During this time in the Arab world, the October 1973 War and the Arab oil embargo were critical. For the first time, Arab oil was used to manipulate the political situation, and this meant that, more than ever, international attention was focused on oil, oil, and oil.

In addition to the West's so-called energy crisis, this period was marked by the Camp David Accords between Israel and Egypt and the subsequent assassination of Egyptian President Anwar Sadat. In the 1970s and 1980s, Lebanon experienced a civil war, and Israeli military operations against PLO strongholds in Lebanon continued, reaching their peak with the 1982 Israeli–Palestinian War in Lebanon.

In this era, whatever Arab common front had existed previously (in variously real, false, and mythical moments), the countries of the Arab world were generally divided into two fronts. Among the matters producing this altered alignment (however loose) were differing policies concerning U.S. military and economic involvement in the area; relations with Israel; support for the PLO; positions on proposed solutions to the Palestinian national cause; and opposing economic interests and drives—capitalist, state capitalist, socialist, state socialist, and so on. In addition, these divisions in the Arab world during the 1970s and 1980s were played out concerning the war between Iraq and Iran (a Persian, not Arab, country), which dragged on with enormous death and destruction from 1984 to 1988. It is with Iraq that we now link up again with *National Geographic*'s representation of the Arab world.

The prosperous Baghdad of 1958, where Chevrolets outnumbered camels, apparently had not ridden its "magic carpet of black gold" very well. In 1985, another *National Geographic* visit found some signs of modernization in the country, but in total it found Iraq lacking: "As recently as 15 years ago Baghdad was patched with shantytowns. The sanitation facilities were antiquated, most of the roads unpaved. There was not a single first-class hotel in the city. Drained of its passions, Baghdad had only its name with which to evoke the sweetness of Arabian Nights."[1] Even with enough money to buy American cars, the Iraqi people remained too backward to improve sanitation facilities. And as usual, Iraq and its people were represented as Baghdad of the *Arabian Nights* (or nightmares), which in turn was represented as an Arab woman.

The magazine continued its description: "For years a recluse, Baghdad is emerging from behind its veils to make a bid as a power broker for the Arab world." As the designated host for the 1982 meeting of nonaligned nations, Iraq embarked on a major construction plan "to design and build a capital city worthy of a nation aspiring to leadership of the Arab world." The war with Iran caused the meeting's venue to be moved to another country; however, "although jilted, Baghdad still wore its wedding gown."[2]

On the whole, Baghdad was represented as a city with little character that did not embrace visitors with warmth. It also suffered from the same contradiction that Rana Kabbani contends Westerners find in the Arab world generally: "Either the Orient was not 'Oriental' enough, or it was *too* 'Oriental.'"[3] Although *National Geographic* pointed out signs of Iraq's backwardness (its Orientalness), it also said, "In truth, Baghdad is a city with great age but little soul. It may be that too much of its historic fabric has been shredded by all the new construction."[4] Adding another layer of contradiction, the magazine reported that foreign firms were "participating in the resurrection of Baghdad from its pit of neglect."[5] However, the author said, shantytowns and poor sanitation were replaced with characterless new construction. There was no way for Baghdad to win when being bounced between these contradictory expectations. In both cases, the country was identified by what were understood, in this context, as markers of the worst of both worlds.

What signified the best of the Arab world, as we have so often seen, was the period of the *Arabian Nights* and what that conjured up within Orientalism.

Fatima Mernissi's interpretation of that so-called Golden Age (the eighth and ninth centuries) is quite different from the Golden Age that was continually called up by authors in *National Geographic* magazine. Mernissi argues that under the Abbasid dynasty the situation of Arab women deteriorated. It was the time of "international conquest for the Muslims and also the arrival of the jawari (women slaves) coming from the conquered countries: Men gave each other jawari. . . . With the economic boom and the expansion of the cities . . . the Arab woman was completely marginalized. . . . She was imprisoned behind locked doors and windows.[6] That is hardly a Golden Age if one applies a gendered critique. Female slavery, the seclusion of women in rich harems, and the world of the *Arabian Nights* stories were signs of the best period of Arab history according to male Orientalism. (I am not suggesting that these circumstances of women were Orientalists' inventions about the Arab world; rather, I am critiquing how they were represented and over-represented in *National Geographic*.)

Even the collection of stories known as the *Arabian Nights* has to be considered a matter of Western representation. As Kabbani argues, these stories were never a definitive text in Arabic literature; they existed as oral folklore in popular quarters long before they were put into writing. It is unclear when written versions of the *Arabian Nights* first appeared, but, Kabbani notes, "the manuscripts that resulted were as amorphous and diverse as the oral versions of the stories had been." In 1704, when the Frenchman Antoine Galland "created a text out of the flexible material he had at his disposal," the *Arabian Nights* became "institutionalized in the way they are known to the West." Kabbani says of Galland: "He is the inventor of a Western phenomenon."[7]

As we have seen, this Western phenomenon surfaced throughout the long history of *National Geographic*'s image of the Arab world. Because this Golden Age was part of the sexual fantasy so integral to Orientalism, it was the rare article on the Arab world that made no mention of *Arabian Nights*. And against this image, the Arab world always fell short: It did not live up to itself, let alone Western standards.

THE DIFFERENCE BETWEEN EAST AND WEST

Most visits to Arab countries produced comparative East and West lists as part of *National Geographic*'s relentless search for difference. This list-making activity was carried out, according to Alison Devine Nordstrom, by "using both text and illustrations to force unfamiliar cultures into patterns of contemporary American values, categories and social relations."[8] These completely arbitrary markers of difference were worked into comparisons that can be truly confounding if one tries to make sense of them. It is useless to look beyond their function to establish East and West difference; there is nothing more there.

For example, Cairo was said to be a mix of influences: "There is a medieval Cairo, and a European Cairo, a Cairo of Arabian Nights ribaldry, and a Cairo of polo and silver-service teas."[9] Beirut was described in a 1970 article as a city of sharp contrasts where, on one side of the city, the author found "a capital of worldly ways, of smartness and cultural richness . . . the renowned American University of Beirut . . . cinemas, . . . fashionable dress shops, . . . restaurants running the gamut of international cuisine . . . many nightclubs and cabarets, . . . [and] the Casino du Liban." The other side of Beirut life had "backgammon boards set up on boxes on the street corners . . . an old quarter where lamb carcasses hang in the butcher shops. Flies own the air there, and garbage fills the gutters; the sidewalks are communal beds, and the coffeehouses are breeding grounds for political coups."[10]

Within this article's framework, everything constructed as good was an example of Westernized Beirut culture, and everything bad remained Arab. Western influence produced worldly ways, the American University, and dress shops; the East had filth, flies, and poverty.

Moreover, no sound comparisons were to be made between, for example, cinemas and garbage or casinos and butcher shops. The most elementary understanding of comparison would suggest, for instance, that the Western cinemas on one side of Beirut be compared with Arab theater on the other side under the category of popular entertainment or the arts. Or that butcher shops be compared with how meat was sold on the other side. The pretense of developing a comparative look at East and West was merely employed to demonstrate (again) the difference between "us" and "them"—a difference that had already been established and just needed repeating.

This difference was so sharp that at times it manifested itself in an abrupt way. Readers learned, in a 1971 article, that Fez, Morocco, had French and native sections. When the author moved from the "new city" into the old, Arab section, he said of the moment: "I turned my back on the familiar world and stepped—as if through the looking glass—into another Fez." Among what he saw there were "women, anonymous under their burnooses." And of the marketplace, he said, "sights, smells, and sounds assault the senses . . . where visitors step from the modern world into a centuries-old way of life." In "exotic Marrakech," the outdoor square "seethes with life, like a huge circus."[11]

The tropes of primitivism and Orientalism were used to construct an image with little other information required. This was all about creating the *essence* of Arab life, not describing its material world. This operation was the same as what Malek Alloula discusses as defining the essence of the harem rather than its inner life.[12] And this attitude was also apparent in a 1973 *National Geographic* article that catalogued some signs of Algeria and France's shared colonial history: "The two faces of Algiers merge into a heady blend—a Christian church with minarets, Arab movies with French subtitles, *Arabian Nights* on the Champs Elysees. . . . Young bureaucrats in Western suits, anonymous women wrapped in crisp white veils, miniskirted co-eds from the nearby University of Algiers, tall, gaunt men from the countryside wearing flowing flannel jellabas with pointed hoods."[13]

The way Arab women dressed was the most often used sign of progress—that is, Westernization or lack of it. "Anonymous women" were those who were not Westernized in dress; on the other hand, a miniskirt apparently gave a woman an identity and a university education. A 1979 article on Bahrain charted what the author called "feminine progress" in three generations of women sighted in the gold bazaar: "Grandma moved like a shadow under layers of black. . . . Mother wore the same black aba, or cloak, but with exposed face and hands. . . . The youngest, in her teens, sported a fashionable red pantsuit."[14] A red pantsuit signified "feminine progress" when compared to the veil. Readers need not know anything more about an Arab woman than that she wore a pantsuit or a veil; dress said it all.

Citing the work of Arjun Appadurai, Clifford speaks of the representational challenge to strategies that localize non-Westerners as 'natives.' They become confined or even imprisoned, "through a process of representational essentializing . . . in which one part or aspect of a peoples' lives come to epitomize them as a whole."[15] When I consider this argument and a century of persistent Orientalist tropes in *National Geographic,* the challenge becomes somewhat daunting, yet all the more necessary. This emblematizing process was most constant and powerful concerning the veil. What Mernissi calls "that piece of cloth" was more often than any other object in the Arab world sighted and loaded with meaning in *National Geographic.*[16] The range of meaning carried by that gendered piece of cloth included aura of mystery, Halloween ghost, oppression, backwardness, modesty, sexual fantasy, and non-Westernness.

SUPERCULTURE

Comparing the East and West by identifying, categorizing, and cataloguing difference in *National Geographic* relied on what Drinnon notes as the

Western use of the term "civilization" to distinguish "Western superculture, or the one true 'civilization,' from so-called primitive cultures."[17] This superculture claim is also known as Eurocentrism.

Eurocentrism is a cultural phenomenon claiming a Western superior model that should be imitated by all peoples. According to Samir Amin, this Eurocentric vision created a history of an "eternal west" that traces its culture and civilization from Ancient Greece to Rome to feudal Christian Europe to capitalist Europe. To support this historical lineage, Ancient Greece and Christianity have to be removed from the Orient and "annexed arbitrarily to Europe."[18] Because the European West, or "Western Christian civilization," boasts material wealth, military power, scientific achievements, and democratic institutions, it becomes justified in taking over the rest of the world. Europeanization is presented as "simply the diffusion of a superior model, function[ing] as a necessary law, imposed by the force of circumstance."

Amin maintains that, since the 1950s, "the 'ideology of development,' founded on the fundamental hypotheses of Eurocentrism . . . [has] not brought about even the smallest reduction in the North–South gap."[19] Development theory ignores the role of colonialism in unequal development and understands the different economic and industrialization histories of European (First World) and non-European (Third World) societies as solely the result of internal factors. However, as Robert Stam argues, Third World countries are "historical victims" of the process of colonization; they are the "colonised, neo-colonised or de-colonised nations of the world whose economic and political structures have been shaped and deformed within the colonial process."[20]

A TIMELESS TABLEAU

If we recall the 1894 Annual Address of National Geographic Society President (see Chapter Two), his division of the world into civilized and uncivilized regions just needed minor adjustments, even more than half a century later, to dovetail ideologically with development theory. Development theory blames the victim. It attributes underdevelopment to non-Western peoples' negative essential characteristics—and, conversely, implies that peoples of developed countries have positive essential characteristics. These negative characteristics are the same used throughout *National Geographic*'s construction of race and the primitive.

A 1982 trip to Sudan quoted a local man reflecting on the conditions in his country to say, "Someday with hard work, *Inshallah,* we will prosper." The author used this statement as a transition to his explaining, with uneasy humor, something of the Sudanese character to *National Geographic* readers. He said, "*Inshallah* means 'God willing,' and that word, along with *bukra* (tomorrow) and *malesh* (never mind), makes an acronym: the IBM system, the code of fatalism by which the Sudanese live."[21] *National Geographic's* uneasy humor was still in play with this IBM joke (insult) that reinforced the hierarchy of technically developed to underdeveloped countries.

An article on Egypt included a full-page, tight close-up of an old woman's face upon which one fly sat at the corner of her right eye and another on the left side of her nose. The caption told readers that she was "serene despite flies" and pointed out that the woman's nose ring and chin tattoo were "now spurned by the young as an anachronism."[22] Flies have had an incredibly long life span in primitivist discourse; in the 1980s they were still among what Alloula refers to as those "redundant signs that serve as the necessary reminders of backwardness."[23] The Arab was still an anachronism. Presumably, only those of the younger generation who spurned tattoos and nose rings (read Arab culture) would be disturbed by flies and find the energy (read Westernization) to shoo them away.

Arabs' laziness and their time warp combined to produce descriptions such as one in 1985 of Mukalla, Yemen. Readers learned that the city, a chief port during the Middle Ages, was "a sleepy town of some 70,000" where "a staggering tidal blend of sewage, garbage, dung, and the remains of dead sharks does to the nose what a blood-curdling scream does to the ears. Such a stench plagued even the noblest cities in antiquity." Keeping in the time warp, the caption to a landscape photograph read: "The riches of Arabia once traveled by caravan through landscapes unchanged in centuries. . . . [an] area almost as isolated as in the first millennium B.C."[24]

A 1986 article on Morocco included a visit to the city of Fez, the country's "1,200-year-old spiritual capital." The author said, "Elsewhere it is still the 20th century; in Fez it is the Middle Ages." And when he walked out of his hotel in what was previously the French colonialists' section, or the "new city," he "turned a blind corner, and entered the 14th century." The center of the city, with its various noises and smells produced a "sensory assault."[25] Much like the earlier description of going through the looking glass, this was an abrupt encounter with another world. There seemed to be no common ground between East and West; they were that different, that separate in time.

While visiting with a store owner in Jordan, in 1984, an author's attention moved in and out of the small store. He said, "Outside, in a timeless tableau, [the store owner's] wife and daughters in long black dresses winnow wheat in the light morning breeze. But from a hand-crank telephone on the wall you can ring up the 20th century—and find turbulent Middle East history still steadily evolving."[26] Here, women's clothing was used as a sign of Arab backwardness and stagnation, and the essentially violent or turbulent Arab was also still in place.

Even an Arab leader could be heard to speak of this time warp. Oman's Sultan Qabus, who, "educated at England's elite Sandhurst brings a modern outlook," was quoted in *National Geographic* as saying, "I am a man with one foot in my country—backward as it is—and the other in the 20th century." The sultan, with British military forces securing his throne, served as Arab legitimation of *National Geographic*'s Orientalism. The magazine, predictably, went on to report an Omani city as "a drowsy place, Nazwa is nevertheless the most important city in the interior."[27] If the interior's most important city was *a* "drowsy place," *National Geographic* readers probably imagined that Oman's lesser cities and villages were comatose.

DEVELOPING DIFFERENCE

An important element in constructing Western development theory was identifying physical differences between peoples of the industrialized West and those of the non-industrialized Arab world—that is, racism. Difference in this context was used for purposes of exclusion or separation and establishing hierarchies of development. Memmi asserts, "It is not the difference which always entails racism; it is racism which makes use of the difference." And when this difference enters what Memmi calls the stage of totalization, we then see the victim, the whole social group, completely characterized by the difference. Herein lies the particular effectiveness of locating difference in the biological— "it is transformed into fate, destiny, heredity."[28]

If, as Kabbani maintains, "nineteenth-century anthropology was predominantly a system for the hierarchical classification of race," it would seem that that tradition still colored us in the late twentieth-century.[29] In the 1970s and 1980s, *National Geographic* reported that in Tunisia there was "skin shading from bronze to jet;"[30] that "the slim, handsome Somalis [were] quick to smile, congenial unless roused;"[31] that a Bahraini falconer had a "hawk profile and his alert, piercing eyes were a match for those of any of his feathered charges;"[32] that Omani sheikhs reminded one author of "proud, disdainful hawks;"[33] and that in Yemen, the male host "looked every inch the hawk-faced desert nomad" and the women were "veiled to their dark and luminous eyes."[34]

In addition to establishing race and the animality of Arabs, there was their closeness, indeed oneness, with nature that separated them from Westerners. This relationhip to nature became a negative characteristic in development theory, while in other contexts it was a positive quality. As Judith Williamson notes in her discussion of "the natural" in advertisements, it is a symbol in culture that signifies a great variety of qualities linked by their being seen as desirable because of their connection to nature. Additionally, these qualities have changed: "There have been periods in the history of our society when 'artificial' was not a pejorative word as it is today; and when 'natural' did not have the bundle of positive connotations which characterizes it now."[35]

In addition to recognizing the variety of qualities linked to "the natural" and their historical changes, we can take Williamson's critique further by recognizing a different understanding of "the natural" when the West constructed primitivist discourse. A certain distance in the relationship to nature was to be achieved so that development could occur. The Western power to master, alter, and exploit (even completely destroy) nature became the natural or correct distance from nature. The relationship of the backward and underdeveloped to nature was unscientific and too close; it did not clearly separate man from his environment or establish a man-to-nature hierarchy.

The primitive's incorrect relationship to nature, what became an unnatural distance from nature in development theory, was represented in both text and visual image in *National Geographic* magazine. An article in which the author embarked on "a kind of personal pilgrimage," trying to follow Moses' footsteps, included a photograph of a robed Arab girl sitting outdoors among large rocks. As photographed, her veiled shape against the rocks produced an image in which the girl and the rocks blended together. It was captioned: "Ringside seat on eternity: A Bedouin girl merges with the rocks and silence of Sinai's wilderness. . . ." Similarly, a photograph of a white-robed Algerian woman showed her as practically indistinguishable from white mounds around her (Photo 26). It was captioned: "Barefoot pilgrim almost disappears as her burnoose blends with a limewashed tomb. . . ." And the caption to a photo of Omani women performing a traditional dance in which they swing their long hair said they were "like swirling desert winds."[36]

These sorts of photographs worked to establish the essentially primitive Arab who was completely attached to the environment—unable to separate into Western categories differentiating man and nature. This defined Arabs all the more negatively by virtue of the Arab world primarily represented as a desert wasteland in *National Geographic*. Arabs were stuck to nature, and a bad

PHOTO 26

"Barefoot Pilgrim Almost Disappears," August 1973
(Photo: Thomas Abercrombie/National Geographic Society Image Collection)

one at that. Finally, it was no coincidence that these pictures were of women. This kind of photograph in the magazine was usually created around women or women and children because gender was at work. Claude Gandelman notes the same in a discussion of bodies, maps, and texts: "Many modern depictions of the body—chiefly of the female body—are anthropomorphic maps or anthropomorphic landscapes."[37] Within the overall construction of gender, women were represented as being at one with nature. At the same time that primitivist discourse put non-Westerners at one with nature, in *National Geographic* the primitive Arab woman was most often seen to merge with nature.

THE MUSLIM'S BIRTHMARK

In a 1971 article on Morocco, the author commented on worshipers coming out of Friday prayers at Fez's Al Qarawiyin Mosque, saying: "Almost everyone . . . bore a round spot—like a faintly visible birthmark—in the center of his forehead . . . many times during each prayer their brows touch the ground. Their devotions have stamped them with a mark as indelible as their faith."[38]

Relying on popular Orientalism, *National Geographic* could expect its audience to believe that the brow of almost every worshipper was dirty from touching the floor (note that the author used the word "ground") of the most historic and well-established mosque in the country. Would readers have believed that worshippers at St. Patrick's Cathedral in New York City were all seen after Sunday church services to have dirty knees? The absurdity of the quotation did not matter; it was used to introduce the idea of a Muslim birthmark, which injected essentialism into Orientalist representations of Arab Muslims. The example bears out Said's statement, "We need not look for correspondence between the language used to depict the Orient and the Orient itself, not so much because the language is inaccurate but because it is not even trying to be accurate."[39]

Aside from Orientalism, how was it that such seemingly suspect accounts passed as truth in *National Geographic?* This process has to do with what Stephen Greenblatt points to as the power of the "claim to personal experience, the authority of the eyewitness." This is "a witnessing understood as a form of significant and representative seeing. To see is to secure the truth of what might otherwise be deemed incredible."[40] And so it was that an author's firsthand account of Muslims with dirtied foreheads that resembled identical birthmarks became believable. Something framed as what a person saw with his own eyes carried weight based on the authority of the eyewitness. *National Geographic* magazine made this discursive choice in its representation of the Arab world: It was around an appeal to the narrator's own presence that articles were constructed.

This marking of Arabs was something of a twist on the operation of marking sights as tourist attractions. It would seem that humans functioned the same way as any other sight to see. George Van den Abbeele discusses the process of "sight sacralization," saying that it is not so much the sight as it is the marker that produces the sight.[41] The marker identifies something as a thing to be seen; the marker makes it a sight. The mark on the forehead would both point to the sight (the Muslim) and be the sight itself (the Muslim birthmark). Knowing, as John Berger argues, "The way we see things is affected by what we know or what we believe," through the power of Orientalist discourse, one could be left with the certainty that the brand of Islam could be "seen."[42]

In a related discussion, Barbara Kirshenblatt-Gimblett looks at how the process of designating objects as ethnographic applies to humans. It is "when people themselves are the medium of ethnographic representation, when they perform themselves . . . when they become living signs of themselves."[43] People performing themselves is not only about ceremony or ritual. Most anything the non-Westerner does becomes performance—like Arabs sitting on the ground or milling about.

Within Orientalism, Arabs are always performing Arabs. For example, the cover of *National Geographic*'s July 1972 issue showed a close-up photograph of an Arab man's face. The same picture was also used inside the issue to introduce the lead article, "The Sword and the Sermon." The man in the picture was dark-complexioned, had a shortly cropped black beard, and was wearing an all-white head covering that was wrapped to frame his whole face. I would describe him as probably in his thirties and with handsome features. He was photographed full-face, carrying a solemn expression, and looking straight into the camera. The cover photo was captioned: "A Saudi Arabian's steely gaze seems to reflect his warrior heritage." And the lengthy caption to the second appearance of the photo within the article read in part: "Eyes fierce as a desert hawk's, a Saudi Arabian mirrors the fervor that spurred Mohammed's first converts. Shouting the name of Allah, Arab armies within 100 years seized a realm that stretched from Spain to Central Asia."[44] This was quite a bundle of Orientalist messages and images to be read from the face of one man.

According to Berger, when we look at a picture and accept the way the photographer saw the subject we do not do so innocently: "We accept it in so far as it corresponds to our own observation of people, gestures, faces, institutions."[45] Therefore, to have looked at a man's face illustrating "The Sword and the Sermon" and have seen a steely gaze reflecting a warrior heritage, or fierce eyes, or religious fervor, or military conquests, was to see through the lens of Orientalism. These meanings were assigned by *National Geographic* and could be seen only by viewers who agreed with the magazine's representation of Arabs. The magazine was producing and reproducing popular Orientalism.

Another reading of this cover photograph could find a "steely gaze" located not in the eyes of the Arab man, but in the eye of the *National Geographic* camera, and the only apparent conquest would be not by Arab armies shouting Allah, but by the camera dominating reality and serving as an instrument of social control. As Norman Denzin notes, the camera operates "as an extension of the oppressor's control over the oppressed. That is, by being able to posture the native in the attitude of the spectrum, the photographer–operator enforces his license to control the actions and movements of the other." By doing this, continues Denzin, the photographer molds the world of the other into an image of his own making.[46]

Additionally, the photograph of the Arab representing Islam's "sword and sermon" carried in it an element that Roland Barthes calls the "*punctum.*" This breaks or punctures what the photographer intended to be in the picture. "*Punc-*

tum is also: sting, speck, cut, little hole—and also a cast of the dice. A photograph's punctum is that accident which pricks." Barthes says of the punctum that it has "a power of expansion" and "paradoxically, while remaining a 'detail,' it fills the whole picture."[47] The punctum is unintentional.

The head cloth worn by the Arab in the photograph is threadbare on the right side lying against his face. The white thread-worn cloth against his black beard made everything *National Geographic* directed me to see about the essential Arab fall apart. Those bits of thread became evidence of a powerful camera. "Eyes fierce as a desert hawk's" were nowhere to be found in the Arab man's face; they were on the other side of the camera.

Additionally, the Arab animality that viewers were expected to see in this photograph brings to mind what Berger says about looking at animals in the zoo: "Nowhere in a zoo can a stranger encounter the look of an animal. At most, the animal's gaze flickers and passes on. . . . They have been immunised to encounter."[48] In the same way we imagine having seen "the look of an animal" at the zoo, *National Geographic* readers would have imagined they saw the animality of Arabs and "the look of an Arab." But there was no Arab and no Muslim there. The gaze of the man representing Islam's sword and sermon passes right by the viewer; he was somewhere else. The man written about in *National Geographic*'s caption was invented by the magazine and readers who went along with its interpretation.

FANTASIA AND FANTASY

National Geographic introduced an article on Morocco with a 10-by-14–inch foldout picture of Arab men on horseback shooting rifles into the air (Photo 27). The text began: "A dozen turbaned riders, twirling and firing their muzzle-loaders, screamed across the plain full-bore toward us. I looked for a place to jump. But, reined in hard, the foaming horses thundered to a stop— seemingly inches away."[49]

The author continued to set this dangerous scene a bit longer before readers learned that what they were looking at in the foldout and reading about in the introduction was a *fantasia*—a traditional Arab riding and shooting performance put on during various celebrations. This particular occasion was the opening of a new hospital, a happy celebration, but the magazine temporarily confused the readers to create the image of a violent and dangerous Arab world. The *fantasia* was used—or misused in the magazine's fantasy of the Arab world; they are two very different things. The author's Orientalist imagination combined with the scene of the *fantasia* in his description of Morocco as "an

PHOTO 27

"Rattle of Gunfire," June 1971
(Photo: Thomas Abercrombie/National Geographic Society Image Collection)

ancient land striving for a modern identity, the Middle Ages galloping wildly through the 20th century, an *Arabian Nights* with a heavy French accent."[50] We have already encountered these images a number of times in this study; they are by now completely predictable.

An article published in 1974 titled "Damascus, Syria's Uneasy Eden," which appeared three years after this account of a *fantasia,* made use of the same device to construct the violent Arab. The article began: "The gun turret slowly revolved; the canon barrel came down to point straight at me. I froze behind the wheel of my car. . . . With Arab-U.S. relations at an all-time low, was I about to become a tragic victim of mistaken identity?"[51] This turned out not actually to be a dangerous situation; rather, it was only a joke played on the author by a friend. The joke and the introduction to the article worked because the essential connection between Arabs and violence was already well known. And with this article, a piece of popular Orientalism was once again produced and reproduced by *National Geographic.*

A 1970 article titled "Lebanon, Little Bible Land in the Crossfire of History" included an account of the funeral of an "Arab commando." The author reported that mourners were "shout[ing] quotations from the Koran and brandish[ing] placards showing machine gun-carrying commandos."[52] The construction of

Islam within Orientalism was in play here with the implication that words from the Koran (shouted, of course) were menacing. In addition, notice that the mourners were said to be "brandishing" pictures of guns. The word choice, in a most manipulative way, turned the demonstrators' pictures into weapons. This was a very direct example of the magazine's ability, which has been examined throughout this study, to turn photographs into very powerful political and cultural weapons.

A 1979 article titled "Volatile North Yemen" included a photograph of several Yemenis examining a machine gun. The caption informed readers that "Yemeni men carry these guns as casually as Westerners carry credit cards." The author reported that when he asked a Yemeni family what they wished to buy with the money coming in from Saudi Arabia, they listed electricity, schools, hospitals, and larger homes. While this may seem a perfectly sound wish list, the author found it indicative of one of Arabs' negative characteristics. He commented that peace was not on their list and speculated that, "with conflict so common among generations of Yemenis, perhaps it has become an accepted part of life."[53] The author ignored what the Yemenis said and instead focused on what he found lacking in their list of needs. With this maneuver he created an excuse to inject the idea of Arabs being so accustomed to fighting that they hardly even take notice of it. (This is an idea that we have already encountered in *National Geographic*.) Fighting has been represented as the Arab way of life throughout the magazine's history.

Decade after decade in *National Geographic* we have read and looked at the same representations of Arabs and violence, and except for the dates, little if anything has altered. Finding these images still circulating in the 1970s and 1980s, one is struck by the resiliency of Orientalism and primitivism. New to Orientalist discourse, as mentioned earlier, was the introduction of oil as part of the general excess surrounding Arabs. In addition, oil was used to make representations of the volatile and unpredictable Arab all the more dangerous.

WHAT *DO* THE ARABS WANT?

In a 1975 article titled, "The Arab World, Inc.: Who Are Those Oil-Rich Arabs, and What Are They Doing with All That Money?" the author said he had visited the Arab world to search for answers to the questions: "What are Arabs doing with their money? Who are the decision makers? And what may we expect of them in the future?" He characterized his trip as following "the trail of Arab billions." During a meeting with the editor of the *Middle East Economic Survey*, the author asked him, "What *do* the Arabs want?"[54]

The big money mystery was conjured up again in a 1980 article on Saudi Arabia. The author said he went to the country "to find out what happens when an Islamic, nomadic, patriarchal, and impoverished society, after hundreds of years of subsistence living, suddenly becomes rich beyond the dreams of Croesus."[55]

These questions constructed Arabs as rich, backward, unpredictable, irresponsible, and irrational. Arabs were unreliable owners of vast oil reserves. As Said notes, in recent decades, the Arab as an oil supplier is added to the list of negative characteristics.[56] The magazine's implication was that Arabs neither deserved nor were responsible enough to control a resource as important as oil.

The Arab world in *National Geographic* was a place where financial "surpluses keep building up" and bankers wonder "What to do with it all?" It was where "once-poor and still little-known lands of the Arabian Peninsula ride a magic carpet of petrodollars" and a "magic wand of money transforms." It was where "consumer goods sop up only a driblet of the oil money flooding Gulf-state coffers," and where "Luxuries unknown a decade ago have become necessities as Gulf Arabs find their pockets jingling." At the same time, this fantastic image of wild excess was presented as disturbing to the West: "To the world financial community, this treasure is a worrisome thing—both threat and opportunity. The sudden shifting of those funds could injure a bank or a nation."[57]

In *National Geographic* magazine, the major problem with oil for the West was that Arabs owned it. A 1974 article on the world's oil supplies and shortages due to Arab cutbacks began: "Not since the depression of the 1930s had the economies of nations around the world suffered such peace-time disruption and strain. Factories shut down, workers were laid off, lights dimmed, buildings chilled . . . Sunday driving was banned." Along with the text of this grim economic account that affected even U.S. Sunday culture was a photograph of an Arab man grinning widely and holding a water pitcher filled with oil (Photo 28). The photograph's caption read: "Pitcher of Kuwait crude and a smiling Arab symbolize the dilemma of the 70s: the economic duel between nations that produce oil and those that must import it to survive."[58]

Through the text and visuals, the magazine produced an image of suffering Westerners and carefree Arabs. In the United States, workers were laid off, buildings chilled, and families were denied their Sunday drives, while oil-rich Arab countries were "faced with so much oil income that it becomes virtually unspendable. . . . Droves of Cadillacs appeared in early days of Saudi prosperity." And in Kuwait there were "miniskirts spawned by sudden wealth." Commenting on such changes, a Saudi was quoted as saying that the Kuwaitis "want to put all civilization in a glass and drink it at a gulp."[59]

PHOTO 28

"Pitcher of Kuwait Crude and a Smiling Arab," June 1974
(Photo: Emory Kristof/National Geographic Society Image Collection)

Arab excess had no limits; it was out of control. Arabs portrayed in Cadillacs and miniskirts—a typically American combination of luxuries—made Arab decadence all the more exaggerated against the West's hardships because of an oil crisis. The power to control—indeed, to put an embargo on—oil to the West would seem a cruel twist of fate after all the good works of the West in the Arab world. Readers were reminded of this colonial history in an article that said of Bahrain: "From the early 1800s until 1971 it was a British protectorate. That presence plus oil—discovered in 1932—paved the way to modernity."[60] (Incidentally, many oil fields in the Arab world had been under the control of various Western governments and companies for decades.) *National Geographic* magazine, in 1979, still pointed to benefits of colonialism and represented former colonial relationships as the West helping Arabs to modernize.

This colonial nostalgia also surfaced in a 1972 article on Egypt titled "Cairo: Troubled Capital of the Arab World." Arab countries without oil were usually portrayed as having trouble, while those with oil were making trouble. The author reported that an Egyptian doctor apologized to him for the condition of Cairo, claiming that it used to be much better. The author explained the doctor's remark to readers by saying that the country started to change after the

1952 revolution, when Egyptians took complete control. Since then, "The once-famous shops no longer stock Paris fashions. The old Shepheard's Hotel, where Englishmen at ease took their gin and tepid Scotch on the verandah, is gone. Bastille Day passes now without scores of French nationals gathering in Ezbekiya Garden for a joyous celebration."[61] Paris fashions and gin signified the cultured, leisured life under Western rule. Such talk about the good old days of colonialism asked readers to acquire what Appadurai calls "nostalgia without memory."[62] The *National Geographic* author recalled a time and a way of life in Egypt that was meant to bring fond memories to the magazine's Western readers, not to Arabs. They were Englishmen sitting on the verandas, not Egyptians, and they were French nationals enjoying celebrations in the garden, not Egyptians. Whose good old days were these?

SHADOWY ROMANCE

National Geographic in the 1970s and 1980s not only blamed Arabs for chilly buildings in the West; it was also still blaming Arab men when it wanted to look at women. As we have seen, among the magazine's alibis for its activities in the Arab world were those specifically enlisted to capture Arab women. These alibis included examining how Arab men dominate Arab women and charting "feminine progress." A picture included in a 1980 article on Tunisia showed a female European tourist sunbathing in a topless bikini (Photo 29). Because it was non-Western women whose breasts were displayed in the magazine, not those of Western women, the sunbather was photographed from the back. Her European breasts were not revealed to viewers of the picture, but they were observed by an Arab laborer who walked in front of the woman. The Arab man's gaze, rather than her exposed breasts on a Tunisian beach, became the subject of the photograph. The picture established Arab lechery.

The message of this visual representation was reproduced in the text a few pages later: "Tunisians are confused about their freespirited visitors. Many . . . do not perceive the distinction between the shedding of inhibitions at the beach and the demands of decorum elsewhere."[63] The author also reported that he had seen Tunisians grab at passing European women as they would dare not do with Arab women. Lecherous Arab men were mistreating free-spirited European women.

National Geographic presented the problem as Arab men acting inappropriately, their not comprehending how to apply "demands of decorum"—of course, that would be Western decorum on an Arab beach. The expectation of European tourists that Western culture should be practiced in the Arab world

PHOTO 29

"More than Veils Are Lowered at Beaches," February 1980
(Photo: David Harvey/ National Geographic Society Image Collection)

was not questioned. *National Geographic* took for granted the right of Westerners to make the Arab world their playground. In addition, what we have here is a case of both Arab and Western men not understanding what Mernissi understands about patriarchy: "While Muslim exploitation of the female is cloaked under veils and hidden behind walls, Western exploitation has the bad taste of being bare and overexposed."[64] *National Geographic* held up Western patriarchy as the better model—white femininity over Arab femininity, the overexposed woman over the underexposed woman.

While Arab men looked at European women on Arab beaches, *National Geographic* in the 1970s and 1980s continued its quest for the harem and Arab women. A 1987 article titled "Women of Saudi Arabia" told about the tradition of veiling that lived on in this "male-dominated culture." Saudi Arabia was described as a country where "most accept the veil for privacy and protection from male harassment, not as a symbol of oppression, and cling to a tradition that defies Western understanding."[65]

Once again, Arab men, unlike Western men, dominated and harassed women. The veil was and is, in fact, a symbol of oppression, just as high heels and silicone breasts are. This really should not defy Western understanding. Throughout *National Geographic*, the veil is revealed in some ways as more a

Western than an Arab obsession. Alloula says, "Thrust in the presence of a veiled woman, the photographer feels photographed; having himself become an object-to-be-seen, he loses his initiative: he is dispossessed of his own gaze."[66] This explains part of the drive to unveil Arab women: The Western male gaze could not rule over veiled women.

And this is what lay behind the magazine's long history of photographs taken inside the harem, whether they were studio-constructed harems or real ones. Before looking at these examples in *National Geographic,* it will be useful to understand the Arab meaning of the veil. Mernissi explains that the concept of the word *hijab* (veil) is three-dimensional: "the first dimension is a visual one: to hide from sight. The root of the verb *hajaba* means 'to hide.' The second dimension is spatial: to separate, to mark a border, to establish a threshold. And finally, the third dimension is ethical: it belongs to the realm of the forbidden. . . . A space hidden by a hijab is a forbidden space."[67] It is against this background that some of the photographs included in the article "Women of Saudi Arabia" must be interpreted.

One picture has an elaborate Arab meal setting as its alibi (Photo 30). The unveiled women standing against the wall or otherwise occupied and not paying attention to the camera reveal that this was really about photographing the harem, not the food. The female American photographer was sent on a masculinist mission. The Arab women, who obviously cleared the way for a view of the lunch spread, were the actual focus of the picture. They stood at the periphery of the room, away from the food, clearly not intending to appear within the picture frame. The caption to this photograph explained: "No men are allowed when guests at the Jiddah mansion of Princess Jawharah, a wife of the late King Faisal, remove the veil for their frequent get-togethers behind closed doors." The women were unveiled only because they were attending a sex-segregated gathering behind closed doors. Did *National Geographic* have the right to open those doors to the world? Photographing these women for mass publication completely disregarded their culture and their rights, and disgraced them.

Another picture in the same article that also resulted in symbolic violence used "the new Arab women" as its alibi to display women (Photo 31). The aerobics class photographed is being held in a Saudi women's center where men would not be allowed free entry. The female photographer took a picture that not only ignored all Arab "demands of decorum" by displaying unveiled Saudi women in leotards, but went even further with a body shot at crotch level. Of all the moments during an exercise class to click the camera, why did the photographer choose this one? What was the purpose of capturing Saudi women this way? The photographer was working within the demands of Orientalism

PHOTO 30

"No Men Are Allowed," October 1987
(Photo: Jodi Cobb/National Geographic Society Image Collection)

and produced an image that reflected a tradition of exposing secluded Arab women.

In addition to asking why the picture was taken, we have to ask: What was the purpose of publishing it? Catherine Lutz and Jane Collins found that "photographers at *National Geographic* have never controlled which of their pictures will be published." They also explain that because the magazine has so much money, photographers are supplied with all the equipment they need to take pictures under almost any conditions and have no limit on the number of rolls of film they use during an assignment.[68] So of all the pictures that this photographer must have taken, why did *National Geographic* choose to publish this one? Male Orientalism's eroticism and exoticism have always been located in inaccessible women's quarters. The essence of what Alloula calls the West's "harem madness" was still between women's legs.[69] This article also established a voyeuristic mood by including pictures of women who are unaware of being watched and photographed.

Another article on Saudi Arabia produced the same kind of photo at an all-women's school. This picture, published in 1980, showed seven young adult women, five of who were unveiled, relaxed and apparently amused by something. The women in this picture, as in the earlier examples from 1987, were

PHOTO 31

"Dancing to a New Tune," October 1987
(Photo: Jodi Cobb/National Geographic Society Image Collection)

not looking at the camera but, rather, directing their attention elsewhere. The caption read: "At ease in the privacy of Jiddah's Dar-el-Hanan School, the kingdom's first and leading girls' educational institution, students go without the veils worn in public by most women older than 12."[70] *National Geographic* magazine invaded their privacy by making public a photograph of these women without their veils. Unveiling Arab women in this way is no less a show of domination than insisting on their veiling. This is Western patriarchy going about its business of exposing women.

This need to unveil women is also tied to what Homi Bhabha points out about colonial discourse producing the colonized "as a fixed reality which is at once an 'other' and yet entirely knowable and visible."[71] The veiled Arab woman is the ultimate symbol of this contradiction. Within the construction of gender, men know women, but at the same time, women are unfathomable. (What *do* women want?) Within the construction of Orientalism and primitivism, Westerners know Arabs (non-Westerners), yet Arabs are a mystery. (What *do* Arabs want?) Arab women, "the other of the other," to borrow Greenblatt's phrase, who are hidden from sight become primary targets, obsessions.[72]

As Alloula remarks, to photograph Arab women "in 'their' quarters, 'their' interior, is tantamount for the photographer . . . to have come, on discreet tippy toes, close to a highly eroticized reality of the Oriental world that haunts him: the harem."[73] That was the place where women were invisible and unknown to Western man, and was therefore the place to penetrate. Within this framework, the veil, identified by Mernissi as "an expression of the invisibility of women on the street, a male space *par excellence*," became in *National Geographic* something of a portable harem that tempted trespassers.[74]

Among the magazine's visual images of Arabs, one of the most symbolically violent is an alley scene taken in Algeria in 1973 (Photo 32). Yael Simpson Fletcher's study on colonial Algeria points out that photographs in books and articles "usually portrayed the Casbah with a view of a heavily veiled woman

PHOTO 32

"Veiled Women, Closed Doors, Secret Thoughts"
(August 1973)

(Photo: Thomas Abercrombie/National Geographic Society Image Collection)

in a narrow passage of steep stone steps."[75] *National Geographic*'s photograph reflects a standard Orientalist image. This picture also corresponds to Sontag's argument that "just as the camera is a sublimation of the gun, to photograph someone is a sublimated murder—a soft murder."[76] A good example of this, given by Sontag, is the photographic safari that replaces the gun with the camera. And much like a safari photograph, the camera trapped two veiled women in an Algerian alleyway between a man in Western clothing entering at one end of the narrow alley and the *National Geographic* eye coming in at the other. Soft murders have often been carried out by *National Geographic*'s camera.

This picture was captioned: "Veiled women, closed doors, secret thoughts. The famous Casbah, heart of old Algiers, still represents shadowy romance to outsiders."[77] Combined, this caption and photograph produce a pornographic structure that agree with Susanne Kappeler's understanding: "The male subject imposes a scenario of violence upon the female subject which eliminates the latter and reduces her to object status."[78] All of this activity in text and visual image was another example of harem madness that reveals *National Geographic*'s understanding the veil and women in precisely the same terms as the tenets of Muslim "orthodoxy." Within that, according to Fatna Sabbah, the veil "represents the denial of the economic dimension of women . . . who are exclusively sexual beings."[79] This common patriarchal ground between *National Geographic* and the most orthodox end of Islam is one of those places where East and West met.

At the same time, we have seen once again how the resiliency and timelessness of Orientalism carried it through a century with remarkably little sign of aging. Closing out the latest period covered in this study of one hundred years of *National Geographic*'s representations of the Arab world, we have seen much of what appeared in earlier eras reproduced. Decade after decade, Arabs were locked into predictable Orientalist interpretations as *National Geographic,* itself veiled and daggered, constructed the Arab world for its millions of readers.

AFTERWORD

THE BAZAAR AND THE BIZARRE

Gardiner G. Hubbard's 1894 "Geographic Progress of Civilization: Annual Address of the President," which was quoted earlier in this study, concluded with the following look to the future of favored countries within the parallels of latitude drawn fifteen degrees north and south of Washington:

> We began with the proposition that in all ages of the past civilization has been confined to the favored regions lying in the temperate zone; but with ever increasing knowledge there seems to be no reason to doubt that man will eventually bring under subjection all the adverse conditions of physical life and become the master of his environment, until the whole earth, even those regions heretofore supposed to be entirely unfit for habitation, shall own his power and become the abode of the highest intelligence and greatest civilization.[1]

We are beginning to learn the destructive results and impossibility of the Western vision to "master the environment" and "bring it under subjection."

The relationship between Hubbard's civilized man and nature has been, and continues to be, shaped by dreams and strategies of domination. This man/nature opposition is not unlike that established with peoples outside the parallels of latitude fifteen degrees north and south of Washington (West/non-West, civilized/uncivilized, developed/underdeveloped, and so on).Throughout this book, we have seen that the history of *National Geographic*'s representation of Arabs reflects the same sort of hierarchical relationship of man over nature that Hubbard was promoting.

A century of so little change regarding the representation of the Arab world in *National Geographic* is disturbing if for no other reason than that one would have liked to think that certain stereotypes and assumptions eventually die of old age. This book demonstrates that some fundamental lines making up Orientalism are as powerful as they ever were within the pages of *National Geographic*. This historical research revealed one hundred years of a remarkable degree of sameness. Orientalism has always been made up of a large and contradictory repertoire of tropes that allow for its chameleonic character while remaining its essential self—timeless, violent, erotic, and primitive—and constructing Arabs within its very own characteristics. That is its magic, its power; the discourse's nature is turned into the Arab's nature. Thus, Orientalism's rhetorical contortions can leave the *National Geographic* reader wondering, "What *do* Arabs want?" rather than wondering what the text or the visual image wants from us. It is always the Arab who is strange or ridiculous, never the discourse.

Orientalism lives on so intact that it has become something of a Western masterpiece. The master's oil painting in the museum survives centuries of a changing world and doesn't lose its position; indeed, it may take on more status and value with time. We still stand reverently in the presence of high culture displayed under precision lighting and behind velvet ropes. It is in these terms that we might understand the timeless discourse of Orientalism. One need not find any more change in the discourse over one hundred years than one would find in the painting on the wall—a new frame, a darkening of hues, some restoration work on one corner, a differnt owner, perhaps, but it remains the old masterpiece. Just as the masterpiece on canvas can be made, decade after decade, to evoke the same aesthetic response, so it is that Orientalism in text and visual image can construct the Arab world in American popular culture and education throughout a century of *National Geographic*.

This study of *National Geographic* brought contemporary critical work around the construction of knowledge squarely into the area of popular educational media. This carries implications for how we approach other popular educational texts that have been taken for granted. Clearly, the large and influential area of popular educational material needs to be examined rigorously within research on curriculum and the sociology of knowledge. My work on one of the foremost producers and transmitters of popular Orientalism on the American educational scene recognizes as objects of analysis those materials that are often considered ideologically neutral.

We should handle *National Geographic* critically and challenge its assumptions. We can use the journal differently from the way it was used in the past by employing strategies of interpretation rather than adopt a blind acceptance to it. And this more generally effects the development of practices related to critical reading and viewing, to creating possibilities of interpretation, and to recognizing multiple perspectives. Further, this work directly links with current work in multicultural curriculum re-evaluation. The door to multicultural critiques of material categorized as factual reference work must be opened farther.

Recently, a university student told me about an assignment given in her social studies methods class. The students were to create a picture file representing themes that included "man adapts to his environment," "man changes the environment," "people and nations are interdependent," and "cultural habits are learned." To demonstrate, the professor pulled out a stack of laminated pictures from *National Geographic.* She informed the students that the magazine was a wonderful source of pictures for social studies classes and said that even back issues were particularly good.

The professor advised her students to laminate their pictures because they would not be handled with care by thirty pairs of hands in their future classrooms. Yes, students should handle the photographs with care; these ideologically laden images demand very delicate treatment. The professor also said, "Most people just look at the pictures and don't really read the articles, and I think that's a shame." I agree; we should *really* read the articles. When viewed and read critically, this magazine, much like many other resources widely available to teachers and students, could from another perspective be well used in the classroom. It is hoped that this book has offered a different way to handle *National Geographic* and a different sort of knowledge to construct from it.

In my criticism of the way the Arab world appears in *National Geographic,* I am not suggesting that we avoid or ignore what we may view as negative aspects of any culture. I have political and social criticisms of the Arab world and criticisms of certain Arab cultural practices. I support democratic struggles and the equality of women in the Arab world. And I don't make excuses for tyrannical Arab regimes. But this is very different from what takes place within Western cultural prejudice practiced against Arabs and Islam. To criticize from within an interpretive process has nothing to do with reproducing stereotypes of Arabs as terrorists, wealthy sheikhs, and downtrodden women. Serious multicultural critique sees the Arab world as having a complex history and culture that calls for rigorous scholarship and cross-cultural collaboration in order to gain understanding. This is very different from the denigration of Arabs within Orientalism, in which the Arab world is all about the bazaar and the bizarre.

Beyond the representation of the Arab world and beyond *National Geographic* magazine, this book asks that we reimagine peoples and places by interpreting texts and pictures from a critical multicultural perspective on "the world and all that's in it." I am familiar enough with articles in *National Geographic* covering India, Africa, and Latin America to know that one could develop a book that is very similar to this one based on any number of countries and areas of the world. And I am familiar enough with educational journals, encyclopedias and other reference books, and many school textbooks to know that this book could have been written based on any number of possible subjects other than *National Geographic.*

But I must also acknowledge that having become so familiar with *National Geographic,* I now understand its unique and almost irresistible power to portray. There is something about *National Geographic* magazine. The photographs are outstanding, and its manner of skipping around the world is fascinating. It is difficult to sustain a critical perspective in the face of such attractive packaging. For instance, I remember that the August 1998 issue contained two pairs of 3D glasses to use for viewing the photographs in articles on Mars and the *Titanic.* The glasses came with instructions to punch out one pair carefully for use now and leave the second in the binding for future use. Suggesting that subscribers put aside a pair of 3D glasses for the future recognizes the common practice of preserving old issues of the magazine, as the social studies methods professor mentioned. I put on my 3D glasses and marveled at the rocky surface of Mars and the eerie underwater photographs of the *Titanic.* The pictures became magical, absolutely breathtaking shots. I immediately called my young son in to share the experience, and he was equally impressed. Yes, we get *National Geographic,* and my son has grown up completely familiar with that ubiquitous yellow-framed magazine. But we are careful not to use it as *National Geographic* wants. In fact, contrary to instructions, we even punched out both pairs of 3D glasses at the same time.

NOTES

INTRODUCTION

1. Gilbert H. Grosvenor, "The National Geographic Society and Its Magazine," *National Geographic,* vol. 69, no. 1. (January 1936), 125.

2. Ibid., 123.

3. Catherine A. Lutz and Jane L. Collins, *Reading National Geographic* (Chicago: University of Chicago Press, 1993), xiii.

4. Wilbur E. Garrett, Editorial, *National Geographic,* vol. 174, no. 1 (July 1988), 1.

5. Fredrick G. Vosburgh, "To Gilbert Grosvenor: A Monthly Monument 25 Miles High," *National Geographic,* vol.130, no. 4 (October 1966), 462, 476.

6. George F. Becker, "The Witwatersrand and the Revolt of the Uitlanders," *National Geographic,* vol. 7, no. 11 (November 1896), 356.

7. Donna J. Haraway, *Primate Visions: Gender, Race, and Nature in the World of Modern Science* (New York: Routledge, 1989), 157.

8. Alison Devine Nordstrom, "Wood Nymphs and Patriots: Depictions of Samoans in *The National Geographic Magazine,*" *Visual Sociology* 7 (1992): 49, 51.

9. Charles McCarry, "Let the World Hear From You," *National Geographic Index, 1888–1988* (Washington, D.C.: National Geographic Society, 1989), 47.

10. Marianna Torgovnick, *Gone Primitive: Savage Intellects, Modern Lives* (Chicago: University of Chicago Press, 1990), 9.

11. Gayatri Chakravorty Spivak, *The Post-Colonial Critic: Interviews, Strategies, Dialogues,* ed. Sarah Harasym (New York: Routledge, 1990), 60.

12. Russell Ferguson, "A Box of Tools: Theory and Practice," in *Discourses: Conversations in Postmodern Art and Culture,* ed. Russell Ferguson et al. (Cambridge, Mass.: MIT Press, 1990), 1.

13. Michel Foucault and Giles Deleuze, "Intellectuals and Power," in *Discourses,* ed. Ferguson et al., 11.

14. Mary Louise Pratt, *Imperial Eyes: Travel Writing and Transculturation* (New York: Routledge, 1992), 7.

15. bell hooks, *Talking Back: Thinking Feminist, Thinking Black* (Boston: South End Press, 1989), 5.

16. James Clifford, *The Predicament of Culture: Twentieth-Century Ethnography, Literature, and Art* (Cambridge, Mass.: Harvard University Press, 1988), 256.

17. Malek Alloula, *The Colonial Harem,* trans. Myrna Godzich and Wlad Godzich (Minneapolis: University of Minnesota Press, 1986), 5.

18. Phil Mariani and Jonathan Crary, "In the Shadow of the West," interview with Edward W. Said, in *Discourses,* ed. Ferguson et al., 94–95.

19. Edward W. Said, "Orientalism Reconsidered," *Cultural Critique* 1 (Fall 1985): 90.

20. Albert W. Atwood, "Gilbert Grosvenor's Golden Jubilee," *National Geographic,* vol.96, no. 2 (August 1949), 261.

CHAPTER ONE

1. Elizabeth Ellsworth and Mariamne H. Whatley, ed., *The Ideology of Images in Educational Media: Hidden Curriculums in the Classroom* (New York: Teachers College Press, 1990), 1.

2. Edward W. Said, *Orientalism* (New York: Vintage Books, 1979), 204.

3. Ibid., 16.

4. Ibid., 255.

5. Alloula, *The Colonial Harem,* 40.

6. Edward W. Said, *After the Last Sky: Palestinian Lives* (New York: Pantheon Books, 1986), 6.

7. Joan Acker, Kate Barry, and Johanna Esseveld, "Objectivity and Truth: Problems in Doing Feminist Research," in *Beyond Methodology: Feminist Scholarship as Lived Research,* ed. Mary Margaret Fonow and Judith Cook (Bloomington: Indiana University Press, 1991), 136.

8. Donna J. Haraway, *Simians, Cyborgs, and Women: The Reinvention of Nature* (New York: Routledge, 1991), 189.

9. Ibid., 155.

10. Joan W. Scott, "Experience," in *Feminists Theorize the Political,* ed. Judith Butler and Joan W. Scott (Routledge, 1992), 37.

11. Elizabeth Ellsworth, "Educational Films Against Critical Pedagogy," in *The Ideology of Images,* ed. Ellsworth and Whatley.

12. Mariamne H. Whatley, "The Picture of Health: How Textbook Photographs Construct Health," in *The Ideology of Images,* ed. Ellsworth and Whatley.

13. Nordstrom, "Wood Nymphs and Patriots": 49.

14. Lutz and Collins, *Reading National Geographic.*

15. Grosvenor, "The National Geographic Society," 149.

16. Vosburgh, "To Gilbert Grosvenor," 450, 476.

17. Ibid., 35.

18. Joseph Judge, "Taking Up the Great Global Issues," *National Geographic Index, 1888–1988* (Washington, D.C.: National Geographic Society, 1989), 52.

19. *"National Geographic* Fact-Finder at Work," *National Geographic,* vol. 114, no. 5 (November 1958), iii.

20. Atwood, "Gilbert Grosvenor's Golden Jubilee," 255.

21. Grosvenor, "The National Geographic Society," 162.

22. Ibid., 123.

23. Vosburgh, "To Gilbert Grosvenor," 484–85.

24. Lutz and Collins, *Reading National Geographic,* 34–35.

25. Vosburgh, "To Gilbert Grosvenor," 468.

26. "President Johnson Dedicates the Society's New Headquarters," *National Geographic,* vol. 125, no. 5 (May 1964), 669.

27. Kenneth F. Weaver, "Of Planes and Men: U.S. Air Force Wages Cold War and Hot," *National Geographic,* vol. 128, no. 3 (September 1965), 349.

28. Vosburgh, "To Gilbert Grosvenor," 469.

29. Ibid., 469

30. Ibid., 474, 447.

31. Melville Bell Grosvenor, "Journey into the Living World of the Bible," *National Geographic,* vol. 132, no. 4 (October 1967), 503.

32. Said, *Orientalism,* 3.

33. James Clifford, "Traveling Cultures," in *Cultural Studies,* ed. Cary Nelson, Paula Treichler, and Lawrence Grossberg (New York: Routledge, 1992), 100

34. Edward W. Said, *Covering Islam* (New York: Pantheon Books, 1981), 134.

35. Pratt, *Imperial Eyes,* 63.

36. Albert Memmi, *The Colonizer and the Colonized* (Boston: Beacon Press, 1967), 85.

37. Myra Jehlen, "Archimedes and the Paradox of Feminist Criticism," in *Feminisms: An Anthology of Literary Theory and Criticism,* ed. Robyn R. Warhol and Diane Price Herndl (New Brunswick, N.J.: Rutgers University Press, 1991), 75.

38. Acker, Barry, and Esseveld, "Objectivity and Truth," 135, 137.

39. Gillian Rose, *Feminism and Geography: The Limits of Geographical Knowledge* (Minneapolis: University of Minnesota Press, 1993), 1, 2.

40. Ibid., 4, 5.

41. Ibid., 94.

42. Ibid., 10.

43. Anne McClintock, *Imperial Leather: Race, Gender and Sexuality in the Colonial Contest* (New York: Routledge, 1995), 124.

44. Julia Clancy-Smith, "Islam, Gender, and Identities in the Making of French Algeria, 1830–1962," in *Domesticating the Empire: Race Gender and Family Life in French and Dutch Colonialism,* ed. Julia Clancy-Smith and Frances Gouda (Charlottesville: University Press of Virginia, 1998), 154, 155.

45. Ibid., 172.

46. Yael Simpson Fletcher, "'Irresistible Seductions': Gendered Representations of Colonial Algeria Around 1930," in *Domesticating the Empire,* ed. Clancy-Smith and Gouda, 194.

47. Ibid., 202–203.

48. Patrick Brantlinger, *Crusoe's Footprints: Cultural Studies in Britain and America* (New York: Routledge, 1990), 71.

49. John Fiske, "British Cultural Studies and Television," in *Channels of Discourse: Television and Contemporary Criticism,* ed. Robert C. Allen (Chapel Hill: University of North Carolina Press, 1987), 254.

50. Mimi White, "Ideological Analysis and Television," in *Channels of Discourse,* ed. Allen, 162–63.

51. Trinh T. Minh-Ha, *When the Moon Waxes Red: Representation, Gender, and Cultural Politics* (New York: Routledge, 1991), 185.

52. Ibid., 227.

53. Robert Stam and Louise Spence, "Colonialism, Racism and Representation—An Introduction," *Screen* 24 (March–April 1983): 9–11.

54. Cris Weedon, *Feminist Practice and Poststructuralist Theory* (Oxford and New York: Basil Blackwell, 1987), 147–48.

55. Stephen Greenblatt, *Marvelous Possessions: The Wonder of the New World* (Chicago: University of Chicago Press, 1991), 7.

56. Homi K. Bhabha, "The Other Question—The Stereotype and Colonial Discourse," *Screen* 24 (November–December 1983): 18–19.

57. White, "Ideological Analysis and Television," in *Channels of Discourse,* ed. Allen, 141.

58. Bill Nichols, *Representing Reality: Issues and Concepts in Documentary* (Bloomington: Indiana University Press, 1991), 116–17.

59. Trinh, *When the Moon Waxes Red,* 189.

60. Alloula, *The Colonial Harem,* 4–5.

61. Lata Mani, "Cultural Theory, Colonial Texts: Reading Eyewitness Accounts of Widow Burning," in *Cultural Studies,* ed. Nelson, Treichler, and Grossberg, 394.

62. Judith Williamson, *Decoding Advertisements: Ideology and Meaning in Advertising* (New York: Marion Boyars, 1984), 17.

63. Bill Nichols, *Ideology and the Image: Social Representation in the Cinema and Other Media* (Bloomington: Indiana University Press, 1981), 2–5.

64. Grosvenor, "The National Geographic," 128.

65. McCarry, "Let the World Hear from You," in *National Geographic Index,* 24.

66. Vosburgh, "To Gilbert Grosvenor," 461.

67. Roland Barthes, *Camera Lucida: Reflections on Photography* (New York: Farrar, Straus & Giroux, 1981), 6.

68. Nichols, *Representing Reality,* 21.

69. Susanne Kappeler, *The Pornography of Representation* (Minneapolis: University of Minnesota Press, 1986), 2–3.

70. Susan Sontag, *On Photography* (New York: Farrar, Straus & Giroux, 1977), 5, 7.

71. Ellen Seiter, "Semiotics and Television," in *Channels of Discourse,* ed. Allen, 23.

72. Kappeler, *The Pornography of Representation,* 17.

73. Keith McElroy, "Popular Education and Photographs of the Non-Industrialized World, 1885–1915," *Exposure* 28, no. 3 (Winter 1991/92): 34, 50.

74. Suzi Gablik, *Magritte* (New York: Thames and Hudson, 1985), 130.

75. Ibid., 135.

CHAPTER TWO

1. Edward W. Said, *Culture and Imperialism* (Vintage Books, 1994), 8.

2. *National Geographic,* "One Hundred Years of Increasing and Diffusing Geographic Knowledge," editorial, vol. 173, no. 1 (January 1988), 1.

3. William H. Goetzmann, "Tell Me If Your Civilization Is Interesting," *National Geographic,* vol. 173, no. 1 (January 1988), 17.

4. Ibid.

5. *National Geographic,* editorial, vol. 171, no. 1 (January 1987).

6. Haraway, *Primate Visions,* 56.

7. Ibid., 57.

8. Ibid., 158.

9. Curtis M. Hinsley, "The World as Marketplace: Commodification of the Exotic at the World's Columbian Exposition, Chicago, 1893," in *Exhibiting Cultures: The Poetics and Politics of Museum Display,* ed. Ivan Karp and Steven D. Lavine (Washington, D.C.: Smithsonian Institution Press, 1991), 344.

10. Robert W. Rydell, *All the World's a Fair: Visions of Empire at American International Expositions, 1876–1916* (Chicago: University of Chicago Press, 1984), 3.

11. Hinsley, "The World as Marketplace," in *Exhibiting Cultures,* ed. Karp and Lavine, 346.

12. Rydell, *All the World's a Fair,* 65.

13. Ibid., 41.

14. Ibid., 155.

15. Ibid., 160.

16. Ibid., 161.

17. Ibid.

18. Hinsley, "The World as Marketplace," in *Exhibiting Cultures,* ed. Karp and Lavine, 351–52.

19. Gardiner G. Hubbard, "Geographic Progress of Civilization: Annual Address by the President," *National Geographic,* vol. 6 (February 1894), 1.

20. Ibid., 1–2.

21. Ibid., 22.

22. Said, "Orientalism Reconsidered": 90.

23. Clancy-Smith, "Islam, Gender and Identities," in *Domesticating the Empire,* ed. Clancy-Smith and Gouda, 158.

24. Frank Edward Johnson, "Here and There in Northern Africa," *National Geographic,* vol. 25, no. 1 (January 1914), 43.

25. Ibid., 22.

26. Ibid., 56.

27. Alloula, *The Colonial Harem,* 53.

28. Fletcher, "'Irresistible Seductions,'" in *Domesticating the Empire,* ed. Clancy-Smith and Gouda, 203.

29. Ibid., 204.

30. Alloula, *The Colonial Harem,* 52.

31. Ibid., 27.

32. Ibid., 28.

33. Albert Memmi, *Dominated Man: Notes Towards a Portrait* (Boston: Beacon Press, 1969), 185.

34. Merian C. Cooper, "Two Fighting Tribes of the Sudan," *National Geographic,* vol. 56, no. 4 (October 1929), 465–86.

35. Ibid., 465-466.

36. Fredrick Simpich, "The Rise of the New Arab Nation," *National Geographic,* vol. 36, no. 5 (November 1919), 375.

37. Frederick Simpich, "Mystic Nedjef, The Shia Mecca: A Visit to One of the Strangest Cities in the World," *National Geographic,* vol. 26, no. 5 (November 1914), 597.

38. Felix Shay, "Cairo to Cape Town, Overland: An Adventurous Journey of 135 Days, Made by an American Man and His Wife, Through the Length of the African Continent," *National Geographic,* vol. 47, no. 2 (February 1925), 127. This entire issue is devoted to the Shays' "adventurous journey."

39. Harriet Chalmers Adams, "Across French and Spanish Morocco," *National Geographic,* vol. 47, no. 3 (March 1925), 332.

40. Shay, "Cairo to Cape Town, Overland," 125.

41. Captain Cecil D. Priest, "Timbuktu, in the Sands of the Sahara," *National Geographic,* vol. 45, no. 1 (January 1924), 77, 79.

42. Shay, "Cairo to Cape Town, Overland," 137.

43. Ibid., 139.

44. Ibid., 140.

45. Ibid., 235.

46. Said, *Orientalism,* 315.

47. Simpich, "The Rise of the New Arab Nation," 373.

48. Cooper, "Two Fighting Tribes of the Sudan," 467–68.

49. Shay, "Cairo to Cape Town, Overland," 141–42.

50. Thomas Cook & Son Cruise Advertisement, *National Geographic,* vol. 46, no. 1 (July 1924), xv.

51. Adams, "Across French and Spanish Morocco," 342.

52. Herbert L. Bridgman, "The New British Empire of the Sudan," *National Geographic,* vol. 17, no. 5 (May 1906), 244–45.

53. Stam and Spence, "Colonialism, Racism and Representation": 5.

54. "The Conquest of the Sahara by the Automobile," *National Geographic,* vol. 45, no. 1 (January 1924), 87, 88.

55. Ibid., 92.

56. Thomas Lindsey Blayney, "A Journey in Morocco: The Land of the Moors," *National Geographic,* vol. 22, no. 7 (July 1911), 750.

57. Rev. S. M. Zwemer, "Notes on Oman," *National Geographic,* vol. 22, no. 1 (January 1911), 91.

58. Adams, "Across French and Spanish Morocco," 327.

59. Stam, "Colonialism, Racism and Representation," 3–4.

60. V. Y. Mudimbe, *The Invention of Africa: Gnosis, Philosophy, and the Order of Knowledge* (Bloomington: Indiana University Press, 1988), 1–2.

61. Frederick and Margaret Simpich, "Where Adam and Eve Lived," *National Geographic,* vol. 26, no. 5 (November 1914), 546, 552.

62. Adams, "Across French and Spanish Morocco," 345, 347, 351.

63. Said, *Culture and Imperialism,* 22.

64. Ibid., 345, 347, 351.

65. Frank Edward Johnson, "Here and There in Northern Africa," *National Geographic,* vol. 25, no. 1 (January 1914), 62.

66. John D. Whiting, "Village Life in the Holy Land," *National Geographic,* vol. 25, no. 3 (March 1914), 261.

67. Nancy Rose Hunt, "Domesticity and Colonialism in Belgian Africa: Usumbura's Foyer School, 1946–1960," *Signs* 15, no. 3 (Spring 1990): 448–49.

68. Ibid., 474.

69. Ibid., 469.

70. Lieutenant-Colonel Gordon Casserly, "The White City of Algiers," *National Geographic,* vol. 53, no. 2 (February 1928), 206–32.

71. Blayney, "A Journey in Morocco," 750, 767.

72. Shay, "Cairo to Cape Town, Overland," 131.

73. Ibid., 133–134.

74. Ibid.

75. Colonel Gordon Casserly, "Tripolitania, Where Rome Resumes Sway: The Ancient Trans-Mediterranean Empire, on the Fringe of the Libyan Desert, Becomes a Promising Modern Italian Colony," *National Geographic,* vol. 48, no. 2 (August 1925), 137.

76. Ibid., 131.

77. Ibid., 132, 133, 135, 149, 156.

78. Major F.A.C. Forbes-Leith, "From England to India by Automobile," *National Geographic,* vol. 48, no. 2 (August 1925), 211, 214–15.

79. Johannes Fabian, *Time and the Other: How Anthropology Makes Its Object* (New York: Columbia University Press, 1983), 63.

80. Ibid., 144–47.

81. Forbes-Leith, "From England to India by Automobile," 215–19.

82. Simpich and Simpich, "Where Adam and Eve Lived," 567.

83. Blayney, "A Journey in Morocco," 765.

84. Adams, "Across French and Spanish Morocco," 331–32.

85. Whiting, "Village Life in the Holy Land," 249.

86. Fabian, *Time and the Other,* 2.

87. Claude Gandelman, *Reading Pictures, Viewing Texts* (Bloomington: Indiana University Press, 1991), 37, 45–46.

88. Casserly, "The White City of Algiers," 223.

89. Johnson, "Here and There in Northern Africa," 32.

90. Simpich and Simpich, "Where Adam and Eve Lived," 573.

91. Adams, "Across French and Spanish Morocco," 343.

92. Commander Francesco De Pinedo, "By Seaplane to Six Continents," *National Geographic,* vol. 54, no. 3 (September 1928), 253.

93. Shay, "Cairo to Cape Town, Overland," 235.

94. Alloula, *The Colonial Harem,* 40.

95. Torgovnick, *Gone Primitive,* 79.

96. Cooper, "Two Fighting Tribes of the Sudan," 481.

97. Irvin Cemil Schick, "Representing Middle Eastern Women: Feminism and Colonial Discourse." *Feminist Studies* 16, no. 2 (Summer 1990): 350.

98. Adams, "Across French and Spanish Morocco," 341.

99. Photo Essay, *National Geographic,* vol. 31, no. 3 (March 1917), 261.

100. Shay, "Cairo to Cape Town, Overland," 131.

101. Said, *Orientalism*, 60.

102. Simpich and Simpich, "Where Adam and Eve Lived," 556.

103. Zwemer, "Notes on Oman," 98.

104. Simpich and Simpich, "Where Adam and Eve Lived," 567, 569.

105. Shay, "Cairo to Cape Town, Overland," 137.

106. Priest, "Timbuktu, in the Sands of the Sahara," 75.

107. Archibald Forder, "Arabia, the Desert of the Sea," *National Geographic,* vol. 20, no. 12 (December 1909), 1045.

108. Rana Kabbani, *Europe's Myths of Orient* (Bloomington: Indiana University Press, 1986), 105.

109. Franklin E. Hoskins, "The Route over which Moses Led the Children of Israel out of Egypt," *National Geographic,* vol. 20, no. 12 (December 1909), 1038.

110. Johnson, "Here and There in Northern Africa," 93.

111. Major Edward Keith-Roach, "Adventures Among the 'Lost Tribes of Islam' in Eastern Darfur: A Personal Narrative of Exploring, Mapping, and Setting Up a Government in the Anglo–Egyptian Sudan Borderland," *National Geographic,* vol. 45, no. 1 (January 1924), 71.

112. Shay, "Cairo to Cape Town, Overland," 137.

113. Sarah Graham-Brown, *Images of Women: The Portrayal of Women in Photography of the Middle East 1860–1950* (New York: Columbia University Press, 1988), 170.

114. Cooper, "Two Fighting Tribes of the Sudan," 480.

115. Casserly, "The White City of Algiers," 230.

116. Kabbani, *Europe's Myths of Orient,* 36.

117. John Berger, *Ways of Seeing* (New York: Penguin Books, 1977), 51.

118. *National Geographic,* vol. 31, no. 3 (March 1917), 267.

119. Alloula, *The Colonial Harem,* 54.

120. Ibid., 89.

121. Norman K. Denzin, "Reflections on the Ethnographer's Camera," *Current Perspectives in Social Theory* 7 (1986): 106.

122. Berger, *Ways of Seeing,* 47.

123. Sontag, *On Photography,* 87.

124. McClintock, *Imperial Leather,* 123.

125. Susan Rubin Suleiman, ed., *The Female Body in Western Culture: Contemporary Perspectives* (Cambridge, Mass.: Harvard University Press, 1986), 2.

126. Samuel R. Delany, "Twilight in the Rue Morgue," *Transition* 54 (1991): 48–49.

127. Lutz and Collins, *Reading National Geographic,* 174.

128. Delany, "Twilight in the Rue Morgue": 48–49.

129. Sander L. Gilman, "Black Bodies, White Bodies: Toward an Iconography of Female Sexuality in Late Nineteenth-Century Art, Medicine, and Literature," in *"Race," Writing, and Difference,* ed. Henry Louis Gates, Jr. (Chicago: University of Chicago Press, 1985), 228, 232.

130. Frantz Fanon, *Black Skin, White Masks,* trans. Charles Lam Markmann (New York: Grove Press, 1967), 170, 177.

131. Berger, *Ways of Seeing,* 15–16.

132. Alloula, *The Colonial Harem,* 105.

133. McElroy, "Popular Education and Photographs of the Non-Industrialized World": 41.

134. Margaret R. Miles, "The Virgin's One Bare Breast: Female Nudity and Religious Meaning in Tuscan Early Renaissance Culture," in *The Female Body in Western Culture,* ed. Suleiman, 203.

135. Keith-Roach, "Adventures Among the 'Lost Tribes of Islam' in Eastern Darfur," 49.

136. George L. Mosse, *Nationalism and Sexuality: Middle-Class Morality and Sexual Norms in Modern Europe* (Madison: University of Wisconsin Press, 1985), 51.

137. Richard Dyer, *Heavenly Bodies: Film Stars and Society* (New York: St. Martin's Press, 1986), 120.

138. Photo Essay, *National Geographic,* vol. 31, no. 3 (March 1917), 263.

139. Kabbani, *Europe's Myths of Orient,* 33.

140. Barbara Kirshenblatt-Gimblett, "Objects of Ethnography," in *Exhibiting Cultures,* ed. Karp and Lavine, 397.

141. Kappeler, *The Pornography of Representation,* 103.

142. Miles, "The Virgin's One Bare Breast," 196.

143. McElroy, "Popular Education and Photographs of the Non-Industrialized World, 1885–1915," 50.

144. Barthes, *Camera Lucida,* 59.

145. Robert L. Chapman, ed., *The New Dictionary of American Slang* (New York: Harper & Row, 1986).

146. Torgovnick, *Gone Primitive,* 79.

147. Photo Essay, *National Geographic,* vol. 31, no. 3 (March 1917), 271.

148. Williamson, *Decoding Advertisements,* 19.

149. Kappeler, *The Pornography of Representation,* 76.

150. Keith-Roach, "Adventures Among the 'Lost Tribes of Islam' in Eastern Darfur," 70.

151. Ibid., 57.

152. Said, *Culture and Imperialism,* 35.

153. Cooper, "Two Fighting Tribes of the Sudan," 483–85.

154. C. Leonard Woolley, "Archeology, The Mirror of the Ages: Our Debt to the Humble Delvers in the Ruins at Carchemish and at Ur," *National Geographic,* vol. 54, no. 2 (August 1928), 226.

155. Ibid., 207.

156. Casserly, "The White City of Algiers," 224.

157. Hinsley, "The World as Marketplace," in *Exhibiting Cultures,* ed. Karp and Lavine, 353.

158. Woolley, "Archeology, The Mirror of the Ages," 211, 224.

CHAPTER THREE

1. M.E.L. Mallowan, "New Light on Ancient Ur," *National Geographic,* vol. 57, no. 1 (January 1930), 100.

2. Pratt, *Imperial Eyes,* 62.

3. Memmi, *The Colonizer and the Colonized,* 79–81.

4. Mallowan, "New Light on Ancient Ur," 111.

5. Ibid., 124.

6. Claude F. A. Schaeffer, "A New Alphabet of the Ancients Is Unearthed," *National Geographic,* vol. 58, no. 4 (October 1930), 498.

7. Clifford, *The Predicament of Culture,* 221.

8. Phyllis Mauch Messenger, ed., *The Ethics of Collecting Cultural Property* (Albuquerque: University of New Mexico Press, 1993), xxi.

9. Karen J. Warren, "A Philosophical Perspective on the Ethics and Resolution of Cultural Property Issues," in *The Ethics of Collecting Cultural Property,* ed. Messenger, 1.

10. Claude F. A. Schaeffer, "Secrets from Syrian Hills," *National Geographic,* vol. 64, no. 1 (July 1933), 100, 126.

11. David Sassoon, "Considering the Perspectives of the Victim: The Antiquities of Nepal," in *The Ethics of Collecting Cultural Property,* ed. Messenger, 70.

12. Aime Cesaire, *Discourse on Colonialism,* trans. Joan Pinkham (New York: Monthly Review Press, 1972, 21.

13. Frederick Simpich and W. Robert Moore, "Bombs over Bible Lands," *National Geographic,* vol. 80, no. 2 (August 1941), 141, 180.

14. Grant Parr and G. E. Janssen, "War Meets Peace in Egypt," *National Geographic,* vol. 81, no. 4 (April 1942), 526.

15. John Van Ess, "Forty Years Among the Arabs," *National Geographic,* vol. 82, no. 3 (September 1942), 385.

16. Memmi, *The Colonizer and the Colonized,* 84.

17. H.G.C. Swayne, "The Rock of Aden," *National Geographic,* vol. 68, no. 6 (December 1935), 732.

18. Willard Price, "By Felucca Down the Nile: Giant Dams Rule Egypt's Lifeline River, Yet Village Life Goes on as It Did in the Time of the Pharaohs," *National Geographic.* vol. 77, no. 4 (April 1940), 445–50.

19. Abdul R. JanMohamed, "The Economy of Manichean Allegory: The Function of Racial Difference in Colonialist Literature," in *"Race," Writing, and Difference,* ed. Gates, 86.

20. Henry Louis Gates, Jr., *Loose Canons: Notes on the Culture Wars* (New York: Oxford University Press, 1992), 49.

21. Henry Field, "Sinai Sheds New Light on the Bible," *National Geographic,* vol. 94, no. 6 (December 1948), 796.

22. Richard Drinnon, *Facing West: The Metaphysics of Indian-Hating and Empire-Building* (Minneapolis: University of Minnesota Press, 1980), 92–93.

23. Field, "Sinai Sheds New Light on the Bible," 811.

24. Said, *Orientalism,* 204.

25. McClintock, *Imperial Leather,* 124.

26. Kabbani, *Europe's Myth of Orient,* 62.

27. Mosse, *Nationalism and Sexuality,* 134.

28. D. Van der Meulen, "Into Burning Hadhramaut: The Arab Land of Frankincense and Myrrh, Ever a Lodestone of Western Exploration," *National Geographic,* vol. 62, no. 4 (October 1932), 402.

29. John D. Whiting, "Petra, Ancient Caravan Stronghold," *National Geographic,* vol. 67, no. 2 (February 1935), 140.

30. Lawrence Copley Thaw and Margaret S. Thaw, "Along the Old Silk Routes," *National Geographic,* vol. 78, no. 4 (October 1940), 475.

31. Kirshenblatt-Gimblett, "Objects of Ethnography," in *Exhibiting Cultures,* ed. Karp and Lavine, 407–409.

32. Herndon Hudson and Mary Hudson, "Ali Goes to the Clinic," *National Geographic,* vol. 90, no. 6 (December 1946), 765.

33. V. C. Scott O'Connor, "Beyond the Grand Atlas: Where the French Tricolor Flies Beside the Flag of the Sultan of Morocco," *National Geographic,* vol. 61, no. 3 (March 1932), 288.

34. Ibid., 280.

35. Swayne, "The Rock of Aden," 726.

36. O'Connor, "Beyond the Grand Atlas," 267.

37. Said, *Covering Islam,* 4.

38. Peter Bruce Cornwall, "In Search of Arabia's Past," *National Geographic,* vol. 93, no. 4 (April 1948), 519.

39. Brown, *Images of Women,* 46.

40. Schaeffer, "A New Alphabet of the Ancients Is Unearthed," 481, 483.

41. Brown, *Images of Women,* 145.

42. O'Connor, "Beyond the Grand Atlas," 290, 297–98.

43. Bhabha, "The Other Question": 18.

44. Alloula, *The Colonial Harem,* xvii.

45. Said, *Orientalism,* 208.

46. O'Connor, "Beyond the Grand Atlas," 261, 264.

47. Cynthia Enloe, *Bananas, Beaches, and Bases: Making Feminist Sense of International Politics* (Berkeley: University of California Press, 1990), 48.

48. Said, *Culture and Imperialism,* 24.

49. O'Connor, "Beyond the Grand Atlas," 302.

50. Ibid., 300.

51. Torgovnick, *Gone Primitive,* 8.

52. O'Connor, "Beyond the Grand Atlas," 280.

53. Maynard Owen Williams, "The Citroen Trans-Asiatic Expedition Reaches Kashmir," *National Geographic,* vol. 60, no. 4 (October 1931), 397.

54. Laura E. Donaldson, *Decolonizing Feminisms: Race, Gender, and Empire-Building* (Chapel Hill: University of North Carolina Press, 1992), 7.

55. Williams, "The Citroen Trans-Asiatic Expedition Reaches Kashmir," 397.

56. Parr and Janssen, "War Meets Peace in Egypt," 523.

57. Ibid., 522.

58. Ibid., 511.

59. Ibid., 511, 517.

60. Margaret Cotter, "Red Cross Girls Overseas," *National Geographic,* vol. 86, no. 6 (December 1944), 755–58.

61. Mary Louise Pratt, "Scratches on the Face of the Country; or, What Mr. Brown Saw in the Land of the Bushmen," in *"Race," Writing, and Difference,* ed. Gates, 151.

62. Van der Meulen, "Into Burning Hadhramaut," 397.

63. Henri de Monfreid, "Pearl Fishing in the Red Sea," *National Geographic,* vol. 72, no. 5 (November 1937), 614.

64. Denzin, "Reflections on the Ethnographer's Camera": 113.

65. Sontag, *On Photography,* 107.

66. Ibid., 55.

67. Maynard Owens Williams, "Time's Footprints in Tunisian Sands," *National Geographic,* vol. 71, no. 3 (March 1937), 362.

68. Ibid., 345.

69. O'Connor, "Beyond the Grand Atlas," 264–65.

70. Van der Meulen, "Into Burning Hadhramaut," 419.

71. De Monfreid, "Pearl Fishing in the Red Sea," 626.

72. Laura Rice, "Nomad Thought: Isabelle Eberhardt and the Colonial Project," *Cultural Critique,* no. 17 (Winter 1990–91): 152.

73. Eric Underwood, "The British Commonwealth of Nations: 'Organized Freedom' Around the World," *National Geographic,* vol. 83, no. 4 (April 1943), 493.

74. Said, *Culture and Imperialism,* 24.

75. Said, *Orientalism,* 121.

76. Underwood, "The British Commonwealth of Nations," 524.

77. Cesaire, *Discourse on Colonialism,* 10, 21.

78. Mudimbe, *The Invention of Africa,* 45.

79. Whiting, "Petra, Ancient Caravan Stronghold," 130.

80. Nelson Glueck, "On the Trail of King Solomon's Mines," *National Geographic,* vol. 85, no. 2 (February 1944), 249.

81. Swayne, "The Rock of Aden," 732.

82. Schaeffer, "A New Alphabet of the Ancients Is Unearthed," 481.

83. Major Edward Keith-Roach, "Changing Palestine," *National Geographic,* vol. 65, no. 4 (April 1934), 493.

84. Gordon Casserly, "Fez, Heart of Morocco: Africa's 'Imperial City' Retains Its Teeming Streets, Cluttered Shops, Glamorous Moorish Homes and Mosques, Amid the Peace of French Rule," *National Geographic,* vol. 67, no. 6 (June 1935), 665, 673.

85. Van Ess, "Forty Years Among the Arabs," 390.

86. Hinsley, "The World as Marketplace," in *Exhibiting Cultures,* ed. Karp and Lavine, 358–59.

87. Frederick Simpich, "Change Comes to Bible Lands," *National Geographic,* vol. 74, no. 6 (December 1938), 721.

88. Van Ess, "Forty Years Among the Arabs," 391.

89. See Gandelman, *Reading Pictures, Viewing Texts.*

90. Pratt, *Imperial Eyes,* 202.

91. Enloe, *Bananas, Beaches and Bases,* 48.

92. Schaeffer, "Secrets from Syrian Hills," 126.

93. Kabbani, *Europe's Myths of Orient,* 89–90.

94. Jane Gaines, "Costume and Narratives: How Dress Tells the Woman's Story," in *Fabrications: Costume and the Female Body,* ed. Jane Gaines and Charlotte Herzog (New York: Routledge, 1990), 187.

CHAPTER FOUR

1. Jean Shor and Franc Shor, "From Sea to Sahara in French Morocco," *National Geographic,* vol. 107, no. 2 (February 1955), 187.

2. Ibid., 161.

3. Gilbert M. Grosvenor, "When the President Goes Abroad," *National Geographic,* vol. 117, no. 5 (May 1960), 647.

4. Helen Schreider and Frank Schreider, "Journey into the Great Rift," *National Geographic,* vol. 128, no. 2 (August 1965), 265, 267.

5. Grosvenor, "When the President Goes Abroad," 642.

6. Elsie May Bell Grosvenor, "Safari from Congo to Cairo," *National Geographic,* vol. 106, no. 6 (December 1954), 748.

7. Thomas J. Abercrombie, "Saudi Arabia: Beyond the Sands of Mecca," *National Geographic,* vol. 129, no. 1 (January 1966), 33.

8. Vron Ware, *Beyond the Pale: White Women, Racism and History* (New York: Verso, 1992), 13–14, 17.

9. Nathaniel T. Kenney, "Africa: The Winds of Freedom Stir a Continent," *National Geographic,* vol. 118, no. 3 (September 1960), 353.

10. Howard La Fay, "Algeria: France's Stepchild, Problem and Promise," *National Geographic,* vol. 117, no. 6 (June 1960), 777.

11. Schick, "Representing Middle Eastern Women": 369.

12. John E. Frazer, "Aladdin's Lamp of the Middle East: Kuwait," *National Geographic,* vol. 135, no. 5 (May 1969), 667.

13. Schreider and Schreider, "Journey into the Great Rift," 257.

14. Harry Hoogstraal, "Yemen Opens the Door to Progress," *National Geographic,* vol. 101, no. 2 (February 1952), 235.

15. Kenneth MacLeish, "Abraham, the Friend of God," *National Geographic,* vol. 130, no. 6 (December 1966), 769.

16. Schreider and Schreider, "Journey into the Great Rift," 263.

17. Alloula, *The Colonial Harem,* 85.

18. *National Geographic,* subscription advertisement, vol. 125, no. 2 (February 1964).

19. Paul Edward Case, "Boom Time in Kuwait," *National Geographic,* vol. 102, no. 6 (December 1952), 799.

20. Abercrombie, "Saudi Arabia," 29.

21. Tay Lowell and Lowell Thomas, Jr., "Flight to Adventure," *National Geographic,* vol. 112, no. 1 (July 1957), 95.

22. Hoogstraal, "Yemen Opens the Door to Progress," 229, 234.

23. Alloula, *The Colonial Harem,* 92.

24. Oskar Luz, "Proud Primitives, the Nuba People," *National Geographic,* vol. 130, no. 5 (November 1966), 678–79.

25. Denzin, "Reflections on the Ethnographer's Camera: 106.

26. Brown, *Images of Women,* 48.

27. Marc DuBois, "The Governance of the Third World: A Foucauldian Perspective on Power Relations in Development," *Alternatives* 16, no. 1 (Winter 1991): 20–25.

28. Ibid., 22–23, 25.

29. Said, *Covering Islam,* 27–28.

30. Hoogstraal, "Yemen Opens the Door to Progress," 213.

31. DuBois, "Governance of the Third World": 22–23, 25.

32. Kenneth MacLeish, "Reunited Jerusalem Faces Its Problems," *National Geographic,* vol. 134, no. 6 (December 1968), 868.

33. MacLeish, "Abraham, the Friend of God," 766.

34. Schreider and Schreider, "Journey into the Great Rift," 267.

35. Ibid., 256.

36. Case, "Boom Time in Kuwait," 802.

37. John Scofield, "Hashemite Jordon, Arab Heartland," *National Geographic,* vol. 102, no. 6 (December 1952), 848.

38. Mariani and Crary, "In the Shadow of the West," in *Discourse,* ed. Ferguson et al., 95.

39. La Fay, "Algeria: France's Stepchild, Problem and Promise," 769.

40. Kenney, "Africa: The Winds of Freedom Stir a Continent," 303–305.

41. Mudimbe, *The Invention of Africa,* 47–48.

42. Donaldson, *Decolonizing Feminisms,* 71.

43. Memmi, *The Colonizer and the Colonized,* 113.

44. Ibid., 3.

45. Elsie May Bell Grosvenor, "Safari Through Changing Africa," *National Geographic,* vol. 104, no. 2 (August 1953): 198.

46. Pratt, *Imperial Eyes,* 7, 61.

47. La Fay, "Algeria: France's Stepchild, Problem and Promise," 780–88.

48. Brown, *Images of Women,* 53.

49. Nordstrom, "Wood Nymphs and Patriots": 51.

50. Harry Hoogstraal, "South in the Sudan," *National Geographic,* vol. 103, no. 2 (February 1953), 272.

51. Ibid., 248.

52. Schick, "Representing Middle Eastern Women": 347.

53. Shor and Shor, "From Sea to Sahara in French Morocco," 149, 184, 186.

54. Cesaire, *Discourse on Colonialism,* 22.

55. Pratt, *Imperial Eyes,* 224.

56. La Fay, "Algeria: France's Stepchild, Problem and Promise," 792.

57. Drinnon, *Facing West,* 372.

58. Mani, "Cultural Theory, Colonial Texts," in *Cultural Studies,* ed. Nelson, Treichler, and Grossberg, 394.

59. JanMohamed, "The Economy of Manichean Allegory," in *"Race," Writing, and Difference,* ed. Gates, 80–81.

60. La Fay, "Algeria: France's Stepchild, Problem and Promise," 794.

61. Shor and Shor, "From Sea to Sahara in French Morocco," 166.

62. Sontag, *On Photography,* 14.

63. MacLeish, "Abraham, the Friend of God," 765.

64. Ibid., 750.

65. Jean Shor and Franc Shor, "Iraq—Where Oil and Water Mix," *National Geographic,* vol. 114, no. 4 (October 1958), 449.

66. Said, *Covering Islam,* xvii.

67. Ibid.

68. Denzin, "Reflections on the Ethnographer's Camera": 108.

69. Ibid., 109.

70. *National Geographic,* "The Arab World," vol. 114, no. 5 (November 1958), 732.

71. Ross Gibson, *South of the West: Postcolonialism and the Narrative Construction of Australia* (Bloomington: Indiana University Press, 1992), 194.

72. Frazer, "Aladdin's Lamp of the Middle East: Kuwait," 637, 643.

73. Shor and Shor, "Iraq—Where Oil and Water Mix," 444, 463.

CHAPTER FIVE

1. William S. Ellis, "The New Face of Baghdad: Iraq at War," *National Geographic,* vol. 167, no. 1 (January 1985), 81.

2. Ibid., 85.

3. Kabbani, *Europe's Myths of Orient,* 137.

4. Ellis, "The New Face of Baghdad," 87.

5. Ibid., 106.

6. Fatima Mernissi, *The Veil and the Male Elite: A Feminist Interpretation of Women's Rights in Islam,* trans. Mary Jo Lakeland (Reading, Mass.: Addison-Wesley Publishing, 1991), 195.

7. Kabbani, *Europe's Myths of Orient,* 23–24.

8. Nordstrom, "Wood Nymphs and Patriots": 51.

9. William S. Ellis, "Cairo: Troubled Capital of the Arab World," *National Geographic,* vol. 141, no. 5 (May 1972), 641.

10. William S. Ellis, "Lebanon: Little Bible Land in the Crossfire of History," *National Geographic,* vol. 137, no. 2 (February 1970), 249, 251.

11. Thomas J. Abercrombie, "Morocco: Land of the Farthest West," *National Geographic,* vol. 139, no. 6 (June 1971), 839–40, 851.

12. See Alloula, *The Colonial Harem,* esp. chap. 8.

13. Thomas J. Abercrombie, "Algeria: Learning to Live with Independence," *National Geographic,* vol. 144, no. 2 (August 1973), 202, 205.

14. Thomas J. Abercrombie, "Bahrain: Hub of the Persian Gulf," *National Geographic,* vol. 156, no. 3 (September 1979), 304–305.

15. James Clifford, "Traveling Cultures," in *Cultural Studies,* ed. Nelson, Treichler, and Grossberg, 100.

16. Mernissi, *The Veil and the Male Elite,* 188.

17. Drinnon, *Facing West,* xvii.

18. Samir Amin, *Eurocentrism,* trans. Russell Moore (New York: Monthly Review Press, 1989), 89–90.

19. Ibid., 106, 107, 112.

20. Stam and Spence, "Colonialism, Racism and Representation": 4.

21. Robert Caputo, "Sudan: Arab-African Giant," *National Geographic,* vol. 161, no. 3 (March 1982), 354.

22. Farouk El-Baz, "Egypt's Desert of Promise," *National Geographic,* vol. 161, no. 2 (February 1982), 204.

23. Alloula, *The Colonial Harem,* 40, 44.

24. Thomas J. Abercrombie, "Arabia's Frankincense Trail," *National Geographic* 168, no. 4 (October 1985): 474–75, 488.

25. Harvey Arden, "Morocco's Ancient City of Fez," *National Geographic,* vol. 169, no. 3 (March 1986), 340–41.

26. Thomas J. Abercrombie, "Jordan: Kingdom in the Middle," *National Geographic,* vol. 165, no. 2 (February 1984), 252.

27. Ibid.

28. Memmi, *Dominated Man,* 187, 189.

29. Kabbani, *Europe's Myths of Orient,* 62.

30. Mike W. Edwards, "Tunisia: Sea, Sand, Success," *National Geographic,* vol. 157, no. 2 (February 1980), 188.

31. Larry Kohl, "Encampments of the Dispossessed," *National Geographic,* vol. 159, no. 6 (June 1981), 765.

32. Abercrombie, "Bahrain," 323.

33. Robert Azzi, "Oman, Land of Frankincense and Oil," *National Geographic,* vol. 143, no. 2 (February 1973), 218.

34. Noel Grove, "Volatile North Yemen," *National Geographic,* vol. 156, no. 2 (August 1979), 251–52.

35. Williamson, *Decoding Advertisements,* 123.

36. Thomas J. Abercrombie, "Oman: Guardian of the Gulf," *National Geographic,* vol. 160, no. 3 (September 1981): 344–45.

37. Gandelman, *Reading Pictures, Viewing Texts,* 81.

38. Abercrombie, "Morocco," 839, 842.

39. Said, *Orientalism,* 71.

40. Greenblatt, *Marvelous Possesions,* 122–23.

41. George Van den Abbeele, "Sightseers: The Tourist as Theorist," *Diacritics* 10 (Winter 1980): 4.

42. Berger, *Ways of Seeing,* 8.

43. Kirshenblatt-Gimblett, "Objects of Ethnography," in *Exhibiting Cultures,* ed. Karp and Lavine, 388.

44. Thomas J. Abercrombie, "The Sword and the Sermon," *National Geographic,* vol. 142, no. 1 (July 1972), 3.

45. Berger, *Ways of Seeing,* 14.

46. Denzin, "Reflections on the Ethnographer's Camera": 113.

47. Barthes, *Camera Lucida,* 27, 45.

48. John Berger, "Why Look at Animals?" in *About Looking* (New York: Pantheon Books, 1980), 26.

49. Abercrombie, "Morocco," 834.

50. Ibid.

51. Robert Azzi, "Damascus, Syria's Uneasy Eden," *National Geographic,* vol. 145, no. 4 (April 1974), 512.

52. Ellis, "Lebanon," 245.

53. Grove, "Volatile North Yemen," 248, 268.

54. John J. Putman, "The Arab World, Inc.: Who Are Those Oil-Rich Arabs, and What Are They Doing with All That Money?" *National Geographic,* vol. 148, no. 4 (October 1975), 498, 530.

55. Robert Azzi, "Saudi Arabia: The Kingdom and Its Power," *National Geographic,* vol. 158, no. 3 (September 1980), 286.

56. Said, *Orientalism,* 286.

57. Putman, "The Arab World, Inc.," 494–523.

58. Noel Grove, "Oil, the Dwindling Treasure," *National Geographic,* vol. 145, no. 6 (June 1974), 792.

59. Ibid., 804.

60. Abercrombie, "Bahrain," 302.

61. Ellis, "Cairo," 653, 656.

62. Arjun Appadurai, quoted in Gates, *Loose Canons,* 191.

63. Edwards, "Tunisia: Sea, Sand, Success," 209.

64. Fatima Mernissi, *Beyond the Veil: Male–Female Dynamics in Muslim Society* (London: Al Saqi Books, 1985), 167.

65. Marianne Alireza, "Women of Saudi Arabia," *National Geographic,* vol. 172, no. 4 (October 1987), 453.

66. Alloula, *The Colonial Harem,* 14.

67. Mernissi, *The Veil and the Male Elite,* 93.

68. Lutz and Collins, *Reading National Geographic,* 66.

69. Alloula, *The Colonial Harem,* 35.

70. Azzi, "Saudi Arabia: The Kingdom and Its Power," 326.

71. Bhabha, "The Other Question": 23.

72. Greenblatt, *Marvelous Possessions,* 50.

73. Alloula, *The Colonial Harem,* 35.

74. Mernissi, *Beyond the Veil,* 97.

75. Fletcher, "'Irresistible Seductions,'" in *Domesticating the Empire,* ed. Clancy-Smith and Gouda, 202.

76. Sontag, *On Photography,* 14–15.

77. Abercrombie, "Algeria," 232.

78. Kappeler, *The Pornography of Representation,* 103.

79. Fatna A. Sabbah, *Woman in the Muslim Unconscious,* trans. Mary Jo Lakeland (New York: Pergamon Press, 1984), 13.

Afterword

1. Hubbard, "Geographic Progress of Civilization," 22.

BIBLIOGRAPHY

Abercrombie, Thomas J. "Arabia's Frankincense Trail." *National Geographic,* vol. 168, no. 4 (October 1985), 474–513.

———. "Jordan: Kingdom in the Middle." *National Geographic,* vol. 165, no. 2 (February 1984), 236–67.

———. "Oman, 'Guardian of the Gulf.'" *National Geographic,* vol. 160, no. 3 (September 1981): 344–77.

———. "Bahrain: Hub of the Persian Gulf." *National Geographic,* vol. 156, no. 3 (September 1979): 300–29.

———. "Algeria: Learning to Live with Independence." *National Geographic,* vol. 44, no. 2 (August 1973), 200–33.

———. "The Sword and the Sermon." *National Geographic,* vol. 142, no. 1 (July 1972), 3–45.

———. "Morocco, Land of the Farthest West." *National Geographic,* vol. 139, no. 6 (June 1971), 834–65.

———. "Saudi Arabia: Beyond the Sands of Mecca." *National Geographic,* vol. 129, no. 1 (January 1966), 1–531.

Acker, Joan, Kate Barry, and Johanna Esseveld. "Objectivity and Truth: Problems in Doing Feminist Research." In *Beyond Methodology: Feminist Scholarship as Lived Research,* ed. Mary Margaret Fonow and Judith A. Cook. Bloomington: Indiana University Press, 1991.

Adams, Harriet Chalmers. "Across French and Spanish Morocco." *National Geographic,* vol. 47, no. 3 (March 1925), 327–56.

Alireza, Marianne. "Women of Saudi Arabia." *National Geographic,* vol. 172, no. 4 (October 1987), 422–53.

Alloula, Malek. *The Colonial Harem.* Translated by Myrna Godzich and Wlad Godzich. Minneapolis: University of Minnesota Press, 1986.

Amin, Samir. *Eurocentrism.* Translated by Russell Moore. New York: Monthly Review Press, 1989.

Arden, Harvey. "Morocco's Ancient City of Fez." *National Geographic,* vol. 169, no. 3 (March 1986), 330–53.

———. "In Search of Moses." *National Geographic,* vol. 149, no. 1 (January 1976), 2–37.

Atwood, Albert W. "Gilbert Grosvenor's Golden Jubilee." *National Geographic,* vol. 96, no. 2 (August 1949), 253–61.

Azzi, Robert. "Saudi Arabia: The Kingdom and Its Power." *National Geographic,* vol. 158, no. 3 (September 1980), 286–333.

———. "Damascus, Syria's Uneasy Eden." *National Geographic,* vol. 145, no. 4 (April 1974), 512–35.

———. "Oman, Land of Frankincense and Oil." *National Geographic,* vol. 143, no. 2 (February 1973), 205–29.

Barthes, Roland. *Camera Lucida: Reflections on Photography.* Translated by Richard Howard. New York: Farrar, Straus & Giroux, 1981.

Becker, George F. "The Witwatersrand and the Revolt of the Uitlanders." *National Geographic,* vol. 7, no. 11 (November 1896).

Berger, John. "Why Look at Animals?" in *About Looking.* New York: Pantheon Books, 1980.

———. *Ways of Seeing.* New York: Penguin Books, 1977.

Bhabha, Homi K. "The Other Question—The Stereotype and Colonial Discourse." *Screen* 24, no. 6 (November–December 1983): 18–36.

Blayney, Thomas Lindsey. "A Journey in Morocco: The Land of the Moors." *National Geographic,* vol. 22, no. 7 (July 1911), 750–75.

Brantlinger, Patrick. *Crusoe's Footprints: Cultural Studies in Britain and America.* New York: Routledge, 1990.

Bridgman, Herbert L. "The New British Empire of the Sudan." *National Geographic,* vol. 17, no. 5 (May 1906), 241–67.

Brown, Sarah Graham. *Images of Women: The Portrayal of Women in Photography of the Middle East 1860–1950.* New York: Columbia University Press, 1988.

Caputo, Robert. "Sudan: Arab-African Giant." *National Geographic,* vol. 161, no. 3 (March 1982), 346–79.

Case, Paul Edward. "Boom Time in Kuwait." *National Geographic,* vol. 102, no. 6 (December 1952), 783–802.

Casserly, Lieutenant-Colonel Gordon. "The White City of Algiers." *National Geographic,* vol. 53, no. 2 (February 1928), 206–32.

———. "Fez, Heart of Morocco: Africa's 'Imperial City' Retains Its Teeming Streets, Cluttered Shops, Glamorous Moorish Homes and Mosques, Amid the Peace of French Rule." *National Geographic,* vol. 67, no. 6 (June 1935), 663–94.

———. "Tripolitania, Where Rome Resumes Sway: The Ancient Trans-Mediterranean Empire, on the Fringe of the Libyan Desert, Becomes a Promising Modern Italian Colony." *National Geographic,* vol. 48, no. 2 (August 1925), 131–61.

Cesaire, Aime. *Discourse on Colonialism.* Translated by Joan Pinkham. New York: Monthly Review Press, 1972.

Chapman, Robert L., ed. *The New Dictionary of American Slang.* New York: Harper & Row, 1986.

Clancy-Smith, Julia. "Islam, Gender, Identities in the Making of French Algeria, 1830–1962." In *Domesticating the Empire: Race, Gender, and Family Life in French and Dutch Colonialism,* ed. Julia Clancy-Smith and Frances Gouda. Charlottesville: University Press of Virginia, 1998.

Clifford, James. "Traveling Cultures." In *Cultural Studies,* ed. Cary Nelson, Paula Treichler, and Lawrence Grossberg. New York: Routledge, 1992.

————. *The Predicament of Culture: Twentieth-Century Ethnography, Literature, and Art.* Cambridge, Mass.: Harvard University Press, 1988.

Cooper, Merian C. "Two Fighting Tribes of the Sudan." *National Geographic,* vol. 56, no. 4 (October 1929), 465–86.

Cornwall, Peter Bruce. "In Search of Arabia's Past." *National Geographic,* vol. 93, no. 4 (April 1948), 492–522.

Cotter, Margaret. "Red Cross Girl Overseas." *National Geographic,* vol. 86, no. 6 (December 1944), 745–68.

de Monfreid, Henri. "Pearl Fishing in the Red Sea." *National Geographic,* vol. 72, no. 5 (November 1937), 597–626.

De Pinedo, Commander Francesco. "By Seaplane to Six Continents." *National Geographic,* vol. 54, no. 3 (September 1928), 247–301.

Delany, Samuel R. "Twilight in the Rue Morgue." *Transition* 54 (1991): 36–56.

Denzin, Norman K. "Reflections on the Ethnographer's Camera." *Current Perspectives in Social Theory* 7 (1986): 105–23.

Donaldson, Laura E. *Decolonizing Feminisms: Race, Gender, and Empire-Building.* Chapel Hill: University of North Carolina Press, 1992.

Drinnon, Richard. *Facing West: The Metaphysics of Indian-Hating and Empire-Building.* Minneapolis: University of Minnesota Press, 1980.

DuBois, Marc. "The Governance of the Third World: A Foucauldian Perspective on Power Relations in Development." *Alternatives* 16, no. 1 (Winter 1991): 1–30.

Dyer, Richard. *Heavenly Bodies: Film Stars and Society.* New York: St. Martin's Press, 1986.

Edwards, Mike W. "Tunisia: Sea, Sand, Success." *National Geographic,* vol. 157, no. 2 (February 1980): 184–217.

El-Baz, Farouk. "Egypt's Desert of Promise." *National Geographic,* vol. 161, no. 2 (February 1982), 190–221.

Ellis, William S. "The New Face of Baghdad: Iraq at War." *National Geographic,* vol. 167, no. 1 (January 1985), 80–109.

————. "Cairo: Troubled Capital of the Arab World." *National Geographic,* vol. 141, no. 5 (May 1972), 639–67.

————. "Lebanon, Little Bible Land in the Crossfire of History." *National Geographic,* vol. 137, no. 2 (February 1970), 240–75.

Ellsworth, Elizabeth. "Educational Films Against Critical Pedagogy." In *The Ideology of Images in Educational Media: Hidden Curriculums in the Classroom.* New York: Teachers College Press, Columbia University, 1990.

Ellsworth, Elizabeth, and Mariamne H. Whatley, ed. *The Ideology of Images in Educational Media: Hidden Curriculums in the Classroom.* New York: Teachers College Press, Columbia University, 1990.

Enloe, Cynthia. *Bananas, Beaches, and Bases: Making Feminist Sense of International Politics.* Berkeley: University of California Press, 1990.

Fabian, Johannes. *Time and the Other: How Anthropology Makes Its Object.* New York: Columbia University Press, 1983.

Fanon, Frantz. *Black Skin, White Masks.* Translated by Charles Lam Markmann. New York: Grove Press, 1967.

Ferguson, Russell. "A Box of Tools: Theory and Practice," in *Discourses: Conversations in Postmodern Art and Culture,* Russell Ferguson et al. Cambridge, Mass.: MIT Press, 1990.

Field, Henry. "Sinai Sheds New Light on the Bible." *National Geographic,* vol. 94, no. 6 (December 1948): 795–815.

Fiske, John. "British Cultural Studies and Television." In *Channels of Discourse: Television and Contemporary Criticism,* ed. Robert C. Allen. Chapel Hill: University of North Carolina Press, 1987.

Fletcher, Yael Simpson. "Irresistible Seductions: Gendered Representations of Colonial Algeria around 1930." In *Domesticating the Empire: Race, Gender, and Family Life in French and Dutch Colonialism,* ed. Julia Clancy-Smith and Frances Gouda. Charlottesville: University Press of Virginia, 1998.

Forbes-Leith, Major F.A.C. "From England to India by Automobile." *National Geographic,* vol. 48, no. 2 (August 1925), 191–223.

Forder, Archibold. "Damascus, the Pearl of the Desert." *National Geographic,* vol. 22, no. 1 (January 1911), 62–82.

———. "Arabia, the Desert of the Sea." *National Geographic,* vol. 20, no. 12 (December 1909), 1062–1117.

Forsyth, George H. "Island of Faith in the Sinai Wilderness." *National Geographic,* vol. 125, no. 1 (January 1964), 82–106.

Foucault, Michel, and Gilles Deleuze. "Intellectuals and Power." In *Discourses: Conversations in Postmodern Art and Culture,* ed. Russell Ferguson et al. Cambridge, Mass.: MIT Press, 1990.

Frazer, John E. "Kuwait, Aladdin's Lamp of the Middle East." *National Geographic,* vol. 135, no. 5 (May 1969), 636–67.

Gablik, Suzi. *Magritte.* New York: Thames and Hudson, 1985.

Gaines, Jane. "Costume and Narrative: How Dress Tells the Women's Story." In *Fabrications: Costume and the Female Body,* ed. Jane Gaines and Charlotte Herzog. New York: Routledge, 1990.

Gandelman, Claude. *Reading Pictures, Viewing Texts.* Bloomington: Indiana University Press, 1991.

Garrett, Wilbur E. Editorial. *National Geographic,* vol. 171, no. 1 (January 1987).

Gates, Henry Louis, Jr. *Loose Canons: Notes on the Culture Wars.* New York: Oxford University Press, 1992.

Gibson, Ross. *South of the West: Postcolonialism and the Narrative Construction of Australia.* Bloomington: Indiana University Press, 1992.

Gilman, Sander L. "Black Bodies, White Bodies: Toward an Iconography of Female Sexuality in Late Nineteenth-Century Art, Medicine, and Literature." In *"Race," Writing, and Difference,* ed. Henry Louis Gates, Jr. Chicago: University of Chicago Press, 1985.

Glueck, Nelson. "On the Trail of King Solomon's Mines." *National Geographic,* vol. 85, no. 2 (February 1944), 233–56.

Goetzmann, William H. "Tell Me If Your Civilization Is Interesting." *National Geographic,* vol. 173, no. 1 (January 1988), 8–37.

Graves, William. "New Life for the Troubled Suez Canal." *National Geographic*, vol. 147, no. 6 (June 1975), 792–817.

Greenblatt, Stephen. *Marvelous Possessions: The Wonder of the New World.* Chicago: University of Chicago Press, 1991.

Grosvenor, Elsie May Bell. "Safari from Congo to Cairo." *National Geographic*, vol. 106, no. 6 (December 1954), 721–71.

———. "Safari Through Changing Africa." *National Geographic*, vol. 104, no. 2 (August 1953), 145–98.

Grosvenor, Gilbert H. "The National Geographic Society and Its Magazine." *National Geographic*, vol. 69, no. 1 (January 1936), 123–64.

Grosvenor, Gilbert M. "When the President Goes Abroad." *National Geographic*, vol. 117, no. 5 (May 1960), 588–649.

Grosvenor, Melville Bell. "Journey into the Living World of the Bible." *National Geographic*, vol. 132, no. 4 (October 1967), 494–507.

Grove, Noel. "Volatile North Yemen." *National Geographic*, vol. 156, no. 2 (August 1979), 244–69.

———. "Oil, the Dwindling Treasure." *National Geographic*, vol. 145, no. 6 (June 1974), 792–825.

Groves, Brigadier General P.R.C., and Major J. R. McCrindle. "Flying Over Egypt, Sinai, and Palestine." *National Geographic*, vol. 50, no. 3 (September 1926), 313–55.

Haraway, Donna. *Simians, Cyborgs, and Women: The Reinvention of Nature.* New York: Routledge, 1991.

———. *Primate Visions: Gender, Race, and Nature in the World of Modern Science.* New York: Routledge, 1989.

Hinsley, Curtis M. "The World as Marketplace Commodification of the Exotic at the World's Columbian Exposition, Chicago, 1893." In *Exhibiting Cultures: The Poetics and Politics of Museum Display,* ed. Ivan Karp and Steven D. Lavine. Washington, D.C.: Smithsonian Institution Press, 1991.

Hoogstraal, Harry. "South in the Sudan." *National Geographic*, vol. 103, no. 2 (February 1953), 249–72.

———. "Yemen Opens the Door to Progress." *National Geographic*, vol. 101, no. 2 (February 1952): 213–44.

hooks, bell. *Talking Back: Thinking Feminist, Thinking Black.* Boston: South End Press, 1989.

Hoskins, Franklin E. "The Route over which Moses Led the Children of Israel out of Egypt." *National Geographic*, vol. 20, no. 12 (December 1909), 1011–38.

Hubbard, Gardiner G. "Geographic Progress of Civilization: Annual Address by the President." *National Geographic*, vol. 6 (February 1894), 1–22.

Hudson, Herndon, and Mary Hudson. "Ali Goes to the Clinic." *National Geographic*, vol. 90, no. 6 (December 1946), 764-66.

Hunt, Nancy Rose. "Domesticity and Colonialism in Belgian Africa: Usumbura's Foyer School." *Signs* 15, no. 3 (Spring 1990): 447–74.

Hussein, H.M. King of Jordan. "Holy Land, My Country." *National Geographic*, vol. 126, no. 6 (December 1964), 784–89.

JanMohamed, Abdul R. "The Economy of Manichean Allegory: The Function of Racial Difference in Colonialist Literature." In *"Race," Writing, and Difference,* ed. Henry Louis Gates, Jr. Chicago: University of Chicago Press, 1985.

Jehlen, Myra. "Archimedes and the Paradox of Feminist Criticism." In *Feminisms: An Anthology of Literary Theory and Criticism,* ed. Robyn R. Warhol and Diane Price Herndl. New Brunswick, N.J.: Rutgers University Press, 1991.

Johnson, Frank Edward. "Here and There in Northern Africa." *National Geographic,* vol. 25, no. 1 (January 1914), 1–132.

Judge, Joseph. "Taking Up the Great Global Issues," *National Geographic Index, 1888–1988.* Washington, D.C.: National Geographic Society, 1989.

Kabbani, Rana. *Europe's Myths of Orient.* Bloomington: Indiana University Press, 1986.

Kaplan, Marion. "Twilight of the Arab Dhow." *National Geographic,* vol. 146, no. 3 (September 1974), 330–51.

Kappeler, Susanne. *The Pornography of Representation.* Minneapolis: University of Minnesota Press, 1986.

Keith-Roach, Maj. Edward. "Changing Palestine." *National Geographic,* vol. 65, no. 4 (April 1934), 493–527.

———. "Adventures Among the 'Lost Tribes of Islam' in Eastern Darfur: A Personal Narrative of Exploring, Mapping, and Setting Up a Government in the Anglo–Egyptian Sudan Borderland." *National Geographic,* vol. 45, no. 1 (January 1924), 41–73.

Kenney, Nathaniel T. "Africa: The Winds of Freedom Stir a Continent." *National Geographic,* vol. 118, no. 3 (September 1960), 303–59.

Kirshenblatt-Gimblett, Barbara. "Objects of Ethnography." In *Exhibiting Cultures: The Poetics and Politics of Museum Display,* ed. Ivan Karp and Steven D. Lavine. Washington, D.C.: Smithsonian Instutution Press, 1991.

Kohl, Larry. "Encampments of the Dispossessed." *National Geographic,* vol. 159, no. 6 (June 1981), 756–75.

La Fay, Howard. "Algeria: France's Stepchild, Problem and Promise." *National Geographic,* vol. 117, no. 6 (June 1960), 768–95.

Lamb, Harold. "Crusader Lands Revisited." *National Geographic,* vol. 106, no. 6 (December 1954), 815–52.

Lowell, Tay, and Lowell Thomas, Jr. "Flight to Adventure." *National Geographic,* vol. 112, no. 1 (July 1957), 49–112.

Lutz, Catherine A., and Jane L. Collins. *Reading National Geographic.* Chicago: University of Chicago Press, 1993.

Luz, Oskar. "Proud Primitives, the Nuba People." *National Geographic,* vol. 130, no. 5 (November 1966), 673–99.

MacLeish, Kenneth. "Reunited Jerusalem Faces Its Problems." *National Geographic,* vol. 134, no. 6 (December 1968), 835–71.

———. "Abraham, the Friend of God." *National Geographic,* vol. 130, no. 6 (December 1966), 739–89.

Mallowan, M.E.L. "New Light on Ancient Ur." *National Geographic,* vol. 57, no. 1 (January 1930), 95–130.

Mani, Lata. "Cultural Theory, Colonial Texts: Reading Eyewitness Accounts of Widow Burning." In *Cultural Studies,* ed. Cary Nelson, Paula Treichler, and Lawrence Grossberg. New York: Routledge, 1992.

Mariani, Phil, and Jonathan Crary. "In the Shadow of the West." Interview with Edward W. Said. In *Discourses: Conversations in Postmodern Art and Culture,* ed. Russell Ferguson, et al. Cambridge, Mass.: MIT Press, 1990.

Matthews, Samuel W. "The Phoenicians: Sea Lords of Antiquity." *National Geographic,* vol. 146, no. 2 (August 1974), 149–89.

McCarry, Charles. "Let the World Hear from You." In *National Geographic Index, 1888–1988.* Washington D.C.: National Geographic Society, 1989.

McClintock, Anne. *Imperial Leather: Race, Gender and Sexuality in the Colonial Contest.* New York: Routledge, 1995.

McElroy, Keith. "Popular Education and Photographs of the Non-Industrialized World, 1885–1915." *Exposure* 28, no. 3 (Winter 1991/92): 34–53.

Memmi, Albert. *Dominated Man: Notes Towards a Portrait.* Boston: Beacon Press, 1969.

———. *The Colonizer and the Colonized.* Boston: Beacon Press, 1967.

Mernissi, Fatima. *The Veil and the Male Elite: A Feminist Interpretation of Women's Rights in Islam.* Translated by Mary Jo Lakeland. Reading, Mass.: Addison-Wesley Publishing, 1991.

———. *Beyond the Veil: Mal–Female Dynamics in Muslim Society.* London: Al Saqi Books, 1985.

Messenger, Phyllis Mauch, ed. *The Ethics of Collecting Cultural Property.* Albuquerque: University of New Mexico Press, 1993.

Miles, Margaret R. "The Virgin's One Bare Breast: Female Nudity and Religious Meaning in Tuscan Early Renaissance Culture." In *The Female Body in Western Culture,* ed. Susan Rubin Suleiman. Cambridge, Mass.: Harvard University Press, 1986.

Mohanty, Chandra Talpade. "Under Western Eyes: Feminist Scholarship and Colonial Discourses." In *Third World Women and the Politics of Feminism,* ed. Ann Russo, Chandra Talpade Mohanty, and Lourdes Torres. Bloomington: Indiana University Press, 1991.

Mosse, George L. *Nationalism and Sexuality: Middle-Class Morality and Sexual Norms in Modern Europe.* Madison: University of Wisconsin Press, 1985.

Mudimbe, V. Y. *The Invention of Africa: Gnosis, Philosophy, and the Order of Knowledge.* Bloomington: Indiana University Press, 1988.

National Geographic. "One Hundred Years of Increasing and Diffusing Geographic Knowledge." Editorial, vol. 173, no. 1 (January 1988).

———. Editorial, vol. 171, no. 1 (January 1987).

———. Busch Gardens Advertisement, vol. 149, no. 2 (February 1976).

———. Subscription Advertisement, vol. 125, no. 2 (February 1964).

———. "President Johnson Dedicates the Society's New Headquarters," vol. 125, no. 5 (May 1964).

———. "The Arab World," vol. 114, no. 5 (November 1958).

———. " *National Geographic* Fact-Finder at Work," vol. 114, no. 5 (November 1958).

———. French Cruise Line Advertisement, vol. 61, no. 3 (March 1932).

———. French Cruise Line Advertisement, vol. 50, no. 4 (October 1926).

———. Thos. Cook & Son Cruise Advertisement, vol. 46, no. 1 (July 1924).

———. "The Conquest of the Sahara by the Automobile," vol. 45, no. 1 (January 1924), 87–94.

———. Photo Essay, vol. 21, no. 3 (March 1917), 257–72.

Nichols, Bill. *Representing Reality: Issues and Concepts in Documentary.* Bloomington: Indiana University Press, 1991.

———. *Ideology and the Image: Social Representation in the Cinema and Other Media.* Bloomington: Indiana University Press, 1981.

Nordstrom, Alison Devine. "Wood Nymphs and Patriots: Depictions of Samoans in *The National Geographic Magazine.*" *Visual Sociology* 7 (1992): 49–59.

O'Connor, V. C. Scott. "Beyond the Grand Atlas: Where the French Tricolor Flies Beside the Flag of the Sultan of Morocco." *National Geographic,* vol. 61, no. 3 (March 1932), 261–319.

Osgood, Wilfred H. "Nature and Man in Ethiopia." *National Geographic,* vol. 54, no. 2 (August 1928), 121–76.

Parr, Grant, and G. E. Janssen. "War Meets Peace in Egypt." *National Geographic,* vol. 81, no. 4 (April 1942), 503–26.

Perdicaris, Ion. "Morocco, 'The Land of the Extreme West' and the Story of My Captivity." *National Geographic,* vol. 17, no. 3 (March 1906), 117–57.

Pratt, Mary Louise. *Imperial Eyes: Travel Writing and Transculturalion.* New York: Routledge, 1992.

———. "Scratches on the Face of the Country; or, What Mr. Brown Saw in the Land of the Bushmen." In *"Race," Writing, and Difference,* ed. Henry Louise Gates. Chicago: University of Chicago Press, 1985.

Price, Willard. "By Felucca Down the Nile: Giant Dams Rule Egypt's Lifeline River, Yet Village Life Goes on As It Did in the Time of the Pharaohs." *National Geographic,* vol. 77, no. 4 (April 1940), 435–76.

Priest, Capt. Cecil D. "Timbuktu, in the Sands of the Sahara." *National Geographic,* vol. 45, no. 1 (January 1924), 73–85.

Putman, John J. "The Arab World, Inc.: Who Are Those Oil-Rich Arabs, and What Are They Doing with All That Money?" *National Geographic,* vol. 148, no. 4 (October 1975), 494–533.

Rice, Laura. "'Nomad Thought': Isabelle Eberhardt and the Colonial Project." *Cultural Critique,* no. 17 (Winter, 1990–91): 151–76.

Rose, Gillian. *Feminism and Geography: The Limits of Geographical Knowledge.* Minneapolis: University of Minnesota Press, 1993.

Rydell, Robert W. *All the World's a Fair: Visions of Empire at American International Expositions, 1876–1916.* Chicago: University of Chicago Press, 1984.

Sabbah, Fatna A. *Woman in the Muslim Unconscious.* Translated by Mary Jo Lakeland. New York: Pergamon Press, 1984.

Said, Edward W. *Culture and Imperialism.* New York: Vintage Books, 1994.

———. *After the Last Sky: Palestinian Lives.* New York: Pantheon Books, 1986.

———. "Orientalism Reconsidered." *Cultural Critique* 1 (Fall 1985): 89–107.

———. *Covering Islam.* New York: Pantheon Books, 1981.

———. *Orientalism*. New York: Vintage Books, 1979.

Sassoon, David. "Considering the Perspectives of the Victim: The Antiquities of Nepal." In *The Ethics of Collecting Cultural Property*, ed. Phyllis Mauch Messenger. Albuquerque: University of New Mexico Press, 1993.

Schaeffer, Claude F. A. "Secrets from the Syrian Hills." *National Geographic*, vol. 64, no. 1 (July 1933), 96–126.

———. "A New Alphabet of the Ancients Is Unearthed." *National Geographic*, vol. 58, no. 4 (October 1930), 477–516.

Schick, Irvin Cemil. "Representing Middle Eastern Women: Feminism and Colonial Discourse." *Feminist Studies*, vol. 16, no. 2, (Summer 1990): 345–80.

Schreider, Helen, and Frank Schreider. "Journey into the Great Rift." *National Geographic*, vol. 128, no. 2 (August 1965), 254–90.

Scofield, John. "Hashemite Jordan, Arab Heartland." *National Geographic*, vol. 102, no. 6 (December 1952), 841–56.

Scott, Joan W. "Experience." In *Feminists Theorize the Political*, ed. Judith Butler and Joan W. Scott. New York: Routledge, 1992.

Seiter, Ellen. "Semiotics and Television." In *Channels of Discourse: Television and Contemporary Criticism*, ed. Robert C. Allen. Chapel Hill: University of North Carolina Press, 1987.

Shay, Felix. "Cairo to Cape Town, Overland: An Adventurous Journey of 135 Days, Made by an American Man and His Wife, Through the Length of the African Continent." *National Geographic*. vol. 47, no. 2 (February 1925), 123–260.

Shor, Jean, and Franc Shor. "From Sea to Sahara in French Morocco." *National Geographic*, vol. 107, no. 2 (February 1955), 147–88.

———. "Iraq—Where Oil and Water Mix." *National Geographic*, vol. 114, no. 4 (October 1958), 443–89.

Simpich, Frederick. "Change Comes to Bible Lands," *National Geographic*, vol. 74, no. 6 (December 1938), 695–750.

———. "The Rise of the New Arab Nation." *National Geographic*, vol. 36, no. 5 (November 1919), 369–93.

———. "Mystic Nedjef, The Shia Mecca: A Visit to One of the Strangest Cities in the World." *National Geographic*, vol. 26, no. 5 (November 1914), 589–98.

Simpich, Frederick, and W. Robert Moore. "Bombs over Bible Lands." *National Geographic*, vol. 80, no. 2 (August 1941), 141–80.

Simpich, Frederick, and Margaret Simpich. "Where Adam and Eve Lived." *National Geographic*, vol. 26, no. 5 (November 1914), 546–84.

Sontag, Susan. *On Photography*. New York: Farrar, Straus & Giroux, 1977.

Spivak, Gayatri Chakravorty. *The Post-Colonial Critic: Interviews, Strategies, Dialogues*, ed. Sarah Harasym. New York: Routledge, 1990.

Stam, Robert, and Louise Spence. "Colonialism, Racism and Representation—An Introduction." *Screen* 24 (March April 1983).

Suleiman, Susan Rubin, ed. *The Female Body in Western Culture: Contemporary Perspectives*. Cambridge, Mass.: Harvard University Press, 1986.

Swayne, H.G.C. "The Rock of Aden." *National Geographic*, vol. 68, no. 6 (December 1935), 723–42.

Sylvester, David. *Magritte: The Silence of the Word.* New York: Harry N. Abrams, 1992.

Thaw, Lawrence Copley, and Margaret S. Thaw. "Along the Old Silk Routes." *National Geographic,* vol. 78, no. 4 (October 1940), 453–86.

Torgovnick, Marianna. *Gone Primitive: Savage Intellects, Modern Lives.* Chicago: University of Chicago Press, 1990.

Treat, Ida. "Sailing Forbidden Coasts." *National Geographic,* vol. 60, no. 3 (September 1931), 357–86.

Trinh, T. Minh-ha. *When the Moon Waxes Red: Representations, Gender, and Cultural Politics.* New York: Routledge, 1991.

Tweedy, Owen. "An Unbeliever Joins the Hadj." *National Geographic,* vol. 65, no. 6 (June 1934), 761–89.

Underwood, Eric. "The British Commonwealth of Nations: 'Organized Freedom' Around the World." *National Geographic,* vol. 83, no. 4 (April 1943), 485–524.

Van der Meulen, D. "Into Burning Hadhramaut: The Arab Land of Frankincense and Myrrh, Ever a Lodestone of Western Exploration." *National Geographic,* vol. 62, no. 4 (October 1932), 387–429.

Van den Abbeele, George. "Sightseers: The Tourist as Theorist." *Diacritics* 10 (Winter 1980): 2–14.

Van Ess, John. "Forty Years Among the Arabs." *National Geographic,* vol. 82, no. 3 (September 1942), 385–420.

Villiers, Alan. "Sailing with Sindbad's Sons." *National Geographic,* vol. 94, no. 5 (November 1948), 675–88.

Vosburgh, Frederick G. "To Gilbert Grosvenor: A Monthly Monument 25 Miles High." *National Geographic,* vol. 130, no. 4 (October 1966), 445–87.

Ware, Vron. *Beyond the Pale: White Women, Racism and History.* New York: Verso, 1992.

Warren, Karen J. "A Philosophical Perspective on the Ethics and Resolution of Cultural Property Issues." In *The Ethics of Collecting Cultural Property,* ed. Phyllis Mauch Messenger. Albuquerque: University of New Mexico Press, 1993.

Weaver, Kenneth F. "Of Planes and Men: U.S. Air Force Wages Cold War and Hot." *National Geographic,* vol. 128, no. 3 (September 1965), 298–349.

Weedon, Chris. *Feminist Practice and Poststructuralist Theory.* Oxford and New York: Basil Blackwell, 1987.

Whatley, Mariamne H. "The Picture of Health: How Textbook Photographs Construct Health." In *The Ideology of Images in Educational Media: Hidden Curriculums in the Classroom,* ed. Elizabeth Ellsworth and Mariamne H. Whatley. New York: Teachers College Press, Columbia University, 1990.

White, Mimi. "Ideological Analysis and Television." In *Channels of Discourse: Television and Contemporary Criticism,* ed. Robert C. Allen. Chapel Hill: University of North Carolina Press, 1987.

Whiting, John D. "Petra, Ancient Caravan Stronghold." *National Geographic,* vol. 67, no. 2 (February 1935), 129–65.

———. "Village Life in the Holy Land." *National Geographic.* vol. 25, no. 3 (March 1914), 249–314.

Williams, Maynard Owen. "Syria and Lebanon Taste Freedom." *National Geographic* 90, no. 6 (December 1946): 729–63.

———. "Time's Footprints in Tunisian Sands." *National Geographic,* vol. 71, no. 3 (March 1937), 345–86.

———. "The Citroen Trans-Asiatic Expedition Reaches Kashmir." *National Geographic,* vol. 60, no. 4 (October 1931), 387–445.

Williamson, Judith. *Decoding Advertisements: Ideology and Meaning in Advertising.* New York: Marion Boyars, 1984.

Woolley, C. Leonard. "Archeology, The Mirror of the Ages: Our Debt to the Humble Delvers in the Ruins at Carchemish and at Ur." *National Geographic,* vol. 54, no. 2 (August 1928), 207–26.

Young, Robert. *White Mythologies: Writing, History, and the West.* New York: Routledge, 1990.

Zwemer, Rev. S. M. "Notes on Oman." *National Geographic,* vol. 22, no. 1 (January 1911), 89–98.

INDEX

Italic page numbers indicate photographs.